Illinois Studies in Communications

Illinois Studies in Communications

Senior Editors
Sandra Braman, James W. Carey, Clifford G. Christians,
Lawrence Grossberg, Thomas H. Guback, James W. Hay, John C. Nerone,
Ellen A. Wartella, and D. Charles Whitney.

Books in the Series

Fifties
Television

William Boddy

Fifties
Television

The Industry and Its Critics

University of Illinois Press
Urbana and Chicago

For my mother
and the memory of my father

© 1990 by the Board of Trustees of the University of Illinois
Manufactured in the United States of America
C 5 4 3 2 1

This book is printed on acid-free paper.

Library of Congress Cataloging-in-Publication Data

Boddy, William, 1953-
   Fifties television : the industry and its critics
   William Boddy.
      p. cm
   Includes bibliographical references.
   ISBN 0-252-01699-8 (alk. paper)
      1. Television broadcasting—United States—History.   I. Title.
PN1992.3.U5B64   1990
384.55'0973—dc20   89-39336
                                                              CIP

Contents

Acknowledgments

I would like to thank Kan Leab, Robert C. Allen, and James Carey for for their generous and active support of this project. Robert Sklar, Brian Winston, Robert Stam, Donna Demac, and Daniel Walkowitz offered important help at earlier stages of the work. Many others have assisted through argument and encouragement, including Margaret Boddy, Janet Staiger, Jay Leyda, William Lafferty, Anne Friedberg, Mary Brosnahan, Jonathan Buchsbaum, Ien Ang, Pennee Bender, and Pam Falkenberg. At the University of Illinois Press, I would like to thank Richard Wentworth and Lawrence Malley, as well as my copyeditor, Mary Giles. Arthur Penn, Herbert Brodkin, Ernest Kinoy, Sidney Lumet, Robert Costello, Bert Briller, and Mel Goldberg helped frame the secondary material on the television industry of the 1950s through a series of interviews they generously granted me.

Several research collections were invaluable to this project, including the National Association of Broadcasters' Television Information Office, where I would especially like to thank Leslie Slocum, Jim Poteat, and Edana McCaffery for their help. Marilynn Dean and Cathy Lim at the NBC Records Administration Library, Roann Rubin and Catherine Foti at the ABC Corporate Relations Office, and Laura Kapnick and her staff at the CBS Reference Library helped me gain access to valuable network materials. Doris Katz at NBC's Research Library made that collection available to me, and Jeanne Dembrowsky at the CBS Script Library and Howard Howarth and his staff at the CBS Records Center provided

access to other important print material. The staffs of the State Historical Society of Wisconsin, the UCLA Department of Special Collections,
Columbia University's Oral History Collection, the Broadcast Pioneers
Library, and the New York Public Library helped locate scripts, business
records, and other material. Viacom International, the Writers Guild of
America, and the Directors Guild of America were all helpful in supplying credit and program information.

Access to early television programming, a special challenge for researchers working in broadcast history, was made easier with the
generous help of Ron Simon at the Museum of Broadcasting, Bob Rosen
at the Academy of Television Arts and Sciences-UCLA Television
Archives, and Emily Sieger at the Motion Picture, Broadcasting, and
Recorded Sound Division of the Library of Congress. I am also grateful
to WPIX-TV for making available syndicated material from the period.

Introduction

The American television industry underwent its deepest and most lasting changes in the middle years of the 1950s, a period represented in the traditional television literature as the transition in prime-time programming from the "Golden Age" of live drama to the rise of Hollywood film series. The shift in dramatic formats was only one of many programming changes in the mid-1950s: prime-time programming also shifted from New York to Hollywood, from anthology programs to continuing-character series, and from the dramatic model of the legitimate theater to that of genre-based Hollywood entertainments. The program changes of the mid-1950s cannot be attributed simply to shifting public tastes or the exhaustion of particular program genres, but underscore fundamental changes in the way in which prime-time entertainment programs were produced, sponsored, and scheduled. For example, the structure of network TV advertising underwent fundamental change in the mid-1950s, from the typical pattern of a single sponsor licensing a program to the present arrangement of many sponsors purchasing simple commercial insertions in programs licensed by networks.

The programming changes of the 1950s represented a repudiation of the aesthetic values promoted by prominent television critics and writers earlier in the decade. Via journalistic reviewing, technical handbooks, and general sociological criticism, writers on television in the early 1950s constructed an unusually explicit and widely shared normative aesthetics of television drama. To these critics and writers, the program changes in the mid-1950s signaled a retreat by the industry from an earlier commitment to aesthetic experimentation, program balance, and free expression. The filmed series, which replaced the autonomous teleplay of the anthology series, challenged the growing prominence and prestige of the television playwright and fundamentally altered the role of the television critic. In the eyes of many critics, television's debt to the legitimate theater in distinction to the motion pictures was renounced, and with it television drama's allegiance to the aesthetics of theatrical naturalism.

The economic and programming trends within the TV industry climaxed at the end of the 1950s, giving American television a relatively stable set of commercial structures and prime-time program forms. Indeed, it was not until the rise of satellite-delivered cable services and proliferating independent stations in the mid-1970s that the relationships among prime-time audiences, advertisers, and networks constructed in the 1950s began to erode, bringing network television its present prospect of sustained economic crisis.

The extraordinary public controversy in 1959-60 over the rigging of TV quiz programs marks a logical end point to the period under study in two ways. First, the direct results of the quiz show scandal reinforced the economic and programming trends established earlier in the decade. Second, the public controversy over quiz show fraud provoked wider debates over the fundamental responsibilities of the television industry regarding program balance and freedom of expression. The spectacular public airing of TV's dirty linen at the end of the 1950s not only provided a forum for prominent television writers and critics to voice their general disenchantment with the medium, but also provoked industry leaders to offer a new public rationale for the American system of commercial broadcasting.

The new industry self-definitions highlighted at the end of the decade provided strikingly different roles for the television writer, critic, and audience and signaled larger changes in the position of television in American cultural life. The disjunction witnessed within a few years between the critics' celebration of network television's Golden Age and their scorning of a "Vast Wasteland" describes not only a shift in TV's program forms and economic practices, but also marks a new cynicism about the commercial imperatives of American television, the quality of federal regulation, and the cultural prestige and aesthetic legitimacy of the medium.

The present study is indebted to the reinvigorated scholarship in film and television history of the last fifteen years. The British film historian Edward Buscombe argues that one imperative of a revisionist television historiography "is [to] pose the question of whether things could have turned out differently. Was the evolution of American television into its present form an inevitable process? To answer this question adequately would require a history of television which goes beyond the mere recording of the various technical, economic, and aesthetic developments, beyond merely noting that certain events occurred." Pointing to the fundamental social choices taken regarding American television, including the dependence upon advertising support, the dominance of a specific set of fiction/entertainment styles in programming, and the definition of the private home as the nearly exclusive arena of viewing, Buscombe notes that these choices often remain implicit and unexamined in conventional accounts of the medium.[1]

Uncovering the logic and consequences of these broad social choices regarding U. S. television requires a wider perspective than generally deployed in the traditional literature, and tracing the threads of continuity and change in program forms and business practices in American television presents unique challenges to the historian. From its origins in the scientific laboratory, commercial television has borne the marks of the distinct and competing interests of electronic manufacturers, networks, and broadcast sponsors. A history of the commercial exploitation of television technology needs to recognize the shifting interests and alliances among the would-be architects of the medium. Four contexts offer avenues of historical inquiry: relations among the distinct sectors of the television industry (including equipment manufacturing, program production, network operation, and television advertising); long-term changes in the advertising and marketing strategies of American business; long-term changes in the motion picture industry; and the history of federal broadcast regulation. A history of television must therefore be in part a history of industrial giants like RCA and AT&T, as well as of Madison Avenue advertising agencies and their corporate clients, and of the major Hollywood studios. Attitudes toward television within these various groups have always been pragmatic and changeable, and an examination of their activities in the medium is likely to yield an account more varied and complex than often supposed.

One special task of the television historian lies in tracing the industry's peculiar relation to the state, including the U. S. Congress, the federal courts, and the Federal Communications Commission (FCC), an independent regulatory agency set up in 1933. Due to television's appetite for space in the electromagnetic spectrum and the technical properties of the portion of the spectrum it occupies, the allocation and station assignment powers of the federal government are qualitatively different for television than for radio broadcasting. Regulatory decisions regarding visual standards and spectrum allocations in the 1930s and 1940s not only set up the still-prevailing technical specifications of American television, but also shaped the terms of entry and competition in the television industry for decades to come. Charting the commercial fortunes of the competing players in the 1950s' television industry therefore requires an appreciation of federal action (and inaction) going back to the 1930s, especially as it concerned such "merely technical" issues as visual standards and frequency allocations.

Attempts by broadcast historians to organize television programming into coherent chronological segments have largely confirmed the significance of the late 1950s as a transition between distinct television eras. In so doing, however, many historians have uncritically reproduced the critical prejudices of 1950s' partisans of the Golden Age. Due to the specific circumstances in the 1950s, the aesthetic defense of live television was largely elaborated by journalistic critics, who also typically served as general reporters and commentators on the medium, a mingling of roles that led to wishful thinking about the television economy and mistaken predictions about the future of television programming. Few attempts have been made to reexamine the aesthetic and ontological claims these critics proposed in defense of their program preferences.

Unpacking the aesthetic and material contexts for television criticism in the 1950s presents some special problems of historical research. The transient nature of television programming and the loss or inaccessibility of original program material make thorough analysis of specific programs, series, formats, and genres difficult. Likewise, the distinct economic interests involved in prime-time television—producers, sponsors, advertising agencies, and networks—are neither monolithic nor static, resulting in contentious and unstable relations of power within the industry. Similarly, the relations of these participants to other interests inside and outside of broadcasting—affiliates and independent television stations, movie producers and exhibitors, TV equipment manufacturers, federal regulators—are also complex. The difficulty of relating TV's programming changes to its economic history has encouraged a personalist bias in television historiography, where program changes are accounted for by the preferences of specific producers or network leaders. Although such historical constructs as "the Weaver era" or "the Silverman years" may have a broad utility, they obviously assume a great deal about the structures and processes of an industry putatively dominated by such "great men."

This study attempts both a reconsideration of the critical consensus surrounding television's Golden Age and a historical analysis of the economic and regulatory ground upon which such programming briefly flourished in the 1950s. It draws upon the extant primary materials—television programs, business documents, the congressional and regulatory record, the trade press—as well as upon the extensive secondary literature on American television. The historical writing on American television ranges from a handful of synthetic accounts of TV programming to a larger number of specialized works from various social science perspectives. One weakness of American television historiography has been the isolation and mutual impoverishment of these strands.

Most important among the general histories is the work of broadcast historian Erik Barnouw. His three-volume history is broadly conceived, well researched, and properly skeptical. However, Barnouw's reliance upon a resolutely narrative historiographic design and his unabashed critical sympathies with the creators and critics of Golden Age programming make his account of 1950s television occasionally veer into polemic, more a piece of the times than an analysis of them. More recent general histories of American television include those by Christopher Sterling and John Kittross, and Harry Castleman and Walter Podrazik.[2]

The myth of television's Golden Age has been remarkably enduring in television literature, perhaps due in part to the paucity of reference works on the medium's programs and the difficulty of access to the great majority of television's programming past. The shallowness of the reference literature on television authorship reflects and perpetuates the popular image of an anonymous telefilm assembly line churning out undifferentiated programming for network moguls. For example, only a single book, written by two *British* historians, addresses the role of the director in American television. Our knowledge of the circumstances of television production, however, has been strengthened recently by a number of published interviews with production personnel, including works by Richard Levinson and William Link, Irv Broughton, Tony Verna, Horace Newcomb and Dick Adler, and Franklin Schaffner. Sociologist Todd Gitlin's *Inside Prime Time* (1985) also profits from access to a great many industry figures in its account of commercial television in the 1980s. A clearer picture of the production process in television has also emerged through the exhibitions and catalogues of the Museum of Broadcasting, which have addressed specific creative careers, broadcast networks, and production studios in American television. *American History/American Television: Interpreting the Video Past* (1983), with articles by fourteen historians, marked the growing seriousness with which television history is viewed from outside the traditional field of broadcast studies.[3]

Perhaps with even greater effect, various scholars in the field of film studies, addressing issues of authorship, genre and textual analysis, have recently challenged conventional accounts of American television. The valuable standard anthology on television criticism, Horace Newcomb's *Television: The Critical View*, now in its fourth edition, has been challenged and supplemented by more theoretically and textual analysis-based readers. The first of these, the 1983 anthology *Regarding Television: Critical Approaches—An Anthology*, joined historical research with work in feminist and psychoanalytic film theory and signaled the growing interest among film scholars in television studies. Following the increased presence of television studies at cinema conferences and in film journals like *Screen, Cinema Journal, The Quarterly Review of Film Studies,* and *Jump Cut,* several anthologies of television theory by film scholars and others were produced in the mid-1980s, including *Television in Transition: Papers from the First International Television Studies Conference* (1986); *High Theory/Low Culture: Analysing Popular Television and Film* (1986); *Studies in Entertainment: Critical Approaches to Mass Culture* (1986) and *Watching Television* (1986). Signs of the maturing of this interest include *Channels of Discourse: Television and Contemporary Criticism* (1987), containing essays enlisting recent film research in semiotics, narrative theory, psychoanalytic theory, and feminist criticism and John Fiske's likewise synthetic *Television Culture* (1987).[4]

Interest in television studies in Great Britain anticipated and paralleled recent work in the United States. Journals of film theory such as

Screen, Screen Education, and *Framework* (and more recently the journal *Media, Culture and Society*) have published work on television since the early 1970s, and the British Film Institute has published a number of pioneering television monographs, dossiers, and books over the past two decades. These works and others from Britain were crucial in integrating television studies with contemporary research in ideology, semiotics, cultural studies, and historiography and have had a great impact on American writing on television. From another context, the critical anthologies edited by John Hanhardt and Peter D'Agostino, while primarily concerned with artists' video, are both broadly conceived and theoretically inclined, indicating a reconsideration of the traditional boundaries between art-world video and broadcast television.[5]

Cinema-influenced research on specific television genres has also revised traditional ways in which American entertainment television has been conceived. Perhaps because the daytime serial or soap opera has seemed a propitious site for work from cinema and literary studies addressing feminism, textual analysis, and reader-oriented criticism, the genre has received the most sustained scrutiny from the field of film studies. Other recent critical works influenced by film studies, literary criticism, and American studies have examined comedy as a television genre.[6]

The historical analysis of the business of entertainment television has lagged behind that of cinema in the United States, although it has profited from the contributions of economists, political scientists, and legal historians who have turned their attention to specific aspects of the industry. A central concern in this literature has been the relation of federal regulation to economic competition in network television, and case studies and dissertations addressing specific technological innovations, network operators, and historical periods provide valuable insights into the nature of economic change in the industry. Although this specialized work has so far made little contribution to more synthetic histories of American television programming, the renaissance of film history in American academia in the 1970s provides signs of a revitalization of the writing and teaching of television history. Evidence of the increasing sophistication of historical writing on American television brought from film studies can be seen in the work of Douglas Gomery, Robert C. Allen, Nick Browne, Edward Buscombe and others. In addition, the 1980s brought debates over methodology and historiography to center stage within the traditional field of communications, witnessed in the *Journal of Communication* and the founding of a new journal, *Critical Studies in Mass Communication.*[7]

While the recent television scholarship is encouraging, the often-proclaimed importance of television in our daily lives and political culture makes imperative a fuller understanding of how the program forms and social institutions of American television came about. The present volume modestly undertakes part of that enormous task. I have tried not only to provide a detailed account of the economic development of the American television industry through 1960, but also to suggest a context for this tale of critical euphoria and disillusionment. If much of the Golden Age critics' theorizing now seems tendentious and their anti-Hollywood biases constricting, their wider critique of the public service performance of commercial television as the industry was assuming its mature place in American culture remains compelling. Regarding the often-claimed intrinsic virtues of live versus film television drama, for example, I remain agnostic, and likewise skeptical of the unqualified aesthetic superiority of "Studio One" over "The Untouchables," or of a typical Rod Serling script for "Playhouse 90" over one written for "Twilight Zone." Such positions would have been heretical to the powerful New York television critics of the 1950s. In any event, I am less interested in righting their critical prejudices than in uncovering the economic and cultural context for their writing and tracing their own role in the economic and regulatory battles in the early television industry. The larger goal is to suggest that the development of American television, and specifically the era of network hegemony which stretched from the mid 1950s to the mid 1970s, was not "natural" or inevitable, but indeed the result of specific economic and political forces and structures with complex determinants.

NOTES

1. Edward Buscombe, "Thinking It Differently: Television and the Film Industry," *Quarterly Review of Film Studies* 9 (Summer 1984): 197.

2. Erik Barnouw, *The History of Broadcasting in the United States*, vol. 1: *A Tower in Babel* (New York: Oxford University Press, 1966); vol. 2: *The Golden Web* (New York: Oxford University Press, 1968); vol. 3: *The Image Empire* (New York: Oxford University Press, 1970); Christopher Sterling and John Kittross,

Stay Tuned: A Concise History of American Television (Belmont Calif.: Wadsworth Publishing, 1978); Harry Castleman and Walter Podrazik, *Watching TV: Four Decades of American Television* (New York: McGraw-Hill, 1982).

3. Christopher Wicking and Tise Vahimagi, *The American Vein: Directors and Directions in Television* (New York: E. P. Dutton, 1979); Richard Levinson and William Link, *Stay Tuned: An Inside Look at the Making of Prime-Time Television* (New York: St. Martin's Press, 1981); Richard Levinson and William Link, *Off Camera: Conversations with the Makers of Prime-Time Television* (New York: New American Library, 1986); Irv Broughton, *Producers on Producing: The Making of Film and Television* (Jefferson, N.C.: Mcfarland, 1986); Tony Verna, *Live TV: An Inside Look at Directing and Producing* (Boston: Focal Press, 1987); Horace Newcomb and Dick Adler, *The Producer's Medium: Conversations with Creators of American TV* (New York: Oxford University Press, 1983); Franklin Schaffner, *Worthington Miner* (Metuchen N.J.: Directors Guild of America Oral History/Scarecrow Press, 1985); Todd Gitlin, *Inside Prime Time* (New York: Pantheon Books, 1985); Museum of Broadcasting, *Lucille Ball: First Lady of Comedy* (1984); *Rod Serling: Dimensions of Imagination* (1984); *KTLA: West Coast Pioneer* (1985); *Produced by . . . Herb Brodkin* (1985); *Metromedia and the DuMont Legacy* (1985); *Television Syndication: Seminars at the Museum of Broadcasting* (1986); *Columbia Pictures Television: The Studio and the Creative Process* (1987); John E. O'Connor, ed., *American History/American Television: Interpreting the Video Past* (New York: Frederick Ungar, 1983).

4. Horace Newcomb, ed., *Television: The Critical View*, 4th ed. (New York: Oxford University Press, 1987); E. Ann Kaplan, ed., *Regarding Television: Critical Approaches—An Anthology* (Frederick Md.: American Film Institute/University Publications of America, 1983); Phillip Drummond and Richard Paterson, eds., *Television in Transition: Papers from the First International Television Studies Conference* (London: British Film Institute, 1986); Colin MaCCabe, ed., *High Theory/Low Culture: Analysing Popular Television and Film* (Manchester: Manchester University Press, 1986); Tania Modleski, ed., *Studies in Entertainment: Critical Approaches to Mass Culture* (Bloomington: Indiana University Press, 1986); Todd Gitlin, ed., *Watching Television* (New York: Pantheon Books, 1986); Mark Crispin Miller, *Boxed In: The Culture of TV* (Evanston, Ill.: Northwestern University Press, 1988); Robert C. Allen, ed., *Channels of Discourse: Television and Contemporary Criticism* (Chapel Hill: University of North Carolina Press, 1987); John Fiske, *Television Culture* (New York: Methuen, 1987).

5. For examples of the recent British literature on television studies, see Richard Dyer, *BFI Television Monograph 2: Light Entertainment* (London: British Film Institute, 1973); Colin McArthur, *BFI Television Monograph 8:*

Television and History (London: British Film Institute, 1978); John Coughie, ed., *BFI Television Monograph 9: Television: Ideology and Exchange* (London: British Film Institute, 1978); Charlotte Brunsdon and David Morley, *BFI Television Monograph 10: Everyday Television: Nationwide* (London: British Film Institute, 1978); Richard Dyer et al., *BFI Television Monograph 13:* Coronation Street (London: British Film Institute, 1982); David Morley, *BFI Television Monograph 11: The Nationwide Audience: Structure and Decoding* (London: British Film Institute, 1982); Jim Cook, ed., *BFI Dossier 17: Television Sitcom* (London: British Film Institute, 1982); Tony Bennett et al., *Popular Television and Film: A Reader* (London: British Film Institute/Open University Press, 1981); Jane Feuer, Paul Kerr, and Tise Vahimagi, *MTM: "Quality Television"* (London: British Film Institute, 1984); Michael Gurevitch et al., eds., *Culture, Society and the Media* (London: Methuen, 1982); several books on television from the publisher Comedia, including Len Masterman, ed., *Television Mythologies: Stars, Shows and Signs* (London: Comedia Publishing Group/MK Media Press, 1984); Jane Root, *Open the Box* (London: Comedia Publishing Group/Channel Four, 1986); John Fiske and John Hartley, *Reading Television* (London: Methuen, 1978); and John Ellis, *Visible Fictions: Cinema Television Video* (London: Routledge and Kegan Paul, 1982). Recent works on independent video and television include John Hanhardt, ed., *Video Culture: A Critical Investigation* (Rochester, N.Y.: Visual Studies Workshop Press/Peregrine Smith Books, 1986); Peter D'Agostino, ed., *Transmission: Theory and Practice for a New Television Aesthetics* (New York: Tanam Press, 1985).

6. See Robert C. Allen, *Speaking of Soap Operas* (Chapel Hill: University of North Carolina Press, 1985); Ien Ang, *Watching Dallas: Soap Opera and the Melodramatic Imagination* (London: Methuen, 1985); Tania Modleski, *Loving with a Vengeance: Mass-Produced Fantasies for Women* (Hamden Coun. Archon Books, 1982). The works on television comedy include David Marc, *Demographic Vistas: Television in American Culture* (Philadelphia: University of Pennsylvania Press, 1984); David Grote, *The End of Comedy: The Sit-Com and the Comedic Tradition* (Hamden Conn.: Shoestring Press, 1983); Mick Eaton, "Television Situation Comedy," *Screen* 19 (1978): 61-89; Mary Beth Haralovich, "Sitcoms and Suburbs: Positioning the 1950s Homemaker," *Quarterly Review of Film and Video* 11 (1989): 61-84.

7. See the contributions of Gomery and Allen to O'Connor's *American History/American Television* and the special television issue of *Quarterly Review of Film Studies* 9 (Summer 1984), which includes articles by Browne, Buscombe, and Gomery. *Journal of Communication* 33 (Summer 1983); see also Todd Gitlin, "Media Sociology: The Dominant Paradigm," *Theory and Society* 6 (1978): 205-53; Willard D. Rowland, Jr., "Deconstructing American Communications Policy Literature," *Critical Studies in Mass Communication* 1

(December 1984): 423-35; Rowland, "The Siren Song of Broadcasting Research," *Public Telecommunications Review* 3 (1978): 31-35; Rowland, *The Politics of TV Violence* (Beverly Hills: Sage Publications, 1983); Garth Jowett, "The Machine in the Text: Technology in Introductory Mass Communication Texts," *Critical Studies in Mass Communication* 1 (December 1984): 442-46; Robert Schmuhl, "American Communications and American Studies," *Critical Studies in Mass Communication* 2 (June 1985): 185–94.

PART ONE

Setting the Stage
for Commercial Television

Debating Television

The 1950s is generally seen as the formative decade of American television, when the medium moved from its scientific origins to its place as a ubiquitous consumer good, developed its unique program forms and production practices, and discovered its regulatory constraints and commercial potential. The 1950s marked the medium's period of most rapid growth, surpassing even that of radio broadcasting in the 1920s. The 1950s, particularly the second half of the decade, also saw an increasingly acrimonious public debate about the nature of commercial television. The public controversy was accompanied by an impressive accumulation of congressional and regulatory reports, investigations, and rule-makings. Surely this was television's crucial decade.

However, appearances are misleading. The years in which the broadest social choices about TV's application were determined, especially that of commercially supported broadcasting to the private home in the place of other commercial and noncommercial uses, were the 1930s and 1940s. Controversies over technical standards and frequency allocations, economic concentration, and commercial practices—issues over which much industry, legislative, and regulatory ink was spilled in the 1950s—all had roots in struggles and decisions made before 1953. Indeed, despite the prodigious amount of congressional testimony, investigations, and reports, actual legislative action in the 1950s relating to television was insignificant. Likewise, despite study groups, special reports, and extended rule-makings by the Federal Communication

Commission concerning television, few regulatory issues in the industry were recast in the middle and late 1950s. A series of critical social choices defining the applications of television technology—from its broad task of delivering commercially supported entertainment to the private home, to the specific regulatory decisions on visual standards, spectrum allocations, and channel assignments—were all made in the 1930s and 1940s.

The development of commercial television was not technologically determined in the sense of awaiting a specific technical invention or innovation. The history of the commercial exploitation of television is a story of patent battles, corporate strategies, and regulatory decisions rather than one of technological breakthroughs that took industry, government regulators, or the general public by surprise. In this regard, television represents a very different case from that of radio broadcasting in the 1920s. Broadcasting was, as the president of RCA put it, the "surprise party" of radio. But the history of commercial television is the story of the deliberate shepherding of a technological apparatus by powerful established interests in electronic manufacturing and broadcasting. As the vice president of Philco, James H. Carmine, remarked in 1945: "Probably never before has a product of a great new industry been so completely planned and highly developed before it was offered to the public as has television."[1]

What seems unanimous among the competing architects of commercial television was their wish to avoid what they saw as the mistakes of the early radio industry. The newly formed Television Broadcasters Association (TBA) asserted in 1944 that its "prime objective . . . is to avoid any repetition of the errors that marked radio's beginnings in the roaring '20s." In 1950 NBC network head and television pioneer Sylvester (Pat) Weaver argued that "Whereas in radio we had to find our way through hit or miss methods, we now have a pattern we believe will enable us, with great economy, to do a tremendous job in television without too much experimentation."[2]

Particularly disturbing to the leaders of the emerging radio industry in the 1920s had been the large number of amateur and other noncommercial broadcasters, as well as the situation in radio manufacturing, where weak patent and commercial barriers to entry failed to prevent the proliferation of what one RCA official derided as "mushroom manufacturers." Before the 1927 Radio Act helped erect barriers to competing broadcasters, operators of the large commercial radio stations saw the airways crowded with amateur, philanthropic, and publicly supported rivals. The leaders of the nascent television industry were determined to avoid such competition in the new broadcast service. As early as 1928, RCA, in applying for a commercial television license, told the Federal Radio Commission that "only an experienced and responsible organization, such as the Radio Corporation of America, can be depended upon to uphold high standards of service."[3]

The sometimes bitter rivalry between amateurs and early commercial broadcasters in radio provoked an intense debate in the 1920s about the proper social uses of radio broadcasting, a debate which leaders in the emerging television industry did not wish to see repeated in connection with television broadcasting.

It is striking that major researchers in the early development of television did not necessarily have broadcasting as their goal. AT&T invested $250,000 in television research in 1924 in the hope of developing the video telephone; the British experimenter John Baird began a series of television demonstrations in 1926, and many experimenters in England and the United States worked on large-screen television in motion picture theaters. With the exception of theater television, which did receive significant industry attention in the late 1930s and 1940s, alternative, nonbroadcast uses of television did not receive general public recognition or debate after the 1920s.

In contrast to the wide-ranging debates of the 1920s over the social uses of radio, the debate over the applications of, and economic support for, television broadcasting was narrow and muted. Notable exceptions include a 1933 article in *Forum* suggesting a system of pay-per-view or receiver license fees in order to "ensure that the abuse of television for commercial purposes is reduced to a minimum." The broadcast critic Gilbert Seldes, noting the lack of public debate over the uses of television, in 1938 warned that "twenty years from now will be much too late for complaints." Ten years later Bernard Smith in *Harper's* agreed, arguing that "patterns of operation will soon become so rigidly fixed that neither the American people who own the channels nor the Congress which represents us will be able to do very much about it."[4]

As Seldes and Smith feared, reasonable hopes of significant change in the industrial structures of television brought about by congressional or regulatory action had faded by 1950. At the same time that the public debate over the proper role for television was muted, federal regulators were preoccupied with other issues. As the historian Robert Stern noted in 1950, the FCC was so occupied with the technical aspects of television "that there has been little time or attention devoted to questions relating to who should be given the use of television facilities, under what conditions and for what purposes."[5]

The debate over the social uses of television was narrow and timid compared to that which had taken place over radio broadcasting in the 1920s. This is apparent in the differing attitudes toward broadcast advertising in the two media. When AT&T began broadcasting advertisements in 1922, the move provoked protests from listeners, amateur broadcasters, other radio firms, and from Secretary of Commerce Herbert Hoover, who directed broadcast regulation until the Radio Act of 1927. The Federal Radio Commission in its 1928 *Annual Report* reflected the reservations about the use of radio for advertising: "Broadcasting stations are not given these great privileges by the United States government for the primary benefit of advertisers. Such benefit as is derived by advertisers must be incidental and entirely secondary to the interests of the public."[6]

The record of television as an advertising medium is very different. As *Sponsor*, a trade journal for broadcast advertisers, pointed out in 1948: "Radio had been operating all over the nation for years before advertising entered the field. This is not, of course, true with television. Stations have commercials during the first week of operation." There were few serious objections in the popular press to television advertising on the ratio model. Likewise, federal regulators of television never seriously questioned its use of advertising. A 1965 FCC report concluded that since the 1930s the commission took it for granted "[t]hat the basic television structure and the programming provided the American home would be paid for by advertising revenue."[7]

Instead, the debate over television advertising remained concerned with narrower issues of appropriate advertising strategies for the new medium. Proponents of television advertising in the 1930s and early 1940s urged sponsors and broadcasters to adapt radio advertising formats to the new visual service. Other observers, less sanguine about the public's acceptance of televised advertising, pointed to advertisers' repeated failures in attempts to exploit theatrical motion pictures for advertising, either in the form of advertising shorts shown in movie theaters or in direct promotional tie-ins with theatrical features. The sceptics argued that television's aesthetic analogies belonged with motion pictures, and feared the television audience would resent the presence of advertising. A 1942 book on television worried that "the eye, trained by motion pictures, might not tolerate advertising on the screen."[8] Debates about the suitability of television advertising turned on notions of the demands on its audience, and it is telling that speculation on television aesthetics in the 1930s and 1940s was found chiefly in the debates regarding advertising strategy within the commercial trade press, not in the critical community or as part of a general public discussion of the medium.

Philip Kerby, in his 1939 *Victory of Television,* warned potential television advertisers that "Experience gained through radio will be of little avail. . . . In television, it is doubtful if the audience sitting in a semi-darkened room and giving its undivided attention to the screen will tolerate interruptions in the program." Kerby, like Seldes in a 1938 *Atlantic* magazine article, argued for indirect, "goodwill" broadcast advertising for television, where sponsors refrained from interrupting programming with direct sales pitches.[9]

The critical distinction for many observers in the early debates over television advertising was the different demands of television and radio for audience attention. Seldes wrote of television in 1938: "The thing moves, it requires complete attention. You cannot walk away from it, you cannot turn your back on it, and you cannot do anything else except listen while you are looking." Irving Fiske wrote in *Harper's* in 1940 that "Television, like the motion picture or the stage, and unlike the radio, requires complete and unfaltering attention."[10]

Television's unique demands on the attention of the broadcast audience made some observers cautious about the prospect of television taking radio's place in the home. In 1935, RCA Chairman David Sarnoff pointed out:

> Television reception is not, cannot be, like sound reception. Today, radio is used as a background for other entertainment, or by the housewife who . . . listens to the music, while she goes on with her work. Television can never be like that, because not only will it require close attention on the part of the onlooker, but it will also be necessary for the room to be somewhat darkened. . . . [L]isteners . . . instead of roaming around as they do now while enjoying a

program, will have to sit tight and pay close attention to whatever is being thrown on their screen. But will they want to do this? . . . I don't know. . . .[11]

Such fears about the rigors of watching television persisted in industry debates into the 1940s; an article in *Fortune* argued in 1939 that "Considering the necessity for close attention from the viewer, it is doubtful that there will ever be more than a 25 percent coverage of the available audience, except in very special cases." One executive warned a group of industry leaders in 1945 that "It is not yet known how many hours a day people will be interested in watching television."[12]

The debate over the commercial utility of television turned on differing conceptions of the home as an arena for broadcasting and a marketplace for electronic hardware. Those most involved in planning television's commercial development—the electronics manufacturers and the commercial broadcasters—defined television simultaneously as itself a consumer product for the home and as an audio-visual showroom for advertisers' consumer goods. Following the model of the radio industry in the 1920s, RCA and the other major manufacturing and broadcast interests in television aimed their marketing strategies directly at the housewife and the family. One analyst in 1945 cautioned that "retuning a television set is far more difficult than a standard broadcast set. Women may not like the mechanics of television tuning." He also wondered anxiously if "the father of the house would be willing to have the lights turned out in the living room when he wants to read because his children want to watch a television broadcast of no interest to him."[13]

The chief concern of leaders of the new television industry, however, was the challenge of integrating television programming into the routines of the housewife's daily chores just as radio had done. The development of commercial television in the model of radio broadcasting—widespread receiver sales to the private home, programming supported by direct advertising—was seen to depend on the housewife as "household purchasing agent" and target of advertising messages. Given television's special demands on the audience's attention, the central question became, according to Lyndon O. Brown, "the degree to which housewives would drop their housework to watch television during the daytime."[14]

The possible conflict between television's perceptual demands on spectators and its tasks as an object and agent of consumer sales in the home was addressed by CBS in 1945. While acknowledging the problem of "eye fatigue" for television viewers and the fears of some observers that television in the home would disrupt the housewife's routine, CBS pointed out that radio broadcasters had adapted daytime programming to serve as "background activity" to household chores. Granting the special demands on the television viewer, CBS argued: that "television's daytime programs, however, can be constructed so that full attention will not be necessary for their enjoyment. Programs requiring full attention of eye and ear should be scheduled for evening hours when viewers feel entitled to entertainment and relaxation."[15] In more elaborate form, Richard P. McDongh, the manager of NBC's script division, in 1948 called for the replication of radio's daytime programming strategies in the new medium:

> [T]he daytime serial appeals mainly to women, and one of its virtues is that day after day the housewife may agonize with her favorite heroines . . . and yet never miss one lick of her housework. . . . [S]he can work in practically any room in the house and get her entertainment as she works. With television, the appeal is to the eye as well as to the ear. . . . [T]he audience must watch a television play in order to receive full enjoyment. And if the housewife does that for too many hours each day and for too many days each week, the divorce rate may skyrocket, as irate husbands and neglected children begin to register protest. Perhaps the answer will lie in the evolution of a new kind of television drama, a combination of the radio and television forms in which, although visual aids are used, clarifying lines of dialogue would accompany them in order to keep that portion of the audience which is unable to watch the program aware of what is transpiring.[16]

Significant in these trade debates over television advertising is the way in which they echo earlier arguments in the debates over radio in the 1920s. The 1920s' debates over broadcast advertising, however, were part of a larger public forum on the social role and economic basis of broadcasting, where the alternatives of public support, license fee, and philanthropic systems of broadcasting were seriously and widely discussed. On the other hand, discussion in the 1930s and 1940s of the prospects of television advertising was generally confined to tactical arguments within the industry and was not part of a larger public debate over the general social role of television.

Just as CBS called for a reconciliation of television's attention demands with its task as sales agent in the home by constructing programs "so that full attention would not be necessary for their enjoyment," the opposing analogies with radio and motion pictures were realigned to serve the existing broadcast model. The leaders of the broadcasting industry urged potential television advertisers to attend to the aesthetic analogies with motion pictures. An RCA executive told a group of businessmen in 1944: "How can you prepare yourself for the coming of television? I recommend that you begin to study its use right now by examining the methods employed by the motion picture to convey ideas. The motion picture producers are experts in the art of visual selling." A contemporary trade journal told its readers: "Go to the movies; analyze everything you see in the picture, every product, be it dress, real estate, transportation; think of it then as if you were trying to sell it. Study your reactions to the pictures of automobiles, food, women's fashions or men's fishing rods. Does the picture show them persuasively, with sales appeal? If it does, then memorize the particular technique as far as you can."[17]

Where some observers saw a conflict between television's aesthetic and perceptual analogies with motion pictures and its role as sales agent in the home in the radio model, the dominant interests in the new television industry succeeded in linking the two views in an instrumental way. They suggested a synthesis of radio's programming philosophies and merchandising goals with the persuasive tools of Hollywood filmmaking, ensuring that the new medium would not shirk its sales-making responsibilities in the general economy.

The chief alternative to television as advertiser-supported, network-distributed programming to the home in the 1930s and 1940s was large-screen theater television. Irving Fiske argued in *Harper's* in 1940 that "[t]he entire basic premise that television's place is in the home is in itself open to doubt." According to Fiske, "[t]elevision's growth need not depend on the extent to which it finds acceptance in the nation's homes." John R. Kirkpatrick, president of Madison Square Garden, told *Variety* in 1939: "I think the future of television is in the theater and not in the home . . . television will be the biggest boon to the theater that ever happened."[18]

Several Hollywood studios pursued significant research and investment in theater television, an interest that peaked in the late 1940s. Paramount and Twentieth Century-Fox were both part owners in the American Scophony Corporation, whose British counterpart had demonstrated successful theater television on an eighteen-foot screen in London before World War II. Fiske wrote in 1940 that "American theater executives have been encouraged by the British experiments to declare that television, within the next decade, would become a permanent feature in all our motion-picture theaters." An executive of RKO outlined the economic possibilities of theater television in 1944: the United States had 18,000 theaters with 11,700,000 seats (one for every twelve Americans), and the U.S. box office took in six times the total national revenues from radio advertising each year. Fiske argued that with the introduction of theater telvision, "the problem of how television is to be paid for will have quietly solved itself."[19]

RCA was also active in research and promotion of theater television during the 1940s. In 1941, the company projected large-screen television images on a theater screen via a coaxial cable from its studios at Radio City. An RCA brochure announced at the time: "Theater television has great promise. . . . It heralds the linking of playhouses in the nation into television networks that can transform every village theater into a Madison Square Garden or a Metropolitan Opera House."[20]

RCA was involved with two different systems of theater television, the first using electronically produced images projected directly on a large screen and the second using a small electronic monitor and a 16mm film camera and rapid film processor that transfered the television images to conventionally projected 16mm film in ninety seconds. Kodak and DuMont Laboratories also worked on film-based projection systems in the 1940s. Paramount's vice president for television argued in 1948 for the film format for theater television, pointing out that it allowed editing and flexible scheduling, as well as the possibilities of theater networks to distribute film programs.[21]

Theater television also triggered early discussions between the radio-electronics giant RCA and the motion picture studios. An RCA promotional brochure that accompanied its 1941 theater television demonstration reported that "David Sarnoff, looking to the possibilities for cooperation between television and the motion picture industry, foresees each able to stimulate the other, with this resulting in an enlarged service to the public." In 1948, both Twentieth Century-Fox and Warner Brothers were working with RCA on theater television, and in 1949 *Sales Management* reported that Sarnoff had proposed a partnership with MGM's Nicholas Schenck.[22]

The overtures by RCA in the 1940s were apparently not warmly received by the major studios, who were making their own plans and investments in television. *Business Week* wrote in 1945 that "the motion picture industry is squaring off with radio broadcasters for a fight to the finish over television." In 1944, Arthur Levey, president of American Scophony, argued, "We may be witnessing the opening skirmishes in warfare between great corporations for the domination of the giant new industry, television."[23]

By 1952, however, it was clear that theater television was to play only a small role in the application of television technology. The equipping of movie theaters never reached more than 1 percent of the nation's theaters, in part because the FCC refused to authorize exclusive broadcast channels for high-definition theater television use. Theater television operators were faced with either duplicating over-the-air programming available free in private homes or leasing AT&T long lines whose costs were usually prohibitive.

By the early 1950s, the commercial applications of theater television consisted of little more than special business presentations and occasional closed-circuit telecasts of prizefights and other athletic events. Theater television has maintained to the present its marginal relationship to broadcast television.[24]

NOTES

1. Indeed, commercial television had been widely prophesied as "just around the corner" since the late 1920s. For a useful discussion of this period, see Robert H. Stern, "Regulatory Influences upon Television's Development: Early Years Under the Federal Radio Commission," *American Journal of Economics and Sociology* 22 (1963): 347-62; J. G. Harbord, "Commercial Uses of Radio," *Annals of The American Academy of Political and Social Science* 142 supplement (March 1929): 57; Carmine is quoted in Lyndon O. Brown, "What the Public Expects of Television," in *Radio and Business 1945: Proceedings of the First Annual Conference on Radio and Business,* ed. John Gray Peatman (New York: City College of New York, 1945), p. 136.

2. "Television Broadcasters Association," *Television,* Spring 1944, p. 9. In

1944, an executive of the newly formed TBA contrasted the industry's careful plans for television with the earlier radio industry where "stations mushroomed indiscriminately across the nation," and "broke out like a rash." Will Baltin, "Television Chaos Avoided," *Televiser*, Fall 1944, p. 52; Pat Weaver, "Television's Destiny," 1950, p. 5, collection of the NBC Records Administration Library, New York.

3. Pierre Boucheron, "Advertising Radio to the American Public," in *The Radio Industry: The Story of Its Development* (Chicago: A. W. Shaw, 1928), pp. 260-70; RCA is quoted in Robert H. Stern, *The FCC and Television: The Regulatory Process in an Environment of Rapid Technological Innovation* (Ph.D. diss., Harvard University, 1950; New York: Arno Press, 1979), p. 56.

4. T. Coulson, "Is Television Ripe for the Picking?" *Forum*, July 1933, p. 36; Gilbert Seldes, "The 'Errors' of Television," *Atlantic*, May 1937, p. 535; Bernard Smith, "Television—There Ought to be a Law," *Harper's*, September 1948, p. 34.

5. Stern, *The FCC and Television*, p. 5.

6. U.S., Federal Communications Commission, Office of Network Study, *Interim Report: Responsibility for Broadcast Matter* (Washington, D.C.: U.S. Government Printing Office, 1960), p. A19.

7. "Sponsor-Agency-Station: Who Is Responsible for What in TV?," *Sponsor*, January 1948, p. 53; U. S., *Federal Communications Commission, Office of Network Study, Second Interim Report:Television Program Procurement*, Part II (Washington, D.C.: U.S.. Government Printing Office, 1965), p. 157. For a useful discussion of the regulatory context of television before 1934, see Stern, "Regulatory Influences upon Television's Development," pp. 347-62.

8. Orrin E. Dunlap, Jr., *The Future of Television* (New York: Harper and Brothers, 1942), p. 12.

9. Philip Kerby, *The Victory of Television* (New York: Harper and Brothers, 1939), p. 84; Seldes, "The 'Errors' of Television," p. 537.

10. Ibid., p. 535; Irving Fiske, "Where Does Television Belong?," *Harper's*, February 1940, p. 268.

11. Owen P. White, "What's Delaying Television?," *Colliers*, November 30, 1935, p. 11.

12. "Television II: Fade in on Camera One!," *Fortune*, May 1939, p. 162; Brown, "What the Public Expects of Television," p. 136. Orrin E. Dunlap, Jr.'s 1942 book on television concluded: "How telecasters can hope to run a continuous show from from morning until midnight, following the radio pattern, is a puzzle. The logical outlook for the radio set of the future is that it will be a combination radio-television, offering on ultra-short waves a continuous broadcast program and pictures on a more limited schedule." Dunlap, *The Future of Television*, p. 45.

13. Brown, "What the Public Expects of Television," pp. 139, 137.

14. Ibid., p. 137.

15. Columbia Broadcasting System, *Television Audience Research* (1945), pp. 4, 6. *Televiser* magazine in 1944 also predicted that daytime and evening programming would be quite different, with daytime programs designed for intermittent visual attention from its viewers, which were expected to be predominantly women. Norman D. Waters, "Has Daytime Video a Future? Of Course It Has!," *Televiser*, Fall 1944, p. 23.

16. Richard P. McDongh, "Television Writing Problems," in *Television Production Problems*, ed. John F. Royal (New York: McGraw-Hill, 1948), p. 39. For a discussion of the role of the television soundtrack in this regard, see Rick Altman, "Television Sound" in *Television: The Critical View* 4th ed., ed. Horace Newcomb (New York: Oxford University Press, 1987), pp. 566-84.

17. T. F. Joyce, "Television and Post-War Distribution," speech to the Boston Conference on Distribution, October 17, 1944, mimeograph; John Black, "What Television Offers as a Selling Medium," *Printer's Ink*, March 30, 1939, pp. 63-68, quoted in Jeanne Allen, "The Social Matrix of Television: Invention in the United States," in *Regarding Television: Critical Approaches—An Anthology*, ed. E. Ann Kaplan (Frederick, Md.: A.F.I./University Publications of America, 1983), p. 112; the president of NBC in 1940 made similar claims of the merchandising power of Hollywood filmmaking, here in an international context: "Economists have already given the motion picture its due as a stimulant to trade. American movies have sold goods everywhere, because movie audiences, the world over, have learned of the existence of useful commodities by the simple process of seeing them as part of the world on the screen. In similar but even more effective fashion, television can demonstrate the existence and utility of goods in the home, where the visualization of the goods in use can be made most effectively. In a word, television can spread to its audience the knowledge of the utility of commodities." Lenox R. Lohr, *Television Broadcasting: Production, Economics, Technique* (New York: McGraw-Hill, 1940), p. 6.

18. Fiske, "Where Does Television Belong?," p. 267; Kirkpatrick is quoted in "Sports Telecasts Hereafter with Special Eye to the Theater BO," *Variety*, July 26, 1939, p. l, cited in Alan David Larson, "Integration and Attempted Integration Between the Motion-Picture and Television Industries Through 1956," Ph.D. diss., Ohio University, 1979, p. 53.

19. "Box Office's Job," *Business Week*, June 17, 1944, p. 90; Fiske, "Where Does Television Belong?," pp. 268-69.

20. Radio Corporation of America, *Television Progress and Promise* (1941), p. 10.

21. Gilbert Winfield, "The Status of Theater Television," *Television*, February 1946, p. 44; Paul Raibourn, "Theater Television Is Here!," *Television*, April 1948, p. 26. In 1947, engineer Alfred Goldsmith announced that theater television "is on

the verge of rapid technical and commercial development." Alfred Goldsmith, "Theatre Television," *Television*, September 1947, p. 39.

22. RCA, 1941, p.10; "Hollywood Report," *Television*, August 1948, p. 55; Fredric Stuart, "The Effects of Television on the Motion Picture Industry: 1948-1960," in *The American Movie Industry: The Business of Motion Pictures*, ed. Gorham Kindem (Carbondale: Southern Illinois University Press, 1982), pp. 293-94.

23. "Hollywood Digs In," *Business Week*, March 24, 1945, p. 92; Arthur Levey, "Who Will Control Television?," *Television*, Spring 1944, p. 25.

24. For an excellent discussion of the relations of Hollywood and the television industry concerning theater television, see Douglas Gomery, "Theater Television: The Missing Link of Technological Change in the U. S. Motion Picture Industry," *Velvet Light Trap*, no. 21 (Summer 1985): 44-54; also see Gomery, "Failed Opportunities: The Integration of the U. S. Motion Picture and Television Industries," *Quarterly Review of Film Studies* 9 (Summer 1984): 219-28; for an account of Zenith Corporation's involvement with theater television, see Robert V. Bellamy Jr., "Zenith's Phonevision: An Historical Case Study of the First Pay Television System," Ph.D diss., University of Iowa, 1985, pp. 61ff.

2

Regulation of the Early Television Industry

The structures of the 1950s television industry arose not only out of the general debates about economic support for the medium, but also out of a series of specific regulatory decisions by the federal government. Indeed, the FCC rulings on television standards and frequency allocations from 1941 to 1952 were the most important determinants of the economic structure of the subsequent television industry. In particular, the FCC decision to locate television service on the limited very high frequency (VHF) band (channels 2–13) set the terms of television service and network competition in the mature industry. Three economists examining American television in 1974 concluded that "Perhaps the most significant event in the history of television regulation was the creation of an artificial scarcity of VHF licenses. The effect of this policy has been to create a system of powerful vested interests which continue to stand in the path of reform and change—particularly change involving in creased competition and viewer choice."[1]

The regulatory decisions involving television, culminating in the FCC's *Sixth Report and Order* in 1952, played a major role in shaping an industry whose economic structures and routines would remain substantially unchanged for twenty-five years. It was not until the growth of cable television, spurred by satellite distribution in the mid-1970s, and the subsequent proliferation of alternate distribution technologies in the 1980s that the basic rules of prime-time television were challenged. When analyzing the changes that *did* occur in television programming and industry economics in the 1950s, it is important to recognize the enduring forces set up in earlier years.

To a striking degree, the technological and commercial structures of American television are the product of a single company, the Radio Corporation of America. RCA assumed this position not chiefly through its network subsidiary, NBC, but instead through its commanding patent and manufacturing position in radio and television equipment. RCA was created in 1919 as a manufacturing patent pool by the dominant makers of radio equipment; through a series of licensing agreements from 1920–23, RCA controlled virtually all radio manufacturing patents in the United States. A 1923 Federal Trade Commission investigation concluded that the patent and marketing practices of RCA violated antitrust laws, illegally gaining the company a patent monopoly in radio receivers. In 1928, a federal court ruled that RCA had used its radio patents in violation of antitrust laws. Despite specific language in the 1927 Radio Act enjoining violators of antitrust laws from holding broadcast licenses, the Federal Radio Commission voted 3–2 not to invoke sanctions against RCA/NBC, ruling that the antitrust violations resulted from activities in radio manufacturing, not broadcasting, and so were not at issue. Around the same time, a civil case against RCA's patent agreements resulted in consent decrees signed in 1932 and 1935. Despite the decrees, RCA's patent control over basic AM receiver manufacturing patents survived substantially intact; a 1939 RCA publication boasted that "practically all domestic manufacturers of broadcast receivers" operated under RCA licenses.[2]

The patent position of RCA in VHF television was even stronger than the one it enjoyed in AM broadcasting. Television research in the 1920s at Westinghouse, General Electric, and other members of the RCA patent pool was consolidated at RCA in 1927, and the company maintained the largest research staff in television through the 1930s. In 1932, the president of NBC told writer Alfred Dinsdale that when the Radio City complex in New York was completed in 1934 its studios would be designed to accommodate both television and radio. Dinsdale wrote that "It is, therefore, not difficult to deduce that . . . RCA expects television to be in a form acceptable to the public by the time Radio City is ready . . . and . . . that . . . RCA intends to be the prime mover in the development of television . . . and to control it commercially. . . . [3]

Although RCA's early schedule for commercial television proved optimistic, by 1940 it estimated its accumulated research expenditures on television at $10 million. The only major competing patents in VHF television were awarded to independent inventor Philo Farnsworth. Because his patents were indispensable to RCA's own television plans, Farnsworth was able to extract unusual concessions from RCA. In the cross-licensing agreements signed with Farnsworth in 1938, RCA agreed to pay continuing manufacturing royalties, an anathema to the company. RCA's vice president reportedly wiped tears from his eyes as he initialed the agreements.[4]

Despite a 1939 FCC legal staff memorandum that noted that RCA, with the new Farnsworth patent licenses, had acquired complete patent control over VHF television receivers, the commission's standards and allocation decisions of 1941 and 1945 located television service in that part of the spectrum where RCA's patent control was strongest. The FCC's decisions, according to the legal historian Bernard Schwartz, set television standards that "could only be met by equipment manufactured under the RCA and Farnsworth patents. Despite warnings by its patent staff that this could lead to an RCA patent monopoly over television, no patent questions were permitted by the FCC during the proceedings and no testimony whatever was adduced respecting patent control of television equipment under the standards to be promulgated."[5]

Manufacturing profits in postwar television equipment sales were extremely high, especially through the early 1950s. Indeed, it was generally predicted before the war that the only profits to be had in commercial television for a number of years were to be in manufacturing, not broadcasting. RCA itself, announcing its plans in 1938 to unveil commercial television, predicted that television networks would operate in the red for five to ten years. Because of chronic overproduction and price-cutting in postwar radio receiver manufacturing, profit margins on retail television set sales were significantly higher than those in other sectors of the industry. Such manufacturing profits were important to the NBC and DuMont television networks in the first years of network expansion.[6]

In 1947, RCA bought from Farnsworth the rights to sublicense television patents and retain royalties. According to an FCC staff memorandum at the time, "This placed complete patent control in RCA of receivers for black and white transmission of television broadcasting stations pursuant to FCC technical standards. After RCA's purchasing of these sub-licensing rights it soon realized a complete monopoly in the business of licensing others to manufacture and sell broadcasting receivers."[7]

By 1949 RCA had eighty-seven licensing agreements with virtually every domestic manufacturer of television sets; RCA received royalties of 3.5 percent of the wholesale price of all receivers. *Fortune* wrote in September 1948 that "It is difficult to dodge the profane thought that RCA stands to make a pile of money out of the television industry." The rapidly expanding U.S. electronics industry owed much of its spectacular postwar growth to television equipment sales. In 1940, the American electronics industry had $500 million in sales; by 1950, the total was $2.5 billion, $1.35 billion of which represented sales of television receivers. RCA's gross profits in 1950 were four times those of 1940.[8]

If the stakes for RCA were high, the regulatory contests over television standards and frequency allocations frequently pitted the company against most of the other television manufacturers and broadcasters. In the regulatory battles over visual standards and frequency allocations from 1941-52, the chief victor was RCA—as manufacturer, patent holder, network operator, and station owner. The victories in these early years would shape the television industry for a long time to come.

From the late 1920s, the federal government had encouraged experimental, noncommercial television broadcasts while declining to fix technical standards for the number of scanning lines in a television image, the frames-per-second rate, or the synchronization system. Unlike AM radio where a single basic transmission system permits listeners with various types of receivers to receive signals from any sufficiently powerful station, in television, transmitters and receivers must employ identical standards for any coherent image to be received. The prospect of competing and incompatible television systems in the hands of the public convinced the industry and the FCC of the need to establish consistent technical standards for the entire industry. There danger was, however, that premature fixing of technical standards that encouraged significant consumer investment in a particular system would create problems of obsolescence. Therefore, the trade-off debated in the television industry in the 1940s was between the benefits of immediate commercialization under prevailing standards or postponed development of an improved system. The costs and benefits of immediate commercial development of television were not evenly distributed within the industry, however, and the debates over the merely "technical" issues of standards and frequency allocations became signals and instruments of corporate self-interest, and for this reason the debates over such technical issues in the 1940s are a valuable record of economic interests within the television industry at the time.

After the Farnsworth patent agreements of 1938 gave RCA a commanding patent position in television manufacturing, the company began pressing the FCC to set technical standards and allow commercial television broadcasting. At an October 1938 RCA board meeting, David Sarnoff revealed plans to introduce television to the public at the 1939 World's Fair. In the same year the RCA-dominated Radio Manufacturers Association (RMA) proposed a 441-line, AM sound television system to the FCC for approval. In response, the FCC set up a three-member Television Committee to examine technical standards and commercialization. The first report of the committee in 1938 recommended against fixing technical standards and wrote that "considerable patience and understanding must be used at this time" regarding television's commercial development. The second report of the Television Committee in 1939, however, was more sympathetic to the RCA-RMA proposals, noting that "It may be that the time is fast approaching when pioneers must secure a return not only on their huge investment but also must secure remuneration for operating expenses."[9]

Following hearings held the previous month, the FCC in February 1940 voted to allow commercial broadcasting beginning in September, but declined to set technical standards for television. At the time, RCA, DuMont, and Philco were each broadcasting using different and incompatible standards. In approving a "semicommercial" basis for television broadcasting while refusing to set technical standards, the FCC, according to Chairman James Lawrence Fly, "begged the industry to move on in a technical research program. We begged them not to fix the standards, not to let them become frozen." An FCC press release of March 23, 1939 warned that "Television is here to stay but conceivably present-day receivers may for practical purposes be gone tomorrow." The commission's 1939 *Annual Report* explained its decision not to fix standards: "Nothing should be done which would encourage a large public investment in receivers which, by reason of technical advances when ultimately introduced, may become obsolete in a relatively short time. Loss to the public by premature purchase in a rapidly advancing field might in a relatively short period exceed many times the present total cost of research."[10]

Despite the commission's warning against premature public investment in television receivers, RCA seized upon the February 1940 ruling as the starting gun in the race for the commercial exploitation of television. In March, the company launched what Commissioner Fly called a marketing and promotional "blitz-krieg" to sell receivers under the RMA standards the FCC had declined to endorse. RCA cut receiver prices 30 percent, offered liberal credit terms and rebates to owners of existing sets and held sales meetings with 450 large retailers in an effort to boost sales. The company placed full-page advertisements in the New York daily press, promising "Thrilling dramas and plays. Exciting boxing bouts. History making parades. Spot news events . . . thrills, excitement, action," at a time, as Commissioner Fly pointed out, when its television receivers were capable of receiving but a single station, broadcasting two to three hours a day.[11]

The industry was sharply divided over RCA's promotional efforts. *Fortune* wrote in 1943: "By getting off to a fast start and attempting to sell as many television sets as possible, RCA, it appeared to the industry, was grabbing for power and control of television too. RCA . . . felt that its research and leadership naturally gave it that privilege." RCA President Sarnoff had threatened to withdraw from RMA if its Television Committee delayed decisions on standards and commercialization, and a February 1940 letter from RCA to the RMA Television Committee disturbed other members of the trade group. In the letter, RCA argued that since 441-line receivers were already in the hands of consumers, any suggestions for technical changes carried the burden of proving a "substantial improvement."[12] Alarmed by what it viewed as RCA's preemptive move to establish de facto standards, Philco resigned from the RMA panel and the remaining members voted, against RCA and Farnsworth, to reexamine the 441-line standards.

Faced with a divided industry and preemptive moves by RCA, the FCC in March 1940 voted to reconsider its earlier approval of commercial television broadcasting, calling RCA's promotional activities "contrary to the public interest by unduly retarding further research and development" in television. Press response to the new FCC action was stridently critical; the *New York Herald-Tribune* called the commission's move "absurd . . . utterly unsound." Within two weeks three different resolutions critical of the commission were introduced in Congress, and in April 1940 Chairman Fly was called before a hostile Senate Commerce Committee. One senator told the commissioner that the FCC's actions had thrown thousands out of work in the television manufacturing industry and had cost the industry $20 million. Meanwhile, Allen DuMont accused Sarnoff of contradicting his own engineers regarding the expense of adapting the RCA sets to possible improved standards. In his testimony, Sarnoff admitted the possibility that new standards might quickly make the RCA TV receivers useless, but pointed out that in that event consumers would still be left with a fine AM radio receiver as part of the appliance.[13]

In the battle over television standards in 1940-41, RCA lost the opening battle and won the war. At the 1940 Commerce Committee hearings Sarnoff laid out the terms of reconciliation with the FCC: "If Chairman Fly and his commissioners would sit down with the industry, we can forget these technicalities and hearings and lock the engineers and executives up in a room and tell them to stay there until they come out with an agreement."[14]

This closed-door, consensual model of regulatory decision making had been established in broadcasting's earliest days with the National Radio Conferences set up by Commerce Secretary Herbert Hoover before the 1927 Radio Act. Chairman Fly was reportedly under pressure from the White House, which feared that in the upcoming 1940 election campaign the Republicans would charge that the commission was holding up television, and the FCC was eager to demonstrate cooperation with the industry after the spring of 1940. The vehicle selected to replace the discredited RMA television panel, the National Television Standards Committee (NTSC), substantially endorsed the earlier RMA standards, according to Philo Farnsworth.[15] The new NTSC standards, which still substantially govern American television, increased the number of scanning lines to 525 and called for the use of FM sound. The NTSC standards were submitted to the commission in March 1941; in May the FCC approved the standards and set the opening of commercial broadcasting for August 1941.

The television standards approved in 1941 and largely unchanged since do more than define the visual quality of television images. The standards also fix the system of electronic synchronization and the frequency bandwidth for television service. While television engineers and the commission itself have readily admitted the possibilities for improvement of the visual and electronic qualities of the NTSC standards, earlier FCC fears have proven prophetic that any set of standards, once endorsed with large public investment in receivers, would discourage technological improvements in American television. As a consequence of the early FCC endorsement of the NTSC standards and its subsequent reluctance to challenge established investments, U.S. television remains technologically inferior to other international television standards. Relative to radio and other uses of the electromagnetic spectrum, television has an enormous appetite for spectrum space or bandwidth. One trade-off of spectrum space is visual quality; as the number of scanning lines in the image increases (or the number of frames per second increases), the demand for bandwidth also rises. In the 1920s, television experimenters worked in the narrow standard broadcast band with systems of sixty lines or less. It was soon clear that television with acceptable visual quality would have to be moved into the more spacious and less-explored high frequencies. Even so, the allocations the FCC made in 1941 for eighteen channels of NTSC-standard television consumed more than 36 percent of the total usable spectrum. The even higher frequencies, the ultrahigh frequencies (UHF) above 300 megahertz (MHz), were labeled experimental and considered by many engineers in the 1930s to be commercially unusable.[16]

It was in the VHF band below the much larger UHF area of the spectrum that RCA placed its plans for television service. The fiercest and most critical battle in the history of television regulation was fought over whether television should be located in VHF or UHF, or a mixture of both. RCA's interests were clear: its manufacturing patents were not fully operative in the UHF portion of the spectrum. It was RCA's specific patent commitment to VHF television that caused the company to pursue an allocation plan bitterly opposed by much of the rest of the industry.

FM radio was another issue never far from the calculations of RCA and other large radio manufacturers and broadcasters when the battle over television allocations was joined. The broadcast historians Erwin Krasnow and Lawrence Longley summarized the fears provoked by FM broadcasting: "The development of FM posed a triple threat—to the dominance of established AM stations and networks, to RCA's hopes for quick post-War development of television, and to RCA's patents." The power of the two major networks, NBC and CBS, was very strong in AM broadcasting; an estimated 97 percent of the total nighttime broadcasting power in the nation was affiliated with one of the networks by the mid-1930s. The broadcast critic Charles Siepmann wrote in 1946: "Only a miracle, one might say, could save us from the projection of present trends into an indefinite future. But a miracle has happened. Radio has a second chance." The miracle, radio's "second chance," was FM broadcasting. Despite demonstrations by FM's inventor and tireless promoter Edwin Armstrong in 1933 and 1935, the FCC did not authorize commercial FM operation until 1940, when it assigned thirty-five channels from 43-58 MHz to the new service. Despite wartime delays, by 1944 there were forty-seven FM stations on the air and an estimated 500,000 receivers in the hands of listeners. In addition, FM broadcasters had set up high-fidelity, low-cost networks using direct-broadcast relays, eliminating the need for AT&T long lines.[17]

Krasnow and Longley title their account of the subsequent contradictory actions of the FCC in relation to the new radio service "smothering FM with commission kindness," and an understanding of the FCC's puzzling actions depends on an appreciation of the relationship of FM radio to television. As an article in *Fortune* noted in 1943: "There is still a big broadcasting group that seems ready to use television as a counter in corporate strategy to hem in FM in the spectrum to maintain the status quo in radio." In 1940, Paul Porter, then chief counsel for CBS (in 1944 he became chair of the FCC) explained: "If there is to be a conflict, as there appears to be, in the allocation problem with respect to television and FM, it is the opinion of the Columbia Broadcasting System that preference should be given to the new public service of television rather than an additional system of aural broadcasting." The conflict between FM and television was a commercial, not an engineering, one, although some participants sought to obscure their larger interests in the regulatory decisions regarding FM and television. Edwin Armstrong viewed the preemptive television marketing moves of RCA in 1940 as an attempt to foreclose FM radio's location in the spectrum permanently.[18]

In spite of the early success of FM on the low band around fifty MHz, the FCC asked an advisory panel, the Radio Technical Planning Board, to study the merits of shifting FM up to the area around a hundred MHz. In 1944, the board voted 25–1 against the proposed shift, arguing that not only would existing FM equipment be made obsolete at an estimated cost of $75 million to set owners alone, but also that transmitters for the proposed high band were not yet available. Nevertheless, the FCC voted in May 1945 to shift the FM service, depending heavily on the classified wartime testimony of a Signal Corps engineer, K. A. Norton, who argued that tropospheric interference on the existing FM band would harm FM reception. There was scant engineering support for Norton's claims, and no witness argued that FM listeners in the lower band were actually troubled by such interference. In a subsequent hearing at the FCC, Norton was pressed on his 1944 testimony to the commission: "But you were wrong?" "Oh, certainly. I think that can happen frequently to people who make predictions on the basis of partial information. It happens every day."[19] More puzzling than Norton's casualness or the commission's credulity was its subsequent decision to turn over the supposedly unreliable, interference-prone channels first over to television and eventually to police and fire emergency services.

The frequency shift was devastating to FM radio. The higher frequencies prevented the use of direct-relay networks, and the FCC's "single market plan" for FM cut allowable transmitter power by as much as 97 percent, shrinking the FM broadcaster's coverage. Under the regulations FM became an adjunct to the commercially monopolized and technically inferior AM system. Also in 1945, the FCC rescinded a 1940 requirement for two hours a day of original FM programming; in that year, 80 percent of FM applicants were AM station operators, primarily from the same market. It was not until 1961 that the number of FM licensees regained the level of 1948.[20]

In 1949 W. Rupert McLaurin offered a charitable view of the FCC's FM radio actions, arguing that if the FCC "had recognized the future importance of FM, the FM allocation would have been more generous." A 1948 Senate Commerce Committee investigation hinted at other explanations of the FCC's actions. One FCC staff member admitted altering a commission report that refuted Norton's testimony but told the committee he was unable to recollect which superior ordered the changes. Other witnesses recalled that during oral arguments in front of the commission, Armstrong was repeatedly interrupted by Chairman Porter, who at one point broke into Armstrong's testimony with the com-

ment "I do not think it is profitable to discuss it further." Senator Charles
W. Tobey, who led the congressional probe into the FCC's FM policies,
concluded: "The Commission could not stand close inspection for the
last ten years . . . a lot of us here . . . know some of the misalliances that
the Commission has had with certain radio interests. The bit was in their
mouth and they 'geed' and 'hawed' for many in the industry."[21]

The television industry lineup on the issue of the FM allocations shift
presents one striking anomaly. Most manufacturers and AM broadcast
interests favored the shift; FM broadcasters and set manufacturers and
most industry engineers opposed the move. However, reversing its position on the 1940 FCC allocation for FM, RCA, at least in its public pronouncements, joined the FM interests in opposing the shift. The reason
had nothing to do with RCA concern for the health of FM radio and
everything to do with its plans for television. Krasnow and Longley conclude in their account of the regulation of FM radio that "[a]lthough the
FCC's policy was suggested and justified on purely technical grounds,
the potential economic effects were quite clear to most participants,
and, in fact, largely defined involvement in the dispute."As *Telescreen
Century* reported in 1945: "Another consideration not highlighted, but
of no small importance, is the fact that most of the patents useable in the
lower frequencies are privately controlled. Those in the higher frequencies are Government-owned." The privately controlled patents in VHF
television were owned by RCA, and for RCA, the allocation stakes for
television were more compelling than the threat to its interests in AM
radio networking and station operation from competition from FM.[22]

NOTES

1. Bruce Owen, Jack Beebe, and Willard Manning, *Television Economics*
(Lexington, Mass.: D.C. Heath, 1974), p. 12.

2. U.S., Federal Trade Commission, *Report on the Radio Industry*
(Washington, D.C.: U.S. Government Printing Office, 1923; New York: Arno
Press, 1974); Bernard Schwartz, "Antitrust and the FCC: The Problem of Network Dominance," *University of Pennsylvania Law Review* 107 (April 1959):
787-88.

3. Alfred Dinsdale, *First Principles of Television* (London: Chapman and Hall,
1932), p. 228.

4. John M. Kittross, *Television Frequency Allocation Policy in the United States*
(Ph.D. diss., University of Illinois, 1960; New York: Arno Press, 1979), p. 91;

Robert H. Stern, *The FCC and Television: The Regulatory Process in an Environment of Rapid Technological Innovation* (Ph.D. diss., Harvard University, 1950; New York: Arno Press, 1979), p. 114.

5. Schwartz, "Antitrust and the FCC," p. 7.

6. "1939—Television Year," *Business Week*, December 31, 1938, p. 17; CBS around the same time predicted networking losses for up to ten years, when it predicted that set penetration would reach 30 percent of the U.S. population. In his 1944 FCC testimony CBS Vice President Paul Kesten predicted that it would take seven years for CBS's New York station to earn a profit and argued: "Television presents the greatest economic problem ever to face broadcasters. Millions of dollars of profits will be made by equipment manufacturers while millions of dollars of loss are being run up by broadcasters." See Paul Kesten, *Postwar Shortwave, FM, and Television* (New York: Columbia Broadcasting Service, 1944), n.p. Also see W. Rupert McLaurin, *Invention and Innovation in the Radio Industry* (New York: Macmillan, 1949), p. 235; "Television! Boom!," *Fortune*, May 1948, p. 193. The article also points out that many of the original RCA radio patents were expiring at the time.

7. Quoted in Schwartz, "Antitrust and the FCC," p. 788.

8. Material on RCA's stakes in postwar television can be found in "Television I: A Three Million Dollar 'If,'" *Fortune*, April 1939, p. 172; for an account of the RCA stakes in the FCC's color television standards, see Schwartz, "Antitrust and the FCC," pp. 789-92; "RCA's Television," *Fortune*, September 1948, p. 81; Lawrence Lessing, "The Electronics Era," *Fortune*, July 1951, pp. 79-80; Robert C. Bitting, Jr., "Creating an Industry," in *Technical Development of Television*, ed. George Shiers (New York: Arno Press, 1977), p. 1017; also see Eugene Lyons, *David Sarnoff* (New York: Harper and Row, 1966).

9. Kittross, *Television Frequency Allocation*, p. 74; U.S., Federal Communications Commission, *Annual Report* (Washington, D.C.: U.S. Government Printing Office, 1939), p. 46; U.S., Federal Communications Commission, Office of Network Study, *Second Interim Report:Television Program Procurement*, Part II (Washington, D.C.: U.S. Government Printing Office, 1965), p. 147. Also see Kittross, *Television Frequency Allocation*, p. 92, on the shift in the two reports of the Television Committee.

10. U.S. Congress, Senate Committee on Interstate and Foreign Commerce, *Hearings: Development of Television*, 76th Cong., 3d. sess. (Washington, D.C.: U.S. Government Printing Office, 1940), p. 18; the FCC press release is quoted in Orrin E. Dunlap, Jr., *The Future of Television* (New York: Harper and Brothers, 1942), p. 29; U.S., Federal Communications Commission, *Annual Report* (Washington, D.C.: U.S. Government Printing Office, 1940), p. 71.

11. Senate Commerce Committee, *Hearings*, 1940, pp. 10, 18, 22.

12. "The Promise of Television," *Fortune*, August 1943, p. 143; Kittross,

12. "The Promise of Television," *Fortune*, August 1943, p. 143; Kittross, *Television Frequency Allocation*, p. 101; U.S., Federal Communications Commission, *Report and Order No. 65: Setting Television Rules and Regulations for Further Hearing*, Docket no. 5086, May 28, 1940, quoted in Stern, *The FCC and Television*, p. 181.

13. For the commission's rationale, see U.S., Federal Communications Commission, *Annual Report* (Washington, D.C.: U.S. Government Printing Office, 1940), p. 71; the *New York Herald-Tribune* is quoted in *Broadcasting*, April 1, 1940, p. 102; Sarnoff's testimony can be found in Senate Commerce Committee, *Hearings*, 1940, pp. 17, 31.

14. Senate Commerce Committee, *Hearings*, 1940, p. 52.

15. Harry W. Sova, "A Descriptive and Historical Survey of American Television, 1937-1946," Ph.D. diss., Ohio University, 1977, p. 182; George Everson, *The Story of Television: The Life of Philo Farnsworth* (New York: Norton, 1949), pp. 252-53.

16. Stern, *The FCC and Television*, p. 186; Kittross, *Television Frequency Allocation*, p. 90.

17. Erwin G. Krasnow and Lawrence D. Longley, *The Politics of Broadcast Regulation* 2d ed. (New York: St. Martin's Press, 1978), p. 114. Longley has published elsewhere a useful narrative account of the FCC's FM policies in "The FM Shift in 1945," *Journal of Broadcasting* 12 (Fall 1968): 353-65; Charles A. Siepmann, *Radio's Second Chance* (Boston: Little, Brown, 1946), p. 238; Vincent Mosco, *Broadcasting in the United States: Innovative Challenge and Organizational Control* (Norwood N.J.: Ablex Publishing, 1979), p. 55; "Armstrong of Radio," *Fortune*, February 1948, p. 209. FCC Commissioner E. K. Jett pointed out in a speech in 1945 that the service area for FM was larger than for AM broadcasters, see E. K. Jett, "FM," in Columbia Broadcasting System, *Forecasts in FM and Television* (New York: Columbia Broadcasting System, 1945), n.p.

18. "The Promise of Television," *Fortune*, p. 144; Porter is quoted in Longley, "The FM Shift in 1945," p. 360; U.S. Congress, Senate Committee on Interstate and Foreign Commerce, *Progress of FM Radio, Hearings on Certain Changes Involving Development of FM Radio and RCA Patent Policies*, 80th Cong., 2d sess. (Washington, D.C.: U.S. Government Printing Office, 1948), p. 15. See also, U.S. Congress, House Committee on Interstate and Foreign Commerce, *Radio Frequency Modulation, Hearings on H.J. Res. 78*, 80th Cong., 2d sess. (Washington, D.C.: U.S. Government Printing Office, 1948), pp. 10-11; also see Eugene Konecky, *The American Communications Conspiracy* (New York: People's Radio Foundation, 1948), especially chap. 7, "The Spectre of the Spectrum," for a discussion of the AM broadcasters' fears of FM and the results of the FCC's FM radio policies.

19. On the FM rule-making, see Lawrence Lessing, "The Television Freeze," *Fortune*, November 1949, p. 127. See also Armstrong's testimony to the Senate

Commerce Committee, *Hearings*, 1948, p. 72; House Commerce Committee, *Hearings*, 1948, p. 13; see also Don V. Erickson, *Armstrong's Fight for FM Broadcasting: One Man versus Big Business and Bureaucracy* (University: University of Alabama Press, 1973), p. 93.

20. For the 1945 figures, see Mosco, *Broadcasting in the United States*, p. 61; Harvey J. Levin, *The Invisible Resource: Use and Regulation of the Radio Spectrum* (Baltimore: Johns Hopkins University Press, 1971), p. 7.

21. McLaurin, *Invention and Innovation in the Radio Industry*, p. 230; Senate Commerce Committee, *Progress of FM Radio, Hearings*, 1948, pp. 173-76, 338-78; Porter is quoted in U.S., Federal Communications Commission, Docket No. 665, Oral Arguments, June 23, 1945, cited in Senate Commerce Committee, *Hearings*, 1948, p. 349; Ibid., *Hearings*, 1948, p. 367.

22. Krasnow and Longley, *The Politics of Broadcast Regulation*, p. 114; "The FCC Allocation Controversy," *Telescreen Century*, Spring 1945, p. 21.

3

UHF, the Television Freeze, and the Network Monopoly

Pressed by increased spectrum demands by military and other government users during World War II, the FCC began a set of general allocation hearings in 1943, a process that led both to the shift of FM radio and the setting of postwar television allocations in May 1945. The critical issue in the television hearings (and for RCA, in the FM hearings as well) was the role of UHF. As early as 1940, CBS proposed a color sixteen-MHz channel television system, using patents not controlled by RCA. CBS told the commission that by 1941 all manufacturing rights would be available to the industry in a nonrestrictive pool. In its original allocations rulings for commercial television in the VHF band in 1941, the commission urged the industry to experiment with high definition and color television on the much larger UHF band set aside for television experimentation.[1]

The battle over UHF television reached center stage in the allocation hearings of 1943-44. In the fall of 1944, CBS pressed a high-definition black and white system on the UHF band employing 750–1,000 scanning lines. The UHF band offered the possibility of higher-definition monochrome and color broadcasting, both then precluded from the VHF band because of their bandwidth demands; more significantly, it offered the possibility for sufficient numbers of conventional six-MHz channels to support the FCC's goal of a "truly nationwide and competitive service." CBS's motives in proposing its UHF system were not to maximize broadcast (or network) competition through freer market entry in the UHF system. Instead, CBS's sixteen-MHz channels would have allowed only twenty-seven UHF channels versus the eighty-two channels possible UHF under the standard six-MHz bandwidth. CBS Vice President Adrian Murphy told the commission: "I would say that it would be better to have two networks in color" instead of the four or more networks possible with narrower bandwidths in UHF.[2]

The television industry was split on the question of UHF in the 1943–44 allocation hearings. Those with significant interests in VHF manufacturing, patents, and broadcasting—RCA, Farnsworth, General Electric, DuMont—supported the immediate commercial expansion of VHF service and opposed the proposed shift to the uncrowded UHF band. In favor of a complete move to UHF were Zenith, Federal Telephone and Radio (IT&T), Westinghouse, CBS, ABC, and Cowles; this group was considered the "comparative newcomers to television."[3]

It was its calculations over UHF television allocation that lay behind RCA's anomalous public position opposing the FM radio shift at the same time. RCA was certainly not interested in encouraging a rival radio service to its enormous manufacturing, patent, and broadcast interests in AM radio, but it feared the precedent of reallocating any set of existing frequencies. Those arguing the shift of FM radio appreciated the implications of any FCC actions for the future of television. RCA's Vice President and Chief Engineer O. B. Hanson told the Senate Commerce Committee in 1943: "If television *or* FM services should be shifted to a higher portion of the spectrum, the designs based on present allocations would be completely obsolete." RCA took an acute interest in the FM allocation hearings; *Business Week* reported that RCA executives "poured thousands of words into the record, backed up by reams of exhibits, extolling the qualities of television in its present location." RCA told the commission it had spent $15 million on television development and was willing to spend "another $10 million if the Commission will reaffirm its present standards." From RCA's position, engineer K. A. Norton's FCC testimony about the dangers of interference in the FM band around fifty MHz threatened VHF television because it occupied the same area of the spectrum and would presumably be even more vulnerable to such interference. Norton's testimony, according to *Business Week*, was "considered a damaging blow to television in the present radio space ... Norton's data supports [*sic*] the contention of the Columbia Broadcasting System that television should be moved to the ultrahigh frequencies (above 300 mc[megacycles])."[4]

According to *Fortune* in 1946, "up to this time, the proponents of low-frequency [VHF] television had looked at CBS principally as a gadfly. Now they began to view it as a saboteur." The position in favor of immediate commercial expansion on the VHF band, according to an earlier article in *Fortune*, was "supported strongly by the business-sales side of the industry . . . with a strong economic and patent interest in the present area of the spectrum," that is, RCA. Consistent with its position against the FM shift, RCA argued that a shift of television to the UHF band would make existing VHF transmitter and receiving equipment obsolete. In response, CBS, in publicity promoting a shift to UHF, quoted Walter H. Johnson, vice president of Marine Midland Trust, in support of UHF: "True, this policy imposes an immediate penalty on certain big companies who have been out in front in this field, but after all, that is the penalty of leadership and one which, in the long run, I think will be more than recompensed by the following of the program which you sponsor."[5]

Zenith President Eugene F. McDonald supported the CBS position in a May 1944 press release that argued: "Until standards are fixed for a television that is worthy of public support, money paid out for a television receiver is money thrown out a window." CBS executive Paul Kesten told the FCC in the allocations hearing of 1944 what he claimed was "often said behind closed doors, . . . [that the] present television standards are simply not good enough to put television over as a real public service or even as a going enterprise. . . . [A] majority of our independent affiliates do not believe present television pictures are good enough to be viewed for more than one hour without eyestrain, or good enough to sell sets in large quantities. . . ."[6]

Unfortunately for CBS, the only strong supporter of UHF on the commission during the allocation hearings of 1943–44 was Chairman Fly, who resigned in the fall of 1944 before the hearings were completed. The broadcast historian John M. Kittross viewed the 1945 allocation hearings of the FCC as the last chance to move television to the UHF band without enormous problems of obsolescence and resistance from entrenched broadcast interests.[7]

A central argument of RCA and others who supported VHF television was the possible delay entailed in setting up a postwar UHF television system. The premier issue of *Television* in the spring of 1944 noted that the huge defense expenditures of World War II had pushed production in the radio manufacturing industry up 1200 to 1500 percent since April 1942. *Television* continued: "The question now arises what to do with these facilities after the war, for the demands of aural radio alone will not be sufficient to keep many of them going. *Only television offers the promise of sufficient business.*" [8]

An RCA executive in 1944, noting employment in the radio industry of 308,000 people, warned that the market for radio sets could sustain such levels no longer than one year after the end of the war. Meanwhile, proponents of UHF conceded that the shift of television service to the higher band would mean a delay of one to two years. *Television* editorialized in 1944: "Both the government and industry are counting heavily on television to absorb a large number of veterans after the war. How will this be possible if television is delayed for even one year after the peace?"[9] More important, proponents of immediate postwar VHF development could point to the critical role it was widely expected to play in fueling postwar economic growth. Even Chairman Fly, an occasional RCA antagonist, wrote in a 1942 letter: "I think it quite likely that during the postwar period television will be one of the first industries arising to serve as a cushion against unemployment and depression."[10]

Not surprisingly, it was RCA, with its huge investment in VHF television, that most vigorously pushed the economic arguments for the immediate development of television. In the last two years of the war, RCA executives argued the importance of immediate postwar VHF television to businessmen and advertisers. One RCA executive told a group of businessmen in 1944 that "Obviously, the postwar problem is not one of production. . . . It is one of demand and distribution. . . . Television has the power to create consumer demand and buying of goods and services beyond anything we have heretofore known."[11]

Another RCA executive, speaking to a group of advertisers in 1944, elaborated: "We believe that television is the only tool that can increase consumer purchasing of all products to a point that is sufficient to produce a satisfactory national income. . . . Television has the power to create in the minds of the people a greater desire for merchandise than they have for their hoarded cash."[12] RCA was able to enlist in its arguments against UHF television—and its promise of higher-quality and more competitive television—the widespread and potent public, government, and business fears of depressed business activity after the war.

RCA executives also responded to the issue of the possible obsolescence of VHF television; C. B. Jolliffe, formerly the FCC's chief engineer and in 1945 vice president in charge of RCA Laboratories, told a trade group that "The bugaboo of quick obsolescence in television has been over-emphasized. Of course, there will be obsolescence; that is the only way the industry can grow. . . . It isn't characteristic of American enterprise to wait. . . . In America, we like to enjoy a new product or service as soon as it has been developed to a point where we can understand and use it. Then, when it has been refined, it is the custom to replace the old with the new. That is how America developed the greatest economy the world has ever known. And that is how we shall continue to thrive."[13]

In May 1945, the FCC approved a thirteen-channel VHF television system along lines supported by RCA and the other VHF interests. RCA prevailed in its argument that with VHF sets already in the hands of the public the penalties of obsolescence were prohibitive, despite the fact that in 1946 there were still only a hundred thousand receivers, half of them in New York City. At the same time that it reaffirmed the modified VHF allocations, however, the FCC also encouraged continued experimentation in the UHF band with an eye toward the possibility of an eventual shift of the entire television service to the higher band. In its May 1945 decision the FCC wrote:

> The Commission is still of the opinion that there is insufficient spectrum space available below 300 mc to make possible a truly nationwide and competitive system. Such a system, if it is to be developed, must find its lodging higher up in the spectrum where more space exists and where color pictures and superior monochrome pictures can be developed through the use of wider channels. . . . It is obvious from the allocations which the Commission is making for television below 300 mc that in the present state of the art the development of the upper portion of the spectrum is necessary for the establishment of a truly nationwide and competitive television system.[14]

The FCC ruling, with its curious logic approving VHF allocations while admitting their inadequacy, did not end the battle within the industry over television allocations. By approving VHF licenses in the short run while threatening an eventual move to UHF, the FCC's 1945 allocation decision led many prospective VHF broadcasters to hold off while awaiting the fate of color and UHF television. Paul Kesten at CBS greeted the FCC's allocation report as at least a partial victory: "[T]he facts in the FCC report on frequency allocations speak *even more clearly than the comments* which accompany them. These facts strip the advocates of low-frequency, low-definition television of all hope that television will remain at that level."[15]

According to the FCC's *Annual Report* of 1946, 80 of the 158 postwar applications for television stations were subsequently withdrawn by the end of that year. In September 1946, CBS submitted a new proposal for a modified UHF color system, and General Electric began warning purchasers of its VHF sets that the receivers could become obsolete in the near future. Meanwhile, CBS's New York VHF station included the following announcement in every broadcast: "We hope you'll enjoy our programs. CBS, however, is not engaged in the manufacture of television receiving sets and does not want you to consider these broadcasts as an inducement to purchase television sets at this time. Because of a number of conditions, we cannot predict how long this television broadcast schedule will continue." In December 1947 there were still only sixteen stations on the air and 185,000 receivers in the hands of the public.[16]

Ironically, given RCA's earlier calls for immediate postwar television, the industry faced a stalemate while the FCC considered the new CBS petition for a UHF shift. In 1943, *Fortune* had hailed television as "one of the brightest stars in the heaven of the postwar planners . . . the hope and beacon of a great new industry"; in 1946, *Fortune* wrote that the television allocation battle threatened to turn television "into the biggest and costliest flop in U.S. industrial history." The magazine quoted a television executive who complained, "If I had sat down and tried to think of some way to screw up this industry, I couldn't have done a better job than CBS has done." A CBS executive admitted, "We found ourselves in a barrage of abuse" from the rest of the industry, and the actions of CBS were viewed by many in the industry as a cynical device to catch up with its broadcast rival NBC. Former CBS network executive Worthington Miner told Franklin Schaffner in 1985 that it was CBS's intention "to cripple television in order to enhance CBS's position in radio."[17]

NBC reacted to the regulatory and commercial uncertainty with plans to scale back its own investments in television. As O. B. Hanson wrote the NBC chairman in October 1945: "with the threat hanging over our heads of a possible shift to some other portion of the spectrum within three to six years, we must consider very carefully the extent to which we wish to commit ourselves with the present television system."[18]

But change came with a new FCC ruling. The regulatory decision that set off the explosion in television station applications and set sales was the March 1947 FCC rejection of the CBS UHF color proposal. As the 1947 FCC *Annual Report* explained: "The Commission's decision served as a go-ahead signal for the expansion of black and white television service on the basis of present rules and standards in the 13 channels between 44 and 216 mc now allocated for commercial television." The FCC reasoning relied heavily on the costs of VHF receiver obsolescence attendant to a UHF shift, although the same argument had not deterred its 1945 FM reallocation, when the number of sets in the hands of the public was much greater. Also in 1947, the FCC rejected a petition from Edwin Armstrong and other FM broadcasters to restore a portion of its original spectrum allocation, which the commission had assigned to television's channel 1 in 1945. Instead, the FCC assigned the frequencies to emergency services. Within six months of the commission's rejections of the CBS UHF proposals and Armstrong's FM petition, FCC Chairman Charles R. Denny resigned to become an NBC vice president at triple his commission salary. A Washington political weekly described the mood at the commission at the time of Denny's departure: "A case of jitters has settled over the FCC. . . . Substantially the FCC is staffed in important positions by those he selected and who are beholden to him for their jobs. The FCC is following policies largely formulated by Mr. Denny and his appointees. Now he goes to NBC as a Vice-President and General Counsel with a duty to advance the interests of RCA. . . . The utmost care on the part of the FCC and NBC will be required or the whole will burst open with a scandal of major proportions."[19]

RCA was the enormous winner in the FCC allocation decisions not merely through its patent and manufacturing position in VHF television, but also in its ownership and affiliation of VHF stations. NBC was the most aggressive seeker of VHF licenses; since the late 1930s Sarnoff and other RCA officials urged NBC's radio affiliates to acquire VHF licenses. NBC itself was by far the largest chain owner of early television stations. In 1940, the FCC ruled that no television licensee could own more than three stations; in 1944, NBC petitioned the FCC to lift the limit to seven, and in May 1944, the FCC raised the limit to five, at a time when there were only five stations on the air in the entire country. From 1948 to 1953, a *majority* of television stations in the U.S. were NBC affiliates.[20]

Network owned-and-operated stations in large markets were (and are) extremely profitable, and their role was especially significant before 1951, when all the networks were losing money on network operations. The most valuable VHF licenses are those in America's largest cities, and early applicants were often granted licenses without FCC hearings. DuMont and ABC were also aggressive early applicants for big-market VHF licenses. ABC followed a strategy of applying for licenses on the higher-frequency channels (channel 7 and higher), considered technically and economically less desirable, and ABC was thus able to avoid license hearings while assembling a group of owned-and-operated stations in the nation's largest markets. By November 1947, NBC, ABC, and DuMont had all acquired their limit of five stations. CBS, its television hopes riding on the rejected UHF system, owned only one VHF station at the time. The alternative for late-starters like CBS and other non-network chain owners was to apply for VHF licenses in less desirable markets or to "trade up" by buying out existing licensees. All three networks followed this path through the 1950s until each of the networks reached around 20 percent of the U.S. population through its five owned-and-operated stations. Another consequence of CBS's late start in VHF television was the difficulty it had in finding New York program production space, primarily leased Broadway and off-Broadway houses; instead, it was forced to rely more than the other networks on live remotes of sporting events and parades.[21] The costs of losing the UHF allocation battle were felt by CBS in many ways.

The FCC's 1945 allocation table, in addition to allocating television's place in the radio spectrum, also assigned television channels to specific cities or markets. In order to avoid interference, the commission in 1945 mandated geographical separations of eighty-five miles for stations on adjacent television channels and two hundred miles for stations on the same channel. Under the plan, the largest 140 cities were assigned at least one channel: Chicago was assigned five channels, New York City four, Washington and Philadelphia three each. The television industry, recognizing the enormous market potential of the large eastern cities, especially New York, put pressure on the FCC to increase the assignments in the largest markets. In May 1948, the FCC compliantly reduced the adjacent channel separation to seventy-five miles and co-channel separation to 150 miles, as well as reducing the number of low-power community station assignments in New York City from three to one.[22]

In reducing the channel separation, the FCC acted against the recommendations of its own engineering staff. The subsequent Hoover Commission Report on the FCC concluded that "Apparently the engineers were convinced that the Commission was going to place seven stations in New York, and as many stations as possible in other large metropolitan centers, whatever the consequences might be. They either wearied of warning the Commission or just were resigned to the probable futility of pressing the point." In any event, the new separation standards were disastrous; the commission heard testimony that the Cleveland and Detroit stations, for example, interfered with each other within two miles of the Detroit transmitter. In September 1948, six months after its decision to narrow station separations, the FCC—faced with four hundred license applications—announced a temporary freeze on license approvals. As an article in *Fortune* chided: "There is something stupendous about the size and proportions of this boner, likely to go down as the engineering botch of the century." Chronic poor communication between the commissioners and the technical staff was exacerbated in the late 1940s by high FCC turnover; at one point in 1948, only one of the seven commissioners had served before 1946.[23]

The television freeze is much more than an illustration of the commission's technical or administrative weaknesses, however. As broadcast economist Stuart Long argues: "What happened during these four years, particularly to the relative strengths of the four networks, profoundly affected the final structure which would emerge in the industry." A generation later, economist Harvey J. Levin argued that "this so-called television freeze operated inadvertently to entrench the first 108 VHF stations with the choicest network and advertising affiliations and has left an impact on industry structure and performance felt almost to this day."[24] The FCC freeze gave a windfall to early VHF station owners and to the two dominant networks, CBS and NBC, at the expense of their weaker competitors, ABC and DuMont.

The term *freeze* is misleading. Although the commission suspended license approvals from September 1948 through April 1952, the number of VHF stations on the air grew from 50 to 108, the number of television sets rose from 1,200,000 to 15,000,000, the percentage of homes with television increased from .4 percent to 34 percent, and television's share of broadcast advertising leaped from 3 percent to 70 percent. As historian Vincent Mosco argues, what was frozen as a result of the FCC's action was not the expansion of the television industry but the ability of the commission to make policy outside the formidable pressures of entrenched VHF television interests. With sales of televisions running at 410,000 sets a month, manufacturers of VHF receivers were not unduly concerned by the freeze, and the two dominant networks, NBC and CBS, had an interest in prolonging the freeze.[25]

The licensing freeze was originally invoked to repair the faulty assignment plan, a task expected to last only six to nine months, but in late 1948 the FCC announced its intention to reexamine the issue of color television. The commission's hearings on color television extended over eighteen months and dragged on in the courts for three years; Allen DuMont maintained that the entire color issue was a CBS red herring designed to prolong the freeze to the advantage of the two dominant networks.[26]

And the freeze did benefit them. According to the economist Barry Litman, the FCC freeze "assured CBS and NBC of an almost impregnable position in television much like the one they had achieved in radio." The dominance of the two networks during the freeze is striking: of the 63 markets served by 108 stations during the freeze, forty markets were served by a single station, eleven by two stations, eight by three stations, and only three by four or more stations. As DuMont told the FCC: "The freeze reserved to two networks the almost exclusive right to broadcast in all but twelve of the sixty-three markets which had television service." In 1948, Mutual, Philco, and Paramount dropped earlier announced plans to operate television networks, and the effects of the freeze were nearly fatal to both ABC and DuMont, pushing the two into continuing and escalating losses in network operations.[27]

The FCC's freeze on station licensing and its continued commitment to the inadequate VHF band, more than any factor of economics or regulation, brought about the restricted competitive structure of network television. In 1954, DuMont quoted 1949 CBS testimony: "It is quite possible that the Commission's allocation plan will as a matter of political necessity permit the development during the critical formative years of only two full nationwide competing networks." Litman concluded that "The Commission knew that powerful networks were inevitable in television, just as they had been in radio; yet it chose policies creating a limited number of powerful stations which would eventually mean a very few powerful networks."[28]

During the freeze, there were signals from a minority at the FCC that a shift to an all-UHF system was still under consideration. The possibility of a move to UHF terrified existing VHF station owners, the two dominant networks, and set manufacturers. RCA engineer Alfred Goldsmith in 1948 objected strongly to discussions of the various UHF proposals: "nor should they even be publicized until that point of definite proof of their usefulness has been reached. Above all, such untried ideas should not become the subject of long and sometimes unhelpful hearings in Washington." Jolliffe told the Senate Commerce Committee in 1948: "There appear to be some who would block the progress of television with charges which misrepresent the purpose and leadership of RCA and NBC in bringing television to the American people. One of these misrepresentations is the assertion that all television should be moved into the higher frequencies. Let us make no mistake about this. If such a move were made at this time, it would not mean more television. It would mean no television at all." The tone of RCA's warning was matched in a 1950 editorial in *Television*, which called on the industry to "strike out against the menace of socialism which is steadily creeping into every phase of our economic life. . . . When men like Commissioner Jones and Commissioner Johnson can talk in terms of 'vested interests' and 'profits for the few,' we have, right in the open, the kind of thinking that can ruin our country. The very basis for free enterprise is profits."[29]

Less threatening than a shift of the entire television service to the UHF band were proposals to create all-VHF or all-UHF local markets instead of intermixing VHF and UHF stations within a given area. These intermixed markets handicapped UHF competitors against the entrenched VHF operators in the same area. In 1948, DuMont presented a complex assignment plan that would have created high-power regional VHF stations, providing at least five VHF stations in the top fifty markets in order to permit at least four national networks. Smaller markets were to be assigned UHF stations. The commission responded to this and other DuMont plans involving wide-coverage regional VHF stations (the only way to allow wide network competition within the restricted VHF band) with statements expressing the FCC's commitment to localism in broadcast licensing.[30]

Other FCC actions during the freeze also hurt the fledgling DuMont and ABC networks. AT&T's time charges for network interconnection, a monopoly granted to the telephone company by the FCC, discriminated against the smaller networks. AT&T charged a flat mileage rate, regardless of the number of affiliates connected; moreover, the rates for one hour per day were almost as high as those for eight hours a day. Finally, AT&T forced television coaxial cable users to rent additional *radio* long lines, discriminating against DuMont, which had no radio network operation. DuMont and ABC protested AT&T's television policies to the FCC, which regulated AT&T's long-line charges, but the commission took no action. The result was that financially marginal DuMont was spending as much in long-line charges as CBS or NBC while using only about 10 to 15 percent of the time and mileage of either larger network.[31]

The television freeze was ended in April 1952 with the FCC's *Sixth Report and Order*, which generally maintained existing VHF assignments and opened a large number of UHF channels, the great majority of which were assigned in intermixed markets, where VHF licenses were also assigned. Not surprisingly, RCA's reaction was favorable, calling the *Sixth Report and Order* "a large distillate of wisdom and sound principle." The *Sixth Report and Order* was optimistic about the economic future of UHF stations in the intermixed markets, and the commission in the 1950s consistently placed its hopes for diversity and competition in network broadcasting in the development of UHF. Douglas W. Webbink, a broadcast economist and later adviser to the FCC, called the commission's optimism regarding UHF an "illusion." The economists Roger Noll, Merton Peck, and John McGowan's 1973 *Economic Aspects of Television Regulation* questioned the sincerity of the FCC's faith in UHF's eventual parity with VHF service: "Such a belief seems entirely without foundation. . . ."[32]

The two dissenting commissioners to the *Sixth Report and Order* had no illusions about the economic problems facing UHF operators. Commissioner Robert F. Jones in his dissent wrote that UHF station owners "had better study astronomy to figure their balance sheets and buy lots of red ink." Jones later explained: "The allocation plan was designed to cause the least disruption to the existing channel assignments of these pre-freeze licensees . . . and gave each licensee a tremendous windfall."[33]

Under the 1952 allocation table, only seven cities received assignments of four or more VHF stations. At the same time, UHF operators in intermixed markets found it difficult to survive against their entrenched VHF competitors. The reasons were circular: UHF stations in intermixed markets were unable to attract network and advertising affiliations given the low penetration of UHF-equipped receivers; without advertising revenues and popular network programming, UHF operators were unsuccessful in attracting viewers or convincing the public to purchase UHF receivers. Of the 1,319 UHF assignments provided in the *Sixth Report and Order,* by 1956 only 363 construction permits had been applied for and approved by the FCC; of these, moreover, 151 never went on the air and an additional 56 stations went bankrupt. In the same period, by contrast, only 4 of 276 post-freeze VHF stations went off the air. Without the marginal and financially precarious UHF stations, a third network depending on VHF outlets could at best reach only thirty-three of the top one hundred markets in the United States, and a fourth network only seven.[34]

The grim situation of many UHF station owners in the 1950s led to intermittent congressional pressure on the FCC to do something about the "UHF problem." Less extreme than proposals to shift television entirely to UHF were various proposals for "selective de-intermixture," that is, creating local markets of either all-VHF or all-UHF stations. The experience of UHF operators in cities without VHF competition proved that UHF was viable if viewers had incentive to purchase UHF sets and networks and sponsors reason to affiliate with UHF broadcasters. In 1953, Senator John Bricker began a Commerce Committee investigation sharply critical of network practices, culminating in a report entitled *The Network Monopoly.* Established VHF station owners and the two dominant networks responded sharply to congressional criticism. *Television* warned that "Insiders agree that action must be taken quickly, before the plight of marginal UHF operators inspires measures that can harm the whole industry." Elsewhere in the same issue the magazine editorialized sternly: "That many UHF stations will fold is a foregone conclusion, and has been ever since the FCC decided to allocate U and V stations within the same markets. Half of the UHF operators should not have gone on the air in the first place."[35]

Between 1953 and 1960, the FCC announced several plans for the de-intermixture of thirteen markets, reversed itself, and eventually carried out limited reassignments in only five markets. Congressman Emanuel Celler, chair of the House Judiciary Committee, who led a long investigation of monopoly problems in the television industry, concluded in 1957 that "The inherent difficulty of correcting the original allocations error which gave rise to the present UHF crisis has been aggravated by regulatory uncertainty, vacillation and lack of leadership." In his dissertation on television allocation policy, Kittross entitled his chapter on FCC television regulation from 1952–59, "Inequality Compounded," and it is clear that by the early 1950s the FCC was unwilling to mount any course of action that would seriously threaten the interests of the entrenched VHF television industry.[36]

Escalating UHF station losses and low sales of UHF television sets in intermixed markets continued through the 1950s, until the percentage of UHF-capable sets manufactured declined to 5.5 percent in 1961. In that year, President Kennedy's new FCC chair, Newton Minow, began to speak more assertively of de-intermixture. The eventual "solution" to the UHF problem negotiated by the industry with Congress and the commission in exchange for relief from threats of de-intermixture was federal intervention in the market for television receivers, requiring manufacturers to equip all television sets with UHF tuners. Webbink estimated the costs to consumers of the 1961 All Channel Receiver Act at $100 million a year, in his view an inefficient form of subsidy to UHF operators. In spite of the All Channel Act, UHF operator losses continued to mount, while most UHF assignments remained unused. It is clear despite the wishful thinking of the FCC regarding UHF television that the economic irrationalities of the 1952 *Sixth Report and Order* were never completely overcome.[37]

The final element of the television industry's mature structure is the three-firm oligopolistic network structure set up by the demise of the DuMont Television Network in 1955. Until 1951, every television network, including NBC and CBS, lost money on network operations, as distinct from owned-and-operated stations. The first years of television networking required large sums of capital difficult to generate solely from advertising revenue. NBC and CBS could draw upon the enormous accumulated and continuing revenues from their AM network operations and owned-and-operated radio stations. NBC and DuMont could also draw from the high-profits gained from electronic manufacturing during the war and television equipment manufacturing through the early 1950s. DuMont, however, was always seriously undercapitalized compared to its larger network competitors. In 1938, after deciding against a large public stock offering, DuMont exchanged 29 percent ownership for a line of credit from Paramount Pictures. The deal with Paramount probably hindered as much as helped DuMont's television plans. Allen DuMont claimed Paramount never put significant amounts of money into DuMont after 1940, and Paramount's own plans for television often worked against DuMont's interests. For example, Paramount itself acquired television stations in Los Angeles and Chicago, and the FCC in 1953 held (against DuMont's protests and the judgement of the FCC hearing officer) that Paramount's interest in DuMont was controlling; therefore DuMont was limited to three owned-and-operated stations. Paramount's checkered antitrust history also probably hurt DuMont in license hearings.[38]

By the early 1950s, the previous super-profits in television manufacturing were disappearing under the pressures of price-cutting and overproduction. DuMont increasingly depended on revenues from its owned-and-operated stations to cover the losses of its network operation. By 1951, half of the network's revenues were coming from two shows, "Captain Video" and "Cavalcade of Stars."[39] In 1954, DuMont sold its Pittsburgh station to Westinghouse for $9,750,000, and the following year it ceased network operations.

The demise of DuMont Television Network was due principally to the allocation and assignment policies of the FCC in its *Sixth Report and Order*, which simply did not permit national competition of four major networks. The final blow to DuMont, however, was the 1953 FCC approval of the ABC-United Paramount Theatres (UPT) merger. As Long argued, "This decision in effect sacrificed the DuMont network in order that at least ABC might survive and prosper to offset the obvious dominance which NBC and CBS had gained in the industry during the freeze years."[40] ABC's merger with UPT brought the network an infusion of $30 million and new leadership under UPT executive Leonard

Goldenson. By the second half of the 1950s, in fact, it was the programming strategies and procurement practices of ABC as developed by Goldenson that provided the model for the rest of the television industry.

The television industry's structure attained its mature form during the mid-1950s, and it remained relatively unchanged for the next two decades.[41] By 1953, approximately 50 percent of total television revenues and 45 percent of industry profits went to the networks. Despite the tremendous increase in the number of television stations after the freeze, the networks' share of television profits and revenues did not greatly change through the next twenty years. The general continuities in the structure of television industry in the 1950s, however, should not obscure the economic shifts that *did* occur during the decade and which brought with them thoroughgoing and traumatic changes in primetime programming.

NOTES

1. Richard W. Hubbell, *Four Thousand Years of Television* (New York: G. P. Putnam and Sons, 1942), pp. 151-52.

2. "Television—A Case of War Neurosis," *Fortune,* February 1946, p. 107; Mildred Steffens, "Postwar Television," *Telescreen,* September 1945, p. 11; FCC, *In the Matter of Petition for CBS Inc. for Changes in Rules and Standards Concerning Television Broadcast Stations,* Hearing Record, Docket 7896, vol. 1, March 18, 1947, p. 27; quoted in Robert H. Stern, *The FCC and Television: The Regulatory Process in an Environment of Rapid Technological Innovation* (Ph.D. diss., Harvard University, 1950; New York: Arno Press, 1979), p. 290.

3. "A Case of War Neurosis," p. 107; for RCA's explanation for its position against the FM shift, see U.S. Congress, House Committee on Interstate and Foreign Commerce, *Radio Frequency Modulation, Hearings on H.J. Res. 78,* 80th Cong., 2d sess. (Washington, D.C.: U.S. Government Printing Office, 1948), pp. 250-51.

4. U.S. Congress, Senate Committee on Interstate and Foreign Commerce, *Hearings on S814 to Amend the Communications Act of 1934,* 78th Cong., 1st sess. (Washington, D.C.: U.S. Government Printing Office, 1943), p. 495, quoted in Stern, *The FCC and Television,* p. 257, emphasis added. "Backing for CBS," *Business Week,* November 4, 1944, p. 88.

5. "A Case of War Neurosis," p. 246; also see an editorial in the opening issue of *Television* magazine: "Television is now entering its most important period— the final planning stage. It is in this period that there must be full cooperation

among the many varied interests." *Television*, Spring 1944, p. 1; "The Promise of
Television," *Fortune*, August 1943, p. 200; Columbia Broadcasting System, *Is
Pre-War Television Good Enough?* (New York: Columbia Broadcasting System,
[1945?]), n.p.

6. Eugene F. McDonald, "The Present Television Controversy," May 16,
1944, quoted in Robert W. Bellamy, "Zenith's Phonevision: An Historical Case
Study of the First Pay Television System," Ph.D. diss., University of Iowa, 1985,
p. 42; Paul Kesten, *Postwar Shortwave, FM, and Television* (New York: Columbia
Broadcasting Service, 1944), n.p.

7. John M. Kittross, *Television Frequency Allocation Policy in the United States*
(Ph.D. diss., University of Illinois, 1960; New York: Arno Press, 1979), pp. 115,
148; see also, "Fly Urges Video in High Frequencies," *Broadcasting*, September
25, 1944, p. 13.

8. "Television—A Test Case for Free Enterprise," *Television*, Spring 1944, p.
36, emphasis in original.

9. T. F. Joyce, "Television and Post-War Distribution," speech to the Boston
Conference on Distribution, October 17, 1944, mimeograph, n.p.; "A Test Case
for Free Enterprise," Spring 1944, p. 4. The editorial warned of the delay of the
shift to UHF: "The very future of television would hang in the balance. There
would be no mass employment in this much 'counted-on' industry. . . . This delay
could conceivably affect our entire post-War economic picture" (pp. 4-5). For
discussion of the delay involved in CBS's UHF system, see "The Promise of
Television," p. 200, Steffens, "Postwar Television," p. 30.

10. In the 1930s, AM radio had grown into a critical advertising medium and
mover of consumer goods. The broadcast critic Gilbert Seldes pointed out in
1937 that "the commerce of America now rests in part on radio advertising; as
businessmen themselves say, their factories are 'geared' to a level production
which would inevitably fall off if the power of radio advertising diminishes."
"The 'Errors' of Television," *Atlantic*, May 1937, p. 533; Fly's letter is reprinted
in Hubbell, *Four Thousand Years*, p. 219.

11. "Television and Post-War Distribution," n.p.

13. C. B. Jolliffe, "An Engineer's Report on Television," speech to the Radio
Executives Club of New York, November 15, 1945, pp. 12, 13, 14.

14. Quoted in Stern, *The FCC and Television*, p. 268.

15. "The FCC Allocation Controversy," *Telescreen Century*, Spring 1945, p.
21, emphasis in original.

16. U.S., Federal Communications Commission, *Annual Report* (Washington,
D.C.: U.S. Government Printing Office, 1946), p. 17; "A Case of War Neurosis,"
p. 250; CBS is quoted in Leo Burnett, Inc., *Report Number 2: Progress of Television: Where the Industry Stands Today Viewed as an Advertising Medium*, July

1946, n.p., collection of the NBC Records Administration Library, New York; Stern, *The FCC and Television,* p. 249.

17. "The Promise of Television," p. 141; "A Case of War Neurosis," pp. 104, 250; CBS Executive Vice President Paul Kesten's FCC testimony is reprinted in Kesten, *Postwar Shortwave,* n.p.; Franklin Schaffner, *Worthington Miner* (Metuchen, N.J.: Directors Guild of America Oral History/Scarecrow Press, 1985), p. 179; also see the account of CBS's chief engineer, Peter Goldmark, on the network's color television plans in Peter C. Goldmark with Lee Edson, *Maverick Inventor: My Turbulent Years at CBS* (New York: Saturday Review Press/E. P. Dutton, 1973), pp. 84-124.

18. O. B. Hanson to Frank E. Mullen, "The Position of NBC in the Present Television Controversy," October 24, 1945, p. 1, collection of the NBC Records Administration Library, New York.

19. U.S., Federal Communications Commission, *Annual Report* (Washington, D.C.: U.S. Government Printing Office, 1947), p. 24; Kittross, *Television Frequency Allocation,* p. 182; *Capitol Radio Reporter,* October 18, 1947, quoted in Don V. Erickson, *Armstrong's Fight for FM Broadcasting: One Man versus Big Business and Bureaucracy* (University: University of Alabama Press, 1973), p. 115. See also the Hoover Commission's Staff Report on the FCC, which concluded: "The Commission seems to have confused private interests with the public interest" and found evidence of "the possibility that some members of the Commission staff have sought to curry favor with the industry in order to obtain more lucrative positions," quoted in Lawrence Lessing, "The Television Freeze," *Fortune,* November 1949, p. 126. For a useful historical analysis of FCC appointments in the period, see U.S. Congress, Senate, Committee on Interstate and Foreign Commerce, *Appointments to the Regulatory Commission: The FCC and the FTC, 1949-79,* James M. Graham and Victor H. Kramer, Committee Print, 94th Cong., 2d sess. (Washington, D.C.: U.S. Government Printing Office, 1976).

20. Gary Newton Hess, *An Historical Study of the DuMont Television Network* (Ph.D. diss., Northwestern University, 1960; New York: Arno Press, 1979), p. 57; Herbert H. Howard, *Multiple Ownership in Television Broadcasting: Historical Development and Selected Case Studies* (Ph.D. diss., Ohio University, 1973; New York: Arno Press, 1979), p. 38; Christopher H. Sterling and Timothy R. Haight, *The Mass Media: Aspen Institute Guide to Communication Industry Trends* (New York: Praeger Publishers, 1978), p. 53.

21. Sterling Quinlan, *Inside ABC* (New York: Hastings House, 1979), p. 4; Hess, *An Historical Study,* p. 53; for a discussion of the economics of constructing versus acquiring a television station, see "High Stakes in a Big Giveaway," *Business Week,* March 22, 1952, pp. 21-22. For an account of a controversial sta-

tion swap of Westinghouse's Philadelphia station with NBC's owned-and-operated station in Cleveland, approved without a hearing by the FCC, successfully challenged by the Justice Department, and restored ten years later, see Bernard Schwartz, "Antitrust and the FCC: The Problem of Network Dominance," *University of Pennsylvania Law Review* 107 (April 1959): 756-72; Roscoe L. Barrow, "Antitrust and the Regulated Industry: Promoting Competition in Broadcasting," *Duke Law Journal*, September 1964, pp. 292-93; and Howard, *Multiple Ownership*, pp. 61-63; for a discussion of CBS's early problems, see "Television Boom!," *Fortune*, May 1948, p. 193.

22. Stern, *The FCC and Television*, p. 277.

23. Ibid., pp. 277, 297, 360; Lessing, "The Television Freeze," p. 124.

24. Stuart Lewis Long, *The Development of the Television Network Oligopoly* (Ph.D. diss., University of Illinois, 1974; New York: Arno Press, 1979), p. 74; Harvey J. Levin, *The Invisible Resource: Use and Regulation of the Radio Spectrum* (Baltimore: Johns Hopkins University Press, 1971), p. 342.

25. Long, *The Development*, p. 85; Vincent Mosco, *Broadcasting in the United States: Innovative Challenge and Organizational Control* (Norwood, N.J.: Ablex Publishing, 1979), p. 74.

26. Kittross, *Television Frequency Allocation*, p. 207; for an excellent and thoroughly researched account of the CBS color proposals, see Bradley Chisholm, "The CBS Color Television Venture: A Study in Failed Innovation in the Broadcasting Industry," Ph.D. diss., University of Wisconsin-Madison, 1987.

27. Barry Russell Litman, *The Vertical Structure of the Television Broadcasting Industry: The Coalescence of Power* (East Lansing: Michigan State University Press, 1979), p. 22; information on network affiliation is found in Long, *The Development*, p. 82; Long quotes DuMont (p. 83), and discusses the effects of the freeze on would-be network operators (p. 57). Ironically, ABC survived only through the profits from its extremely valuable large-market VHF stations, whose profits were considerably enhanced by the station scarcity enforced by the freeze.

28. For DuMont's testimony, see U.S. Congress, Senate Committee on Interstate and Foreign Commerce, *Status of UHF and Multiple Ownership of Television Stations*, 83rd Cong., 2d sess. (Washington, D.C.: U.S. Government Printing Office, 1954), pp. 228-29, cited in Hess, *An Historical Study*, p. 175; Litman, *The Vertical Structure*, p. 21. Lawrence Lessing wrote that "The restrictive very highs [frequencies] have been conducive from the start to monopolistic tendencies—the same tight arrangement as in AM radio, with about the same number of national networks, controlled by about the same corporations— the FCC's new proposals seem to strengthen everywhere the status quo," "The Television Freeze," p. 164.

29. Alfred Goldsmith, "Stability vs. Chaos," *Television,* October 1948, p. 24; U.S. Congress, Senate Committee on Interstate and Foreign Commerce, *Progress of FM Radio, Hearings on Certain Changes Involving Development of FM Radio and RCA Patent Policies,* 80th Cong., 2d sess. (Washington, D.C.: U.S. Government Printing Office, 1948), p. 42. Asked if he expected that television services would ever be moved to the UHF band, Jolliffe replied, "I doubt if they ever will be, sir" (p. 72); F. A. Kugel, "Threat to Our Economy," *Television,* February 1950, p. 11.

30. Hess, *An Historical Study,* p. 156; On the FCC's inconsistent use of the criterion of localism in broadcast licensing, see Roger C. Noll, Merton J. Peck, and John McGowan, *Economic Aspects of Television Regulation* (Washington, D.C.: Brookings Institution, 1973) and Nicholas Johnson and Kenneth Cox, *Broadcasting in America and the FCC's License Renewal Process: An Oklahoma Case Study* (Washington, D.C.: Federal Communication Commission, 1968).

31. Hess, *An Historical Study,* p. 140. The Barrow Commission's *Network Broadcasting* report for the FCC (U.S. Cong., House Committee on Interstate and Foreign Commerce, *Report,* 85th Cong., 2d sess., 1958) concluded: "The AT&T service changes are, therefore, a substantial barrier to gradual entrance to the network industry" (p. 203).

32. RCA's reaction is quoted in Douglas W. Webbink, "The Darkened Channels: UHF Television and the FCC," *Harvard Law Review* 78 (June 1962): 1585. Webbink's characterization is found on p. 1593. For the text of the FCC's *Sixth Report and Order,* see U.S. Congress, House, Committee on the Judiciary. *Monopoly Problems in the Regulated Industries, Hearings, before the Subcommittee on Antitrust,* 84th Cong., 2d sess.(Washington, D.C.: U.S. Government Printing Office, 1956), pp. 3785-808; Noll, Peck, and McGowan, *Economic Aspects,* p. 96.

33. Commissioner Jones is quoted in Kittross, *Television Frequency Allocation,* p. 294. Kittross concludes: "It is difficult to see how the majority of the Commission could have arrived at its optimistic conclusions on the future of the ultra-high frequencies" (p. 295); Robert F. Jones to *Harvard Law Review,* October 20, 1961, quoted in Webbink, "Darkened Channels," p. 1582.

34. Hess, *An Historical Study,* pp. 170, 173.

35. *Television,* September 1954, p. 8; "The UHF Dilemma," *Television,* September 1954, p. 27.

36. For a discussion of FCC UHF policy in the 1950s, see Erwin G. Krasnow and Lawrence D. Longley, *The Politics of Broadcast Regulation,* 2d ed. (New York: St. Martin's Press, 1978), pp. 118-26; Emanuel Celler, "Antitrust Problems in the Television Broadcasting Industry," *Law and Contemporary Problems* 22 (Autumn 1957): 554; Kittross, *Television Frequency Allocation,* p. 286.

37. Krasnow and Longley, *The Politics of Broadcast Regulation*, pp. 119, 121; also see Douglas W. Webbink, "The Impact of UHF Promotion: The All-Channel Television Receiver Law," *Law and Contemporary Problems* 34 (Summer 1969): 545, 552-53.

38. Hess, *An Historical Study*, pp. 33, 105; George Bauer, *Government Regulation of Television* (New York: New York University Graduate School of Public Administration, 1956), p. 44. On DuMont's troubles with, and on account of, Paramount, see Hess, *An Historical Study*, pp. 89-128.

39. Hess, *An Historical Study*, p. 202.

40. Long, *The Development*, p. 101.

41. Ibid.

PART TWO

The Television Industry in the Early 1950s

4

Early Film Programming
in Television

The most basic questions about television—the formats and aesthetic forms of programs, the responsibility for program production, the structures of distribution and sponsorship—were subject to both aesthetic speculation and commercial conflict in the first half-decade of the medium. If by the mid-1950s critics spoke with increasing assurance of the fundamental artistic strengths of the medium, it was due in part to their sense of growing prosperity and stability in the television industry. By the end of the decade, however, the critics' hopes for a harmony of aesthetics and market forces in commercial television had turned into a cynicism characteristic of more contemporary attitudes toward television. An understanding of the current precarious position of television in American intellectual life would profit from an appreciation of the earlier hopes of critics of television, as well as the historical reasons for the unmaking of those hopes.

The early years of television witnessed considerable speculation about the appropriate forms and sources of television programming, speculation informed by wider social and cultural attitudes toward contemporary culture and business life. Like the early debates over television advertising, many of the arguments over the appropriate forms of television programming, especially between live and film programming, were poised between the competing models of radio and the motion pictures. John Western wrote in the *Public Opinion Quarterly* in 1939: "About the only point on which program authorities are in agreement is the belief that film will fill a major portion of telecasting hours. Estimates range from forty to more than ninety percent."[1]

Parallel to the contemporary trade debates over television advertising, some commentators argued that the situation of the television audience in the private home made full-length theatrical films unsuitable for television. C. J. Hylander and Robert Hardy, Jr., in the 1941 *Introduction to Television* argued that television and motion pictures dealt with essentially different products because the television audience could not be expected to stay at home for long programs. Western agreed, arguing that "Most critics of television programs agree that the one-hour dramatic program is too long for in-the-home entertainment."[2]

There was also early concern that the economics of advertiser-supported television broadcasting to the home could not support the program costs of Hollywood-style film entertainment. Bernard Smith in *Harper's* in 1948 offered some possible consolation for such fears: "People will look at and listen to television programs for the same reason that they now listen to the radio: the television set is placed where it will form a part of the living habits of the American people. They will accept a much poorer level of entertainment in their own homes than they will demand if they have to leave the house or apartment to attend a public performance."[3]

Notwithstanding such hopes for diminished expectations on the part of the television audience, many observers believed that the per-minute program costs of even low-budget Hollywood material would be too expensive for the television market. A 1940 book on television argued that "The expense to be faced is almost terrifying. Translated into terms of running time on the screen, a motion-picture play may cost from $1,000 to $35,000 a minute, with $1,000 representing about the worst that the public will tolerate. If we are to have every day a new television comedy and tragedy lasting an hour and a half, the studio incurs an outlay that dwarfs anything with which producers are familiar."[4]

NBC President Lenox R. Lohr voiced similar fears in 1940: "any plan for recording programs with standard movie-studio techniques and equipment appears doomed to failure, since the figures indicate that the hope of bringing costs within practical limits is rather remote. If, by new methods, costs could be cut to even one-tenth their present amount, they would still be excessive for television purposes until a very large audience had been built up." A private research report on television in 1948 endorsed the common belief that programs should be limited to thirty minutes in length, argued that television's intimacy precluded both feature films and full-length theatrical works, and predicted that television would revive vaudeville and variety formats.[5]

Another problem foreseen in film programs for television was the expectation that the reuse of film material would have limited audience appeal and commercial value. Western wrote that "Rarely does a moviegoer see a film more than once. There is no reason to believe that the looker will consent to see a telecine transmission more frequently. Afterwards, the film must be relegated to the vaults." Lohr shared similar doubts over the viability of film reruns, arguing in 1940: "It appears to be inadvisable to broadcast most programs more than once. On the second broadcast, the audience is likely to become hypercritical and to lose interest."[6]

Traditional historical accounts need to be revised that suggest a mutual lack of interest and collaboration between the film industry and the television networks in the early years of the TV industry. Despite doubts about the viability of either feature films or original film programming in the early years of the medium, the major Hollywood studios followed events in the television industry very closely. Beginning in the late 1930s, motion picture studios became active in television research and manufacturing and made significant investments in television production companies, broadcasting stations, and networks. In the 1940s, Paramount, Twentieth Century-Fox, and Warner Brothers were active in the development of theater television. As early as 1936, Warner Brothers bought a 65 percent interest in Trans-American Television and Broadcasting Company, a production firm. By 1944, Paramount owned and operated television stations in Los Angeles and Chicago; controlled a theater-television firm, American Scophony; held a 29 percent interest in the DuMont Television Network; and controlled significant patents on the television cathode-ray tube. Paramount executive Paul Raibourn sat on the boards of Scophony and DuMont Television Network. By 1951, Paramount was syndicating film and live programs from its Los Angeles station to forty-three stations.[7]

Several major studios expressed interest in producing original material for television in the 1940s, at the same time RCA was showing its interest in producing or purchasing film material for the medium. The radio manufacturer, eager to consolidate its interests in VHF television to discourage the threatened shift of television to the UHF band, approached the major studios in the mid-1940s for production commitments. In 1944, Arthur Levey, president of American Scophony, wrote that RCA warned that studios that did not enter productions deals would be cut out of the market when the network made its own arrangements. Levey called for studio unity in the face of what he saw as an RCA attempt to play one producer against another, arguing that Hollywood was in a strong bargaining position with its experience in visual communication, its control of talent and story material, and the potential of more than six thousand movie theaters available for conversion to theater television. In December 1944, *Television* magazine reported that RCA was looking for telefilm production deals with major studios, and that the company warned it would turn to independent producers if frustrated.[8]

Several studios in the 1940s declared an interest in producing programming for television. In 1944, the head of RKO Television Corporation told *Television* that his firm was interested not only in theater television, but also in producing and packaging material for broadcast television. In 1948, *Fortune* reported that RKO was "ready to produce film for television as soon as sponsors and agencies decide what they want." George Shupert, director of commercial television development for Paramount, in August 1949 saw "a new Klondike" for telefilm producers.[9]

There clearly was a market for film programming in the early years of television. For the new station operator, film programming was attractive not only because it was cheap to acquire but also because it required few technical facilities and personnel compared to live programming. "Some new stations do seventy-five percent or more of their programming on film," William I. Kaufman and Robert C. Colodzin reported in 1950. Furthermore, as Shupert noted, film represented the only medium with which to reach all forty-seven television markets, less than half of which were served with coaxial cable.[10]

While both Columbia Pictures and Universal-International set up subsidiary telefilm production units in the early 1950s, most of the television plans of the major studios remained unrealized. Some of the problems for the studios resulted from actions of the FCC. Because the advertising revenues in the early years of television were too small to support original production by the major Hollywood studios, and were less than the value of theatrical rerelease of existing features, the studios investigated the alternate means of exploitation of theater television and pay television. In these two services the FCC consistently moved against the studio interests, refusing allocations or assignments for either service throughout the 1950s. Paramount, one of the studios moving most aggressively into television, held out the longest for the alternative systems, in the meantime withholding talent and material from broadcast television. In the spring of 1950, the FCC issued a warning to the Hollywood motion picture studios against withholding product and talent from broadcast television, in what motion picture exhibitors denounced as "a bullying statement."[11]

The studios had reasons to be cautious about supplying programming for the new medium in addition to the still-unfavorable economics of television program fees. Although the first of the federal antitrust consent decrees separating the major Hollywood studios from their theater chains was signed by Paramount in 1948, divorcement at all the studios was not completed until 1959; in the meantime, the still-integrated companies feared injury to their exhibition business by release of their feature films to television or by a precipitous move to telefilm production. At the same time, threats of theater owners to boycott the theatrical product of studios that moved too emphatically into television inhibited some producers; the telefilm units of both Columbia and Universal-International, for example, used casts and crews separate from theatrical production in part to insulate the studio from such reprisals.[12]

These constraints on the major Hollywood studios did not deter smaller independent producers from entering the telefilm business. Independent producers William Pine and William Thomas set up a telefilm company, Telecom Incorporated, in 1944. In 1946, *Television* reported "new companies forming every day" to supply television stations. In 1948, the largest packager and syndicator of radio programs in the country, Frederick W. Ziv, entered telefilm production, and Jerry Fairbanks, Jr. became the first Hollywood producer to make a series sale to television with "The Public Prosecutor" to NBC. By 1951, "hundreds" of new firms were producing telefilms, led by independents such as Fairbanks, Hal Roach, Jr., Walter Wagner, and Bing Crosby Productions. These independent producers either packaged existing features films for television ("Hopalong Cassidy" was an early success) or produced original material for television (such as the telefilm series "Roy Rogers"). The sound stages and backlots of Hollywood's "Poverty Row" of B-film production companies and some of the major studios were rented out to independent telefilm producers. In spite of this activity, in 1952 there were only twelve substantial telefilm companies, among them Crosby, Fairbanks, Roach, Motion-Picture TV Center, Flying-A Production (Roy Rogers), General Service Studios, and Frank Wisbar Productions.[13]

Producing telefilm was an unstable business with special challenges facing early participants. The television networks were regarded as hostile to film programming, fearing it would loosen the network's arrangements with sponsors and affiliates by encouraging station managers to make independent deals with advertisers and film producers. Because networks controlled the most valuable prime-time positions available for programming, syndicators of independent telefilms had to settle for fewer markets and less desirable time periods, both of which meant much smaller advertising revenues and license fees compared with network-supplied programming. Furthermore, distribution costs in placing telefilm programs in independent stations were high, requiring a national sales force with the attendant imperative of supplying enough product to obtain efficiencies of scale. Telefilm producers also complained that advertising agencies were hostile to film programming; as *Newsweek* explained: "Television had after all grown up in New York in the care of executives who neither knew nor cared about film techniques, an ignorance encouraged by advertising men unwilling to shift East Coast power to Hollywood and dubious of receiving their fifteen percent cut on shows turned out by movie magnates."[14]

Commercial banks, accustomed to dealing with theatrical motion picture producers, were reluctant to lend to independent telefilm producers; not until 1952 were commercial banks willing to discuss telefilm financing, according to *Television*. The field was also very competitive: in 1951, *The Saturday Evening Post* pointed to a pool of two hundred unpurchased pilots produced for $10,000 each. *Time* in 1954 wrote that of five hundred telefilm firms recently established in Hollywood, only forty-six survived and only six made substantial profits. In 1951, *Television* warned that it was difficult for independent producers to make a telefilm series sale without at least thirteen completed episodes; in

1952, it reported that some sponsors demanded twenty-six episodes in the can, requiring a speculative investment by the producer of $500,000. Finally, without a network sale, producers could not expect to recoup their investment in less than two or three years.[15]

Few feature films of any vintage from the major studios were available to television before 1955, and the available American theatrical films tended to be low-budget and from minor studios. Another reason feature films were held in low esteem in early television is suggested in a 1950 *Sponsor* article, "How to Use TV Films Effectively," which advised station managers and sponsors how to edit feature films for television use: "Far from ruining a picture, expert editing can make it even better for TV. Obviously, twenty-five minutes hacked indiscriminately from any film will leave viewers confused and annoyed. How do you snip out thirty percent of a carefully made product and have it make sense? First eliminate all dark scenes that won't show up on a TV tube, and then all the long shots in which distant objects get lost."[16]

There was also criticism within Hollywood of much of the early film programming for television. In 1952, *Newsweek* quoted Fairbanks's complaints about the gold-rush atmosphere of the telefilm industry where "everyone who could buy or borrow a little drugstore movie camera announced himself as a TV-Film producer." The magazine went on the describe the scene in Hollywood:

> Movie actors financed "pilot" shows which paraded their aging charms—and which got no closer to the small screen than an advertising agency's shipping room. Assistant directors and senior office boys from the movie studios made the transcontinental trek to New York, carrying bags full of scripts and shooting schedules and announced they were "Hollywood producers. . . . " [T]he Hollywood hills became littered with dead and dying telefilm creators. Some of the casualties were long-time motion-picture executives temporarily "at liberty" who announced that they were available to bring their tremendous "know-how" into TV films, "just for the experience." One guess on the number of pilot films turned out in Hollywood: 2,000.[17]

Sponsor magazine wrote in 1953 of the unhappy experiences of many advertising agencies that came to Hollywood for early television film programs: "These top agencies somehow got the idea that they had bought what constituted Hollywood. . . . They found out that what they had bought in the main were a lot of out of work producers, directors, and writers—not the real genius that had made Hollywood a world byword in entertainment."[18]

Faced with the speculative investment and slow payback of telefilm production, most producers specialized in the low-budget, mostly action-adventure genres, including the Western, crime and mystery, science-fiction, and situation comedy. With a few exceptions, anthology drama, which was becoming an increasingly important part of the networks' live programming from New York in the early 1950s, was not represented in Hollywood telefilm. Frederick Ziv explained the reasoning behind his launch of "The Cisco Kid," the first television series sold by his company: "It was obvious to all of us who had our fingers on the pulse of the American public that they wanted escapist entertainment. . . . We did not do highbrow material. We did material that would appeal to the broadest segment of the public. And they became the big purchasers of television sets. And as they bought television sets, the beer sponsors began to go on television. And the beer sponsors, for the most part, wanted to reach the truck and taxi driver, the average man and woman. They were not interested in that small segment that wanted opera, ballet or symphony."[19]

Furthermore, the small budgets of independently syndicated telefilms were modest even by the standards of Poverty Row studios. *Business Week*, in a 1951 article, "Hollywood Cameras Grind Out Film Fare for TV," described the routine at Louis B. Snader's Telescriptions studios: sixty-minute films were completed on shooting schedules of one and one-half to three days; thirty-minute telefilms reached TV stations five days after shooting was completed; and single performers would shoot seven short television films in a morning and five more in an afternoon of a single day. Roach's telefilm studios by 1954 were consuming more film stock than MGM, Twentieth Century-Fox, and Warner Brothers studios combined, with a highly rationalized production process and a staff of thirty writers: "It's like the auto business," Roach told *Time*. Ziv recalled that "In the early days of television, we had to produce these things cheap. There's just no question about it, and cheap is the word. Not inexpensive, but cheap."[20]

Given these financial constraints and management attitudes, it was little wonder among most television critics of the early 1950s that film programs in general enjoyed a poor reputation compared to network-supplied live programs. Schedules of early television stations, both network affiliates and independents, contained a good deal of both kinds of programming. Researcher George Bauer wrote that for the typical independent station, even in a large television market, "[a]bout sixty percent of its programs are on film which are cheaper than live shows and which it shows up to six times each." Kaufman and Colodzin complained of the role of film programming in most program schedules: "Most of the feature films presently shown seem to have been scraped from the cutting room or dragged unwilling from their musty cinema tombs. They range in quality from mediocre to extremely bad. They have, however, the unquestionable attraction of being cheap."[21]

The comparison of film versus live program formats became the central element in the highly prescriptive critical discourse of television's Golden Age. Critics seized on weaknesses of the cheap, genre-based thirty-minute telefilms, comparing them to the big-budget sixty-minute network spectaculars and dramas to support claims of television as an essentially live medium. The aesthetic opposition of film and live programming in the writings of television critics in the 1950s inevitably mingled with more general attitudes toward the motion picture industry, New York versus California as production centers, the value of differing dramatic styles, and arguments over television's freedom from commercial censorship. A common thread through the positions of most prominent critics on these issues was the role of the television networks in safeguarding artistic quality in the medium.

As widely reported in the trade press, the television networks were publicly cool to film programming in the early 1950s, fearful that affiliates would make independent deals with producers of film programming and sell time directly to sponsors, cutting out the network entirely. The self-interest on the part of the networks was often cloaked in the endemic anti-Hollywood rhetoric of the time. In 1956, Bauer cited "early network exponents of live television" who argued: "When Hollywood gets its hands on anything, mediocrity immediately reigns. The Hollywood touch. . . . " *Time* magazine in 1954 quoted NBC Vice President John K. West on film programming: "Keep it the hell off the networks."[22]

Radio and film actress Lucille Ball was approached by CBS to develop a comedy series for the 1951 television season, and when Ball insisted on doing the series on film, the network sold back its interest in the idea to the actress.[23] CBS Vice President Harry Ackerman explained the network's attitude: "We are primarily in the live TV business. We definitely wanted to shoot 'I Love Lucy' live. But the sponsor made us go to film. You can say that we went into the film business at the whim of the sponsor."[24]

In *The History of Broadcasting in the United States,* Erik Barnouw wrote that in 1953 "in spite of 'I Love Lucy,' the dominance of live production was expected to continue. David Sarnoff of RCA was said to be determined that it should; so was William Paley of CBS." The defense of live drama by the leaders of CBS and NBC was undoubtedly encouraging to those critics who argued for the special place of live drama in television. In a 1952 *New York Times* article, "A Plea for Live Video," Jack Gould, probably 1950s' television's most influential daily critic, wrote at length against the use of Hollywood telefilm by the networks: "The decision of television to put many of its programs on film has turned out to be the colossal boner of the year. On every count— technically and qualitatively—the films cannot compare with 'live' shows and they are hurting video, not helping it. . . . There is simply no substitute for the intangible excitement and sense of anticipation that is inherent in the performance that takes place at the moment one is watching. . . . To regard the medium as merely a variation on the neighborhood picture house is to misunderstand the medium." Gould called the growing use of film in network schedules "a step backwards," and denounced the "dog-eared films that Hollywood is turning out for television, the pedestrian little half-hour quickies that are cluttering up the facilities of even the best of networks."[25]

The opposition between live and film programming was often couched in network versus Hollywood terms by critics and by the networks themselves. As Gilbert Seldes wrote in the *New York Times Magazine* in 1956, "It is ungrateful to bring up such things, but the lack of pungent characters, of the excitement of discovery, all trace back to the principle of playing it safe by imitating whatever has been successful. This is the cynical method of Hollywood, which did more than television to keep the people away from movie houses." Television writer Rod Serling spoke for many writers and critics when he argued in 1957:

> It is . . . unquestionable that in the golden days of live television's ascendancy its filmed counterparts on the West Coast were pretty much uninspired, formulated, hackneyed assembly-line products that could boast fast production and fast profit, but little strain in the cre-

ative process. Whatever memorable television moments exist were contributed by live shows. Whatever techniques were developed that were television's own are live techniques. Whatever preoccupation there was with quality and with the endless struggle against sponsors' dicta, fears and endless interference existed in New York and Chicago—not in Los Angeles.[26]

Serling's language was echoed in private and public statements by network executives. The *New Yorker* quoted a 1953 memorandum from the head of NBC, Pat Weaver, to his programming staff: "movies and radio point the horrible path that looms before us. . . . The conformity and carbon copy boys are hard at work. This is not satisfactory. Television must be the shining center of the home."[27]

The networks' anti-Hollywood rhetoric reached a peak in 1955-56 in response to complaints from telefilm producers and others that network treatment of affiliates and advertisers had the effect of unfairly discriminating against independent program producers. In hearings before the Senate Commerce Committee, network representatives presented the issue as one of defending television programming from the corrupting influence of Hollywood. An NBC submission argued that the independent program producers in fact represented a lobby of Hollywood film interests eager to unload a flood of telefilms and features on television:

> It was the networks which developed the facilities and skills and undertook the financial risks of building a national television service—not the film-come-latelys or the promoters with Hollywood backlogs in their portfolios. While the networks were chalking up annual losses of millions of dollars to develop the new medium, the film interests withheld their product from it, and turned to television only after it had been built by others. [If network commercial practices were restricted] the accumulated product in Hollywood's vaults—most of it musty and out-dated—would hit television with the impact of a tidal wave. The American public would literally drown in a celluloid sea.[28]

By the mid-1950s, however, the anti-film rhetoric of the networks was seriously at odds with their own programming practices, by then less a statement of principled program philosophy than a handy public shield against competitive and regulatory threats. In any event, the networks in the mid-1950s found it useful to enlist the rhetoric of critical defenders of live television for their own commercial battles. The informal alliance of the early and mid-1950s between television critics and the major networks helped set the tone of public discussion of the medium in the age of live drama. The dissolution of the alliance in the second half of the decade provoked bitterness and recriminations in a critical community that felt betrayed by a medium and its commercial leaders.

The opposition of the Hollywood telefilm with the networks' live programs was only one element in the critics' hierarchy of dramatic programming of the early 1950s. The complex criteria—live versus film, the drama of character versus that of plot, an aesthetic of theatrical naturalism versus Hollywood genre and spectacle, anthology versus continuing character series, sixty-minute versus thirty-minute programs, the television writer as legitimate playwright versus motion picture studio employee—all operated to reinforce the opposition between the networks and Hollywood. The critics' prescriptive hierarchies were argued simultaneously as products of inductive practical criticism and of deductive reasoning following from the fundamental aesthetic strengths and demands of the television medium. Together, the two forms of argument produced widely held and sharply defined assertions about television's proper program forms, assertions that defined artistic achievement in the Golden Age of television.

NOTES

1. John Western, "Television Girds for Battle," *Public Opinion Quarterly* 3 (October 1939): 557. Philip Kerby, in his 1939 *Victory of Television* (New York: Harper and Brothers, 1939) predicted that radio-style networks would not be economically feasible in television because of the prohibitive expense of telephone long lines. Instead, he predicted, "telestars" would tour the nation to perform on local live television shows, and the bulk of programming would be circulated on film, making television the largest consumer of Hollywood film (p. 58). Radio inventor Lee DeForest in *Television Today and Tomorrow* (New York: Dial Press, 1942) likewise argued that high interconnection costs made it doubtful that permanent national television networks would ever be feasible and foresaw instead a market of syndicated film programs, chiefly produced by Hollywood (p. 36).

2. C. J. Hylander and Robert Harding, Jr., *An Introduction to Television* (New York: Macmillan, 1941), p. 201; Western, "Television Girds for Battle," p. 559.

3. Bernard B. Smith, "Television—There Ought to Be a Law," *Harper's*, September 1948, p. 37.

4. "1939—Television Year," *Business Week*, December 31, 1938, p. 27; the president of NBC, Merlin Aylesworth, told *Broadcasting* in 1936: "Television will never be a competitor to the regular screen. They will not televise feature pictures produced expressly for the purpose of a single television broadcast because of the enormous sums required for production. Imagine any advertiser spending $500,000 to broadcast a production of 'Little Women'!," Merlin Aylesworth, "Radio Is Movies' Best Friend," *Broadcasting*, August 1, 1936, p. 9, cited in Alan David Larson, "Integration and Attempted Integration Between the Motion-Picture and Television Industries Through 1956," Ph.D. diss., Ohio University, 1979, p. 130; John Porterfield and Kay Reynolds, eds., *We Present Television* (New York: W. W. Norton, 1940), p. 29.

5. Lenox R. Lohr, *Television Broadcasting: Production, Economics, Technique* (New York: McGraw-Hill, 1940), p. 101; Curtis Publishing Company, *The Television Industry* (Philadelphia: Curtis Publishing, 1948), p. 23. In 1948, *Fortune* expressed skepticism that Hollywood filmmaking would ever be viable for television, arguing that quality films would remain prohibitively costly. "Television! Boom!" *Fortune*, May 1948, p. 197.

6. Western, "Television Girds for Battle," p. 558; Lohr, *Television Broadcasting*, p. 5.

7. For a discussion of early involvement of the motion-picture industry in television, see "1939—Television Year," p. 30; Douglas Gomery, "Failed Opportunities: The Integration of the U.S. Motion Picture and Television Industries," *Quarterly Review of Film Studies* 9 (Summer 1983): 219-28; "Box Office's Job," *Business Week*, June 17, 1944, p. 94; "California as a Program Source," *Television*, April 1951, p. 38; William Lafferty, "Television Film and Hollywood: The Beginnings," in *Columbia Pictures Television: The Studio and the Creative Process* (New York: Museum of Broadcasting, 1987), pp. 7-15.

8. Arthur Levey, "Who Will Control Television?," *Television*, Spring 1944, pp. 25-26; complicating negotiations over telefilm production was the jockeying over theater television between RCA and the motion picture industry. "What About Hollywood?," *Television*, December 1944, p. 5.

9. "Box Office's Job," p. 94; "Television! Boom!" p. 196; George Shupert, "Film for Television," *Television*, August 1949, p. 22.

10. William I. Kaufman and Robert S. Colodzin, *Your Career in Television* (New York: Merlin Press, 1950), p. 41; Shupert, "Film for Television," p. 22.

11. Milton MacKaye, "The Big Brawl: Hollywood vs. Television," *The Saturday Evening Post*, January 26, 1952, part 2, p. 121.

12. Amy Schnapper, "The Distribution of Theatrical Feature Films to Televi-

sion," Ph.D. diss., University of Wisconsin-Madison, 1975, p. 25; MacKaye, "The Big Brawl," part 2, p. 121.

13. For a discussion of the role of independent telefilm producers in early television, see Stanley R. Lane, "Films as a Source of Programming," *Television*, May 1946, p. 14; "California as a Program Source," p. 38; Frederick Kugel, "The Economics of Film," *Television*, July 1951, p. 45; "Film vs. Live Shows," *Time*, March 29, 1954, p. 77; MacKaye, "The Big Brawl," part 2, p. 119. For an account of conditions in the early telefilm industry from the president of a production firm, see Everett Crosby, "Film Package Syndication for Television," in Irving Settel and Norman Glenn, *Television Advertising and Production Handbook* (New York: Thomas Y. Crowell, 1953), pp. 302-25.

14. Kugel, "Economics of Films," p. 13; "Filmed TV," *Newsweek*, February 12, 1951, p. 78; also see "California as a Program Source," p. 38.

15. For accounts of the financial situation of early telefilm producers, see MacKaye, "The Big Brawl," part 2, pp. 119-20; "Syndicated Film," *Television*, July 1952, p. 27; "Film vs. Live Shows," p. 78; in July 1951, *Television* reported that the Bank of America and a few other commercial banks were now "willing to discuss" telefilm financing, see Kugel, "The Economics of Film," p. 13.

16. "How to Use TV Films Effectively," *Sponsor*, June 19, 1950, p. 33.

17. "Film for '52," *Newsweek*, August 11, 1952, p. 137; Bob Chandler compared the early telefilm industry with the "wild and woolly" early years of the motion picture industry in "TV Films: An Updated Version of Freewheeling Picture Pioneers," *Variety*, January 4, 1956, p. 9, quoted in Helen B. Schaffer, "Movie-TV Competition," *Editorial Research Reports*, January 18, 1957, p. 54.

18. "Have TV Show Costs Reached Their Ceiling?," *Sponsor*, September 21, 1953, p. 106.

19. Interview with Frederick Ziv, quoted in Morleen Getz Rouse, "A History of the F. W. Ziv Radio and Television Syndication Companies, 1930-1960," Ph.D. diss., University of Michigan, 1976, p. 119.

20. "Hollywood Cameras Grind Out Film Fare for TV," *Business Week*, November 24, 1951, p. 125; "Film vs. Live Shows," p. 78; Ziv is quoted in Rouse, "A History of the F. W. Ziv Radio," p. 79.

21. George Bauer, *Government Regulation of Television* (New York: New York University Graduate School of Public Administration and Social Service, 1956), p. 38. Gilbert Seldes reported in the summer of 1948 that of the ninety-four hours of local live programming presented on New York City stations, more than 50 percent was devoted to sports. One reason for the early reliance on live *remote* broadcasts by local stations was that such programming was inexpensive, but another motivation may have been demographic: a 1949 NBC survey revealed that 14 percent of its audience watched television in bars. Gilbert

Seldes, "Television: The Golden Hope," *Atlantic,* March 1949, p. 35; National Broadcasting Company, *NBC Television Profile April 1950* (New York: National Broadcasting Company, 1950), collection of the NBC Research Library, New York; Kaufman and Colodzin, *Your Career in Television,* p. 42.

22. On the economics of network attitudes toward telefilm, see Kugel, "Economics of Film," p. 13; "TV and Film: Marriage of Necessity," *Business Week,* August 15, 1953; "Film vs. Live Shows," pp. 77-78; Bauer, *Government Regulation,* p. 96.

23. Max Wilk, *The Golden Age of Television: Notes from the Survivors* (New York: Delacorte, 1976), p. 251.

24. "Film vs. Live Shows," p. 78; in her dissertation on television syndication, Barbara Moore concluded that through 1952, "[w]ith the exception of a few shows, networks still seemed wedded to the idea of live programming." Barbara Ann Moore, "Syndication of First-Run Television Programming: Its Development and Current Status," Ph.D. diss., Ohio University, 1979, p. 16.

25. Erik Barnouw, *The History of Broadcasting in the United States,* vol. 3: *The Image Empire* (New York: Oxford University Press, 1970), p. 21; Jack Gould, "A Plea for Live Video," *New York Times,* December 7, 1952, sec. 2, p. 17; in 1956, Gilbert Seldes contrasted the enlightened networks to the greedy station operator and film packager: "It is known that the first TV station ever to operate in the black from the day it went on the air began to transmit before the coaxial cable reached it and the owners, making a tidy fortune out of old movies, looked with distaste to the day when public demand for created programs would force them to join a network." Gilbert Seldes, *The Public Arts* (New York: Simon and Schuster, 1956), p. 180.

26. Gilbert Seldes, "A Clinical Analysis of TV," *New York Times Magazine,* November 23, 1954, p. 60; Rod Serling, "TV in the Flesh vs. TV in the Can," *New York Times Magazine,* November 24, 1957, p. 49.

27. James Whiteside, "The Communicator I: Athens Starts Pouring In," *The New Yorker,* October 16, 1954, pp. 58, 60.

28. National Broadcasting Company, *Statement of Facts,* reprinted in U.S. Congress, Senate, Committee on Interstate and Foreign Commerce, *The Television Inquiry,* vol. 4: *Network Practices, Hearings before the Committee on Interstate and Foreign Commerce, Senate,* 84th Cong., 2d sess. (Washington, D.C.: U.S.. Government Printing Office, 1956), p. 2279; also see Val Adams, "Network Accuses Film Syndicators," *New York Times,* May 28, 1956, p. 51.

5

Live Television: Program Formats and Critical Hierarchies

Aesthetic distinctions offered by television critics in the early 1950s were often argued on essentialist grounds. Gilbert Seldes's 1952 *Writing for Television* was typical: "On the controversy on the merits of live and filmed television programs, it is possible to hold that one is better or cheaper or more effective than the other, but it is not possible to maintain that they are identical. Common experience tells us that two things produced by different means, under different material and psychological conditions, will probably not be the same."[1]

According to many early writers on television, the essential technological feature of television versus the motion picture was the electronic medium's capacity to convey a simultaneous distant performance visually. In this regard, the medium was a unique synthesis of the immediacy of the live theatrical performance, the space-conquering powers of radio, and the visual strategies of the motion picture. In 1956, Jack Gould wrote of live television: "Alone of the mass media, it removes from an audience's consciousness the factors of time and distance. . . . Live television . . . bridges the gap instantly and unites the individual at home with the event afar. The viewer has a chance to be in two places at once. Physically, he may be at his own hearthside but intellectually, and above all, emotionally, he is at the cameraman's side." The critical feature of live television, according to Gould, is that "both the player in the studios and the audience at home have an intrinsic awareness of being in each other's presence." Seldes described this metaphysic of presence in live television: "The essence of television techniques is their contribution to the sense of immediacy. . . . The tension that suffuses the atmosphere of a live production is a special thing to which audiences respond; they feel that what they see and hear is happening in the present and therefore more real than anything taken and cut and dried which has the feel of the past."[2]

The opposition between film's "feel of the past" and the immediacy of live television created different putative audience paradigms for film and live programs, in which viewers of a live performance were seen as more highly involved than those of film programs. Gould argued in his 1952 article, "A Plea for Live Video," that film programs on television "lack that intangible sense of depth and trueness which the wizardry of science did impart to 'live' TV. . . . The lasting magic of television is that it employs a mechanical means to achieve an unmechanical end." The polemical linking of technological immediacy to more metaphysical notions of authenticity, depth, and truth reached an apotheosis in Gould's 1956 essay, where he excoriated "the ridiculous conceit of film perfectionists who think they can be better than life itself. . . . In their blind pursuit of artificial perfectionism, the TV film producers compromise the one vital element that endows the home screen with its own intangible excitement: humanness. Their error is to try to tinker with reality, to improve upon it to a point where it is no longer real. In so doing, they break the link between human and human. The viewer loses his sense of being a partner and instead becomes a spectator. It is the difference between being with somebody and looking at somebody."[3]

The linking of a technological essentialism in the service of a implicit liberal humanism can also be seen in a 1952 text by Edward Barry Roberts, script editor for "Armstrong Circle Theatre": "More than prose, more than the stage, more than motion pictures—oh, so much more than radio—television, with its immediacy, gets to the heart of the matter, to the essence of the character, to the depicting of the human being who is *there,* as if under a microscope, for our private contemplation, for our approval, our rejection, our love, our hate, our bond of brotherhood recognized." Television script editor Ann Howard Bailey in 1953 described the unique capabilities of the television camera for dramatic storytelling and concluded: "As the television writer learns to look within himself and those around him for the eternal and infinitely variable human conflicts, he will learn how the television camera can serve as the scalpel with which to lay bear the human heart and spirit."[4]

If the metaphysics of presence was one element of the ontology of television argued by early television critics, another was the medium's practical situation of production and reception. William I. Kaufman and Robert S. Colodzin argued in 1950: "Unlike both the movies and the theatre, television does not play to the mass audience . . . it plays to a group of perhaps five or six people at a time." The intimacy of the viewing group had implications for television dramaturgy, directing techniques, and performance style. Kaufman and Colodzin explained that "Emphasis must be on quick character development, on revealing close-ups which make the lift of an eyebrow or the flash of a smile more important than the sweep of an army. Dialogue must be carefully written and sincere in tone because of the intimacy of the audience and the actors and the constant scrutiny of the main characters of the play by an audience which is practically 'on top of' the performers."[5]

Writer Donald Curtis elaborated on the special demands on the television performer in a 1952 essay: "The actor in television must visualize the conditions under which his performance is being viewed. He is coming into a home and joining an intimate family group which averages from two to six persons. There is no place for acting here. He must 'be' what he represents. . . . The television camera goes inside of an actor's mind and soul, and sends the receiving set exactly what it sees there."[6]

Broadcast critic Charles Siepmann in 1950 saw in television drama the development of a new performance style, "not, as in the film, predominantly physical, but psychological—both sight and sound serving to give overt support to the covert expression of the mind." In an introduction to a collection of television plays, William Bluem observed that "In some ways TV is the penultimate technological extension of the naturalistic drama and its rejection of romantic superficiality in favor of the inner revelation of human character. The entire theatrical movement towards realism in acting and staging seems to culminate upon the small screen, where it can work out its own absolutes of form and style."[7]

Like the prescriptions on performance style in television, commentary on television staging and direction found a rationale for theatrical naturalism in the concrete production and viewing circumstances of the medium. As Seldes explained, "Every television program is in a sense an invasion; you turn on your television set and someone comes into your living room, and you tune in one station or another according to whom you want in your room at any particular moment."[8]

The early literature on television production constantly emphasized the necessity for naturalist performances, frequent close-ups, and simplified, naturalistic staging. A 1945 CBS publication explained that "because viewers express a natural wish to 'get a good look' at a character, producers should whenever possible use close-ups to introduce all characters on a program." In a 1946 article in *Television*, ABC executive Harvey Marlowe argued that television drama had no need for elaborate sets and that 80 percent of the typical television play would be shot in close-up. In 1950, Kaufman and Colodzin advised would-be television playwrights that "[a] good television script must be simple to produce," with sets that are "few and inexpensive." The cast "should be limited to a small number of characters," and "[s]pecial effects should be avoided in instances where simpler methods would be just as dramatic." An example of a rigorous application of the reductive design of television's theatrical naturalism was Albert McCleery's "Cameo Theatre," in which a small cast sat on stools on an arena stage without scenery, costumes, or props. In his *Best Television Plays 1950-51*, Kaufman called the McCleery program "pure television."[9]

For the TV playwright as well, the special properties of the television medium seemed to support a new kind of dramatic realism. Paddy Chayefsky wrote in 1955 that "lyrical writing, impressionistic writing and abstract and expressionistic writing are appalling in television whereas they might be gauged exciting in the theatre." In his contribution to the 1952 anthology, *How to Write and Direct for Television*, Chayefsky elaborated:

> In television, there is practically nothing too subtle or delicate that you cannot examine with your camera. The camera allows us a degree of intimacy that can never be achieved on stage. Realism in the theatre is a stylized business; what one achieves is really the effect of realism. In television, you can be literally and freely real. The scenes can be played as if the actors were unaware of their audience. The dialogue can sound as if it had been wiretapped. . . . The writer has a whole new, untouched area of drama in which to poke about. He can write about the simplest things, the smallest incidents, as long as they have dramatic significance.[10]

Television's ability to bring intimate details of a performance to its audience, along with the practical constraints of staging live television drama, also led the critics to suggest the most appropriate forms of dramatic structure for the medium. For Erik Barnouw, the structural principles of early live drama on television meant that "The structure of these plays related to circumstances under which they were produced." As a result there emerged "plays of tight structure, attacking a story close to its climax—very different from the loose, multi-scene structure of film."[11]

Barnouw's juxtaposition of the dramatic structures of film and television was widely echoed in the early television literature. The same distinction was often cast in terms which opposed the drama of character to the drama of plot. Edward Barry Roberts argued in 1952, for example, that "the new playwriting inescapably is founded on character.... The most successful 'live' television plays, therefore, would seem to be those which do not have much plot." Another script editor advised would-be television writers in 1953: "Live TV is limited in scope: that is, it cannot depend upon broad panorama, colossal montages, or the thrill of the hunt or chase to help the limping script. Literally, the 'words are the thing,' and in nine out of ten TV shows, the climax depends upon what the characters say rather than what they do."[12]

Seldes argued that television's technological immediacy gave the medium an "overwhelming feel of reality": "The result is that television can render character supremely well and it is not theoretical or idealistic but very practical to say that it should not abandon its prime quality." Seldes wrote that until 1952, television drama seemed to be following the theatrical model of a drama of character over one of plot, but warned that "This may not always be true of television drama because *the conditions in which television is received make it a prime medium for communicating character*, but as a lot of TV drama is being made in Hollywood by people in the Hollywood tradition, the struggle for character drama may be a bitter one." Like the essentialist rationale for naturalism in staging and acting in television, Seldes's defense of character drama derived from the technological and phenomenological premises of the medium: the casual environment and attitude of viewers at home detracted from the effectiveness of complicated plot structures, he argued.

Beyond the criteria of live versus film and character versus plot, critics also placed the unique teleplay of the anthology series above works in the continuing series and dramatic serial. Seldes called the sixty-minute original teleplay in an anthology series the "top of the prestige pyramid of all television drama." The critic identified in the sixty-minute original teleplay "something like a new dramatic form . . . slowly emerging," and in a 1956 look at the first ten years of television programming Seldes found "the most honorable accomplishments of television . . . in the hour-long play. . . ."[13]

The thirty-minute program was consistently compared unfavorably to the hour-long dramatic program on television. In 1955, Don Sharpe of Four Star Productions compared the thirty-minute and sixty-minute programs in an article in *Television* and concluded that "The half-hour dramatization is primarily a stunt and frequently a trick." For Sharpe, "The viewer of the hour program is satisfied to sit and wait for something to happen, as he would in the legitimate theatre." But on the other hand, argued Sharpe, "unless a thirty-minute show develops an almost immediate impact . . . there is a good chance that many viewers will switch channels or take the pooch for a stroll." Vance Bourjaily wrote in *Harper's* that "the half-hour show is too brief, and it is interrupted by a commercial too soon after it begins, to be anything but a hook, a gimmick, and a resolution." Jack Gould argued that "the half-hour program with the middle commercial inevitably puts a premium on the contrived plot and on action for its own sake. . . . there can be almost no characterization and the emphasis is more on stereotypes than on real people."[14]

In sum, most prominent television critics of the early 1950s denigrated the program forms and dramatic values they associated with Hollywood in favor of those they linked with the New York-based television networks. The opposition is nowhere more stark than in the critical perception of the differing roles for the television writer in the two contexts. Like the critical debates over the aesthetic proclivities of the two media, the image of the writer was colored by long-standing cultural attitudes toward the motion picture industry. In the context of pre-auteurist American film criticism, individual contributions by writers or directors in the Hollywood studio system tended to be devalued by sociological or belletrist accounts of Hollywood as a monolithic dream factory where faceless contract writers toiled in confining genres at the whim of autocratic and philistine moguls. The image of the serious writer in Hollywood in mid-century American literature and popular criticism was that of a figure compromising or renouncing the autonomy and artistic possibilities available in other literary forms. These general cultural attitudes toward the writer in Hollywood played an important part in setting a tone for the debates over television program forms in the 1950s.

Broadcast writer and critic Goodman Ace in a 1952 article, "The Forgotten Men of TV," characterized the expectations of writers in Hollywood telefilms by citing an unattributed quotation from Lucille Ball regarding the writers' contribution to "I Love Lucy": "We never see them. We never discuss anything with them. After two readings we get on our feet and throw the scripts away." A 1954 article, "Writer Is a Dirty Word," described Ace's trip to Hollywood, where, he wrote, "for the most part, television writers, especially comedy writers, are considered a necessary but evil part of the TV set-up."[15]

The employment situation and critical reputation of the writer in live television drama were very different, although it took some time before the TV writer earned the prominence associated with most accounts of television's Golden Age. An article in the premier issue of *Television* in 1944, for example, lamented that "The program end of television has been an arid wasteland, almost devoid of imagination, showmanship, and (what is equally important) any indications of a knowledge of the nature of television. . . . The big bottleneck will be in good writers and directors, artists and executives with imagination and showmanship who understand their medium." In May 1947 an article in the magazine was still complaining: "Capable actors are available, good original scripts are not. . . . Perhaps it would be better for television to forego dramatic production unless top scripts are available, for television will only suffer in comparison to other media when mediocre productions are staged."[16]

The manager of NBC's Script Department wrote in 1948: "Television's primary need is for material, and the one who provides that material in a suitable form may be said to be one of the most important, if not *the* most important, person in the television picture—the writer." Charles Underhill, head of CBS television programming, in 1950 wrote succinctly of the television programmer: "Greatest need: material. Solution: uncover young writers, woo Hollywood and Broadway writers."

Variety concluded that the development of writing talent suited "specifically for TV looms as the most necessary ingredient for programming in 1950."[17]

Seldes described the new market for television scripts: "For writers, the turning point in television came somewhere in the early spring of 1951." The number of Writers Guild of America members reported working in television grew from 45 in February 1951 to 110 by the end of that year. In 1952, Edward Barry Roberts, an NBC script editor, wrote: "The centers of production are swarming with would-be television writers. The competition is killing, although paradoxically there aren't enough really good writers to supply the demand. . . . Yet it is only through good writing that television will grow, and fulfill its potential destiny as the most fascinating and the most important means ever known of communicating information, entertainment and education. . . . We are all waiting hopefully and impatiently for the television artist-playwrights to appear."[18]

The title "artist-playwright" attached to the work of the writer in live television drama suggests the importance and prestige frequently associated with the new craft. In a June 1952 episode of the ABC public-affairs program "Horizons," entitled "The Future of Television Drama," producer Alex Segal argued that "I think TV eventually, if given time to develop, if not rushed, and if not sidetracked, will do the wonderful thing we always wished for, that of bringing the legitimate theatre into the home in its final stage." Most TV critics and many of the other creative personnel in television saw the writer at the center of television drama. In 1952, Herbert Spencer Sussan, a CBS producer-director called the writer "truly the creative artist" in television and described the work of the TV director as "akin to the director of a symphony orchestra, fusing many elements into harmonious unity." Chayefsky later recalled how the prestige associated with TV writing could ignite the career of a young writer of live drama of the mid-1950s: "Right at that time, it was a writer's medium. Think of all those shows that were done in New York—'Philco,' 'Studio One,' 'Kraft Television Theatre,' 'Robert Montgomery Presents,' 'U.S. Steel Hour'—all those other weekly half-hour shows, perfect for writers. If you could come in at the right time and do something that caught on, it was the beginning of a career." Indeed, the best known writers of television drama—Paddy

Chayefsky, Rod Serling, Reginald Rose, Horton Foote, Robert Alan
Aurthur—came not from established careers in the motion picture industry but achieved first public notice through their work in
television.[19]

The prominence and prestige accorded to writers in live television
drama—TV's new artist-playwrights—were often contrasted with the
plight of writers working in feature films and filmed television. In 1957,
Serling compared the role of the writer in live and filmed television:

> Probably most fundamental in any discussion of the differences be-
> tween live and filmed television is the attitude reserved for their
> creators. It is rare in Hollywood that a filmed show will make anything
> but a perfunctory reference to its author. Hollywood television took a
> leaf out of the notebook of the motion pictures and shoved its authors
> into a professional Siberia. The writer of the filmed television play was
> never and is not now an identifiable name in terms of the audience.
>
> This is in sharp contrast to the New York live television writer who
> has been granted an identity, an importance and a respect second
> only to the legitimate playwright. For this reason, it is rare that a "live"
> playwright will write for filmed shows, despite that fact that, in the
> long run, the half-hour film may bring him almost ten times the total
> price of the live script.[20]

Writers of live television drama often maintained a significant degree
of control over their material. Television writer Ernest Kinoy looked
back at the position of the television writer in the mid-1950s:

> The general practice in live television of this time was to accept the
> notion of the writer as the original instigator-creator of a particular
> play. . . . This was picked up from Broadway, where the author is con-
> sidered the man who has produced the work, who has done the thing
> which is going to be presented. Therefore, you would, in most cases,
> continue with it in a relatively respected position, along through the
> rehearsals to the final presentation on the air. And your opinion was
> sought and listened to with varying degrees of attention. But as a pat-
> tern, the writer was considered to belong with his property until it was
> finally presented.[21]

In addition to a measure of control from the completed script through
the production process, the live television writer was accorded a position by critics and the public closer to that of the legitimate playwright
than the Hollywood contract-writer. Gore Vidal, who wrote seventy

television plays over a two-year period in the mid-1950s, recalled a few years later: "If you did a good show on 'Philco,' you would walk down the street the next morning and hear people talking about your play." In an interview in the *New York Times* in 1956, thirty-one-year-old Serling pointed to television's appeal to a writer interested in social commentary: "I think that of all the entertainment media, TV lends itself most beautifully to presenting a controversy. You can just take a part of the problem, and, using just a small number of people, get your point across."[22]

Serling is perhaps the best example of a young writer who achieved prominence through a series of live drama scripts in the mid-1950s. His first major teleplay, "Patterns," was hailed by the *New York Times* as "one of the high points in the television medium's evolution," and was repeated in live performance on "Kraft Television Theatre," the first time a live drama was restaged for the medium. Within two weeks after the airing of "Patterns," Serling told an interviewer: "I received twenty-three firm offers for television writing assignments. I received three motion picture offers for screenplay assignments. I had fourteen requests for interviews from leading magazines and newspapers. I had two offers of lunch from Broadway producers. I had two offers to discuss novels with publishers."[23]

Serling won a Peabody Award in 1956 and Emmy awards for his television plays in 1955, 1956, and 1957. *Vogue* magazine described the writer in 1957 as a "revved-up, good-looking playwright of thirty-two," and *Cosmopolitan* profiled Serling in 1958 as the most conspicuous member of "a new class of millionaire writers in America." Serling's sudden success and visibility in the popular press was only one indication of the cultural position of the television writer and the original television play in the era of live drama. New York television critic John Crosby wrote in a 1973 recollection:

> Does TV generate that kind of excitement any more? Certainly not over the author of a TV play. In the 1950s everyone was *interested* in TV—the educated and the featherbrains alike. It was new and we were very innocent. . . . I remember walking into "21," a fairly sophisticated beanery, one day in the 1950s and finding the whole restaurant buzzing with talk about another Rod Serling play, "Requiem for a Heavyweight". . . . The important thing was that "Requiem" set the whole town talking in much the same way Al Jolson used to do when he'd walk out on the stage of the Winter Garden and knock 'em

dead in the 1920s. Television was *the* medium of the moment and it attracted all the brilliant young kids. . . . [24]

The TV writer, then, stood at the center of the artistic promise of live television drama, and many playwrights became widely reported commentators on the medium and its programming in the rest of the decade. For many television critics in the 1950s, the television playwright symbolized the medium's commitment to the live format and to the dramatic forms to which they were fiercely attached. The rising debate within the industry and in the popular press over the role of the television writer in the 1950s therefore becomes one marker of a shift in general cultural attitudes toward the medium. Television writers were at once the objects of, and often acute commentators upon, the enormous changes in commercial television in the second half of the 1950s.

NOTES

1. Gilbert Seldes, *Writing for Television* (New York: Doubleday, 1952), p. 30.

2. Jack Gould, " 'Live' TV vs. 'Canned,'" *New York Times Magazine,* February 5, 1956, p. 27; Seldes, *Writing for Television,* p. 32

3. Jack Gould, "A Plea for Live Video," *New York Times,* December 7, 1952; Gould, " 'Live' TV," p. 34.

4. Edward Barry Roberts, "Writing for Television," in *The Best Television Plays, 1950-1951,* ed. William I. Kaufman (New York: Hastings House, 1952), p. 296, emphasis in original; Ann Howard Bailey, "Writing the TV Dramatic Show," in Irving Settel and Norman Glenn, *Television Advertising and Production Handbook* (New York: Thomas Y. Crowell, 1953), p. 226.

5. William I. Kaufman and Robert Colodzin, *Your Career in Television* (New York: Merlin Press, 1950), p. 62.

6. Donald Curtis, "The Actor in Television," in *The Best Television Plays, 1950-1951,* ed. Kaufman, pp. 319-20.

7. Charles Siepmann, *Radio, Television and Society* (New York: Oxford University Press, 1950), p. 357; William Bluem and Roger Manvell, eds., *TV: The Creative Experience: A Survey of Anglo-American Progress* (New York: Hastings House, 1967), p. 17.

8. Seldes, *Writing for Television,* p. 79. Seldes continued: "In a dramatic program you are inviting a group of people to live a portion of their lives with you. The closer their lives come to the tenor of the lives of yourself and your friends, the more the invasion has taken on the nature of a visit; the characters must be

with you without reservation and without pressure, so that in the end you can move from your living room into their lives."

9. Columbia Broadcasting System, *Television Audience Research* (New York: Columbia Broadcasting System, 1945), p. 7; Harvey Marlowe, "Drama's Place in Television," *Television*, March 1946, p. 17; Kaufman and Colodzin, *Your Career in Television*, p. 61; Kaufman, ed., *The Best Television Plays, 1950-1951*, p. 263.

10. Paddy Chayefsky, "Good Theatre in Television," ibid., p. 45.

11. Erik Barnouw, *The History of Broadcasting in the United States*, vol. 3: *The Image Empire* (New York: Oxford University Press, 1970), p. 31.

12. Roberts, "Writing for Television," pp. 296-97; Baily, "Writing the TV Dramatic Show," p. 214.

13. Seldes, *Writing for Television*, 1952, pp. 105, 138, 148, 151, 152, emphasis in original; Gilbert Seldes, "A Clinical Analysis of TV," *New York Times Magazine*, November 23, 1954, p. 55.

14. Don Sharpe, "TV Film: Will Economics Stifle Creativity?," *Television*, April 1955, p. 39; Vance Bourjaily, "The Lost Art of Writing for Television," *Harper's*, October 1959, p. 152; Jack Gould, "Half-Act Drama," *New York Times*, February 10, 1952, sec. 2, p. 13.

15. Goodman Ace, *The Book of Little Knowledge: More Than You Want to Know About Television* (New York: Simon and Schuster, 1955), pp. 8, 18.

16. "Programming," *Television*, Spring 1944, p. 21; "Programming," *Television*, May 1947, p. 31.

17. Richard P. McDongh, "Television Writing Problems," in *Television Production Problems*, ed. John F. Royal (New York: McGraw-Hill, 1948), p. 28; "The Programmers," *Television*, February 1950, p. 14; "Video's '50 Accent on Writing," *Variety*, December 21, 1949, p. 27.

18. Seldes, *Writing for Television*, p. 9; Milton MacKaye, "The Big Brawl: Hollywood vs. Television," *The Saturday Evening Post*, January 26, 1952, Part 2, p. 119; Roberts, "Writing for Television," p. 300.

19. Alex Segal, "The Future of Television Drama," "Horizons," June 6, 1952, collection of the Museum of Broadcasting, New York; Herbert Spencer Sussan, "The Voice Behind the Cameras," in *The Best Television Plays, 1950-1951*, ed. Kaufman, p. 302; Max Wilk, *The Golden Age of Television: Notes from the Survivors* (New York: Delacorte, 1976), p. 132.

20. Rod Serling, "TV in the Flesh vs. TV in the Can," *New York Times Magazine*, November 24, 1957, pp. 52, 54.

21. U.S., Federal Communications Commission, Office of Network Study, *Second Interim Report:Television Program Procurement, Part II* (Washington, D.C.: U.S. Government Printing Office, 1965), p. 630.

22. Ibid., p. 626; Vidal went on: "It was a strange feeling . . . you have this

audience, and writers—at least my kind of writer—wants as large an audience as he can possibly get, to do as much damage as they can to the things they think stand in want of correction to society." Rod Serling, interview with J. P. Shanley, *New York Times*, April 22, 1956, sec. 2, p. 13.

23. The original reaction to "Patterns," its restaging, and play's effect on Serling's career are discussed in J. P. Shanley, "Notes on 'Patterns' and a Familiar Face," *New York Times*, February 6, 1955, sec. 2, p. 15. Rod Serling, *Patterns* (New York: Simon and Schuster, 1957), p. 30.

24. "People Are Talking About," *Vogue*, April 1, 1957, p. 138; T. F. James, "The Millionaire Class of Young Writers," *Cosmopolitan*, August 1958, p. 40; John Crosby, "It Was New and We Were Very Innocent," *TV Guide*, September 22, 1973, p. 6.

6

The False Dawn of a Golden Age

The debates in the 1950s over suitable program forms for television and over freedom of expression for writers in the medium were inseparable from the fundamental question of who would control television programming: the networks or the broadcast sponsors and their advertising agencies. As in the contemporary debates over live versus film programming, the commercial battles over program control often were couched in terms of the public interest, program aesthetics, or similar high-minded goals. In addition, the lessons of the network radio industry of the 1930s had a complex and powerful effect upon the debates as well as upon the outcomes of commercial battles within the young television industry.

While RCA was launching its public relations campaign for the immediate development of postwar VHF television and approaching the Hollywood studios for early telefilm production deals, it also encouraged advertisers and advertising agencies to enter commercial television. One RCA official told a group of advertising executives in 1944 that agencies risked their 15 percent commissions if they failed to move promptly into television, warning them that sponsors might instead negotiate directly with program producers. The RCA official lamented what he described as a "lack of interest in the agency in the business of television." A 1949 U.S. Commerce Department report also noted the reluctance of many advertising agencies to enter television; given the still-small television audience and meager advertiser billings, the medium was generally unprofitable for agencies faced with the high costs of servicing clients. Echoing RCA officials, the premier issue of *Sponsor* in 1946 urged agencies to experiment in the still-unprofitable medium in order to gain prestige, experience in programming, and the privileges of early arrival. Chief among these privileges was a "time franchise," the control by the agency of a particular time slot in the network program schedule for its client. One TV station manager explained in 1953: "A good time spot is a property to protect and hold. Some advertisers have spent years getting outstanding spots on the air, changing from relatively poor positions to better ones as they become available."[1]

Although the networks encouraged advertising agencies to move into the new medium, they were also fearful of repeating the pattern of network radio of the 1930s, when the agencies gained substantial control over network prime-time programming. Advertising executive Fairfax M. Cone later explained that the networks had lost programming control to advertising agencies in radio before World War II, "and they were determined not to let the same thing happen in TV." An article in *Televiser* in 1945, noting network opposition to outside program production, concluded, "who'll produce television is still any man's guess."[2]

Despite network wishes to retain program control in the new medium, the first few years of network television were marked by high levels of direct sponsor involvement in the production and the scheduling of programming. An advertising executive told the FCC's Office of Network Study in 1960: "In the beginning television was completely in the hands of advertising agencies like ours. That was essential to all programs because there was no money allocated for television and the advertising agency controlled the advertising monies of the country." The networks typically delegated program direction to an agency-employed director who instructed the network technical director and crew. In 1947, *Sponsor* reported a shift in program production from the networks to advertising agencies despite network wishes because of a shortage of network personnel to keep up with expanding television schedules. *Television* reported in 1949 that five of the ten most popular television programs were produced in-house by a single advertising agency, Young and Rubicam.[3]

After the FCC's rejection of the CBS UHF proposal in 1947, television advertising advanced rapidly: in November 1947, *Television* proclaimed television a serious advertising medium, no longer simply representing "a chance to experiment."[4] In spite of the FCC freeze on applications for station construction from 1948-52, television audiences grew quickly, and with increased circulation came higher time charges for television sponsors and a change in relations between networks and advertisers.

By 1950, the networks were attempting to regain program control. Frank Stanton at CBS argued that the key to successful network operation in television would lie in control of popular programs, not in affiliate transmitter power or coverage, as was the case in network radio. The desire of CBS to produce and schedule its own prime-time programming was explained in its 1950 *Annual Report:* "[P]rograms that have been developed by CBS are owned by CBS; they can be scheduled at times that are best for their own maximum growth; and once established, they can be held at strategic points throughout the week's schedule, in time-periods that then become 'anchor-points' in the winning of a great network audience. Carefully placed throughout the schedule, these anchor-points naturally attract other audience-seeking programs."[5]

There were similar moves at NBC. In 1954, NBC network head Pat Weaver described the situation when he became network chief at the end of 1949, determined to take programming control away from the agencies: "The programming just had no direction. Programs landed next to each other by mere chance with each agency building its own show in a way that was aimed at nothing more than keeping its client happy. There was no planned relationship of one program and another or to the competition, and no particular attempt to create a lasting pattern for the people at home."[6]

In a January 1950 article, "Packaging Returns to the Networks," *Sponsor* discerned a trend from agency-controlled to network-controlled shows. The network not only gained greater control over its program schedule in order to create block programming (a succession of programs designed to maximize program adjacencies and audience flow over a single evening) and counterprogramming (strong or complementary programs matched against those of another network in the same time slot), but also ensured long-term network talent commitments to a successful series or performer. Advantages for advertisers moving out of direct program production and licensing, according to *Sponsor,* included the stability of an established program with a ratings history and the possibility of favored status from the network in program scheduling and promotion. Another incentive for sponsors to abandon program production were the steeply rising costs of the medium. An article in *Sponsor* in 1949 explained that television audiences were growing so rapidly that costs-per-thousand (the sponsor's cost of reaching a thousand viewers) were actually declining, but in the early 1950s time and production charges for sponsors rose even more sharply, encouraging sponsors and agencies to shift the risks of program development to independent packagers and the networks. A 1952 *Sponsor* article reported that the networks were curtailing their previous subsidies of program production costs; the result was sharply higher sponsor charges. The end of the FCC station freeze in 1952 also led to increased time charges for the much-enlarged roster of network affiliates sold to the sponsor.[7] All these economic forces encouraged the concentration of program control in the hands of the networks in the mid–1950s.

Network attempts to wrest program control from sponsors and agencies in the 1950s generally cast the advertiser in selfish pursuit of the lowest cost-per-thousand in contrast to the broader interests of the network, including "balanced" programming over the entire television schedule. This opposition between narrow-minded sponsors and enlightened networks began in the era of network radio before World War II, when programming was split between the "sponsored" programs supplied directly by advertising agencies and the "sustaining" or unsponsored programs produced by the networks. In the 1950s' battles over program control in television, the networks could therefore enlist earlier dissatisfaction with radio broadcasting. Like the arguments of network executives against film programming, network attempts to assert control over television programming were often couched in public-interest terms. And like the debates over television aesthetics and film programming, the battles between the networks and the agencies over program control made for some curious bedfellows and much subsequent bitterness.

Much of the rhetoric in the early debates over the control of television programming is a legacy of the widespread criticism of network radio in the 1930s and 1940s. In 1945, Ira Hirshman, vice president of Metropolitan Television, told a conference on radio and business: "I hope we will have the self-control and the sense of standards to start television on a better path than that on which oral radio was started. . . . The way that radio has . . . aimed at the least common denominator . . . is something which is not a compliment to our people."[8]

The FCC's interest in the question of program control was initiated by the chain broadcasting investigations of the late 1930s, which culminated in the famous "Blue Book" of 1946, *Public Service Responsibility of Broadcast Licensees*. The "Blue Book" underscored the disparity between the mass-appeal sponsored programs and the unsponsored sustaining programs offered by the radio networks. Sustaining programming, according to the "Blue Book," had five features serving the public interest: 1) sustaining programs provided balance to the broadcast schedule, supplementing the soap operas and popular music programs that gained the highest ratings and readiest commercial sponsors; 2) they allowed for the broadcast of programs which by their controversial or sensitive nature were unsuitable for sponsorship; 3) they supplied cultural programming for minority audiences; 4) they provided limited broadcast access for non-profit and civic organizations; and 5) they made possible artistic and dramatic experimentation shielded from the pressures of short-run ratings and commercial considerations of the commercial sponsor. The rhetorical opposition between the censorious sponsor in single-minded pursuit of maximum audience versus the more enlightened, artistically innovative network is suggested in the language of the "Blue Book": "If broadcasting is to explore new fields, . . . it is clear that the sustaining program must . . . have the fullest scope, undeterred by the need for immediate financial success or the imposition on writers of restraints deriving from the natural, but limiting, preoccupations of the sponsor."[9]

The commission found network radio dominated by a small group of large sponsors and advertising agencies that produced or licensed programs and negotiated with networks for air time. In the view of the FCC, these sponsors had a natural fear of offending any members of their audience. The "Blue Book" noted that "Procter and Gamble, probably the largest sponsor in American broadcasting, has been described as having 'a policy never to offend a single listener.'" The FCC report quoted the president of the American Tobacco Company, another major network radio advertiser, about his company's programming philosophy: "We are commercial and we cannot afford to be anything else. I don't have the right to spend the stockholders' money just to entertain the public."[10]

The control of radio programming by advertising agencies, according to the "Blue Book," caused widespread frustration among radio writers. The report quoted a 1945 *Variety* article that described a growing exodus of writers dissatisfied with the commercial constraints of the radio medium: "Radio script writers are turning in increasing numbers to the legitimate field . . . as long as radio remains more or less a 'duplicating machine' without encouraging creative expression and without establishing an identity of its own, it's inevitable that the guy who has something to say will seek other outlets." With this evidence in mind, the FCC encouraged the networks to assert greater control over radio schedules to advance the public interest values associated with the network's sustaining programs. The "Blue Book" concluded that "The concept of a well-rounded structure can obviously not be maintained if the decision is left wholly or preponderantly in the hands of advertisers in search of a market, each concerned with his particular half hour, rather than in the hands of stations and networks responsible under the statute for overall program balance in the public interest."[11]

There was ready evidence of the fear of controversy among early advertisers in television. Edward Barry Roberts advised would-be television writers in 1952: "The sponsor will lay down the policy of what can be written about, or, at least, what he is willing to pay for on his program." A 1951 article in *Sponsor* elaborted on the advertiser's role in monitoring program content: "Censorship is integral to the critical purpose of creating good will, pleasant association, popular feelings of gratitude. In the logic of the marketplace and the business man's accenting of the positive, the commercial side of American radio favors the gay, amusing, harmless, neutral and avoids the sharp, acid, hateful. Typically, the business man chooses to reflect and echo public taste as commonly interpreted. In so choosing, he plainly censors the opposite values, has no association with political, artistic or literary avant garde."[12]

Even the large "institutional" advertisers of television's early years kept a close eye on potentially troublesome program content. An example is "Theatre Guild of the Air," sponsored on radio since 1935 and brought to television in 1953 by the U.S. Steel Company. According to an article in *Sponsor* in 1955, the purpose of the program for the advertiser was straightforward: to raise the company's public image from its poor reputation in the 1930s. Hired by U.S. Steel as a public relations advisor, advertising man Bruce Barton told the company: "You are being advertised whether you like it or not, because people talk about you. The only channel to the public which you can control is the one you pay for." *Sponsor* reported that "U.S. Steel believes it must have absolute control if the public relations purpose is to be properly fulfilled," and noted that the company directly oversaw all aspects of "Theatre Guild of the Air," selecting scripts, supervising casting, and attending rehearsals. The company's preference, the magazine explained, was "for stories with power but outside controversial areas. . . . Company and agency deplore writer tendencies to be grim, look for endings with a lift." *Sponsor* concluded: "The client is never further away than the sponsor's booth, right down to show time."[13]

There were also external pressures on the television sponsor to "avoid association with political, artistic or literary avant garde" in its programs. Most significant and sustained was the systematic political censorship and blacklisting of television personnel objectionable to the organized, anticommunist Right. Inspired by earlier congressional investigations in Hollywood and the increasingly anticommunist mood of the country, political blacklisting in television began in earnest in 1950 with the publication by a small right-wing organization of *Red Channels: The Report on the Communist Influence in Radio and Television.* The targets of the report were not only Communist party members in the broadcast industry, but also what *Red Channels* called the "dupes" and "innocents" among the "so-called 'intellectual' classes." The report singled out several network-produced dramatic anthologies and explained: "Dramatic programs are occasionally used for Communist propaganda purposes. . . . Several commercially sponsored dramatic series are used as sounding boards, particularly with reference to current issues on which the Party is critically interested: 'academic freedom,' 'civil rights,' 'peace,' the 'H-bomb,' etc. These and other subjects, perfectly legitimate in themselves, are cleverly exploited in dramatic treatments which point up current Communist goals."[14]

Jack Gould said in 1961 that *Red Channels* "set off the most shocking panic I've ever seen in my life." An important ally to the *Red Channels* group was Syracuse grocer Lawrence Johnson, who led a campaign against CBS's dramatic anthology series "Danger" by threatening its sponsor, Block Drugs, with the prospect of red-baiting displays next to the company's products on Johnson's supermarket shelves. The politically offending actors were removed from the program. Johnson's tactics of pressuring the television sponsor were effective because, as the historian Erik Barnouw pointed out, "Products sold through super-markets accounted for more than 60 percent of broadcast revenue. Manufacturers of such products were especially vulnerable to pressures that threatened their place on supermarket shelves."[15]

Another early case establishing the power of the political blacklist in television was examined in a three-part article, "The Truth About *Red Channels*," in *Sponsor* in 1951. Actress Jean Muir was removed from a popular program by sponsor General Foods after right-wing pressure; admitting it made no efforts to investigate the validity of the accusations against Muir, the sponsor argued that the presence of charges itself was sufficient justification for her dismissal: "Using her would have been akin to sending out a poor salesman in an area where the salesman was disliked," General Foods explained.[16]

These early and well-publicized blacklisting cases convinced many industry observers that television sponsors were unreasonably sensitive to such organized pressure groups, and some expressed faith that net-work organizations would be in a stronger position to resist such pressures. Max Wilk wrote in 1951: "When the sponsor stays on his side of the curtain, currently the door to the studio, and allows his producers, directors and writers to function unhampered by his amateur opinions, television drama will improve overnight." Paddy Chayefsky wrote in the introduction to his published television plays in 1955 that "The advertis-ing agencies are interested only in selling their client's products, and they do not want dramas that will disturb potential customers. This limits the choice of material markedly. You cannot write about adultery, abor-tion, the social values of our times, or almost anything that relates to adult reality. . . . Downbeat-type drama is almost as taboo as politically controversial stories."[17]

Throughout the red-baiting and blacklisting that marked the televi-sion industry during the 1950s, the networks generally succeeded in presenting themselves as victims of, or at worst, reluctant partners in, program censorship and restrictive employment practices. Pat Weaver told a group of Dartmouth students on a 1955 NBC program, "Youth Wants to Know":

[T]he basic management groups in large part are very conservative and . . . do not wish to associate the sale of their product with anything controversial. . . . I know that we had trouble in getting certain shows accepted by certain clients who took a line that we thought was not even liberal. . . . Those of us who run communications know that America is based on the sanctity of dissent, that anything which pressures for uniformity or conformity is a block that is building a wall that ends our whole way of life. I think generally speaking . . . the attitude of management is one for dissent and for the unpopular idea and for the use of controversial issues.[18]

In addition to pressure from the organized Right, the live drama and variety programs produced in New York by the networks were targets of more general complaints in the early years of television. Many of the complaints were couched in issues of program taste, often opposing the "big city" sensibility of the networks' New York programming to the standards of the rest of the country. The friction goes back even before commercial television operations were underway. Due to commercial television's abortive prewar start and its subsequent suspension during the war, the only television broadcast service through the mid-1940s came from a handful of New York stations. Lee DeForest in his 1942 *Television Today and Tomorrow* decried this dependence on New York as a laboratory for early television programming: New Yorkers, according to DeForest, were "too sophisticated to become television-minded." Nevertheless, DeForest optimistically predicted that the success of television would cause a reinvigoration of family ties, spark an exodus from the large cities in a massive suburban migration, and lead to "the gradual razing of these ridiculous structures," the urban skyscrapers.[9]

In a less speculative manner, the complaints of other critics about network-produced, New York-based programming revealed a similar antiurban animus. A 1951 article in *Sponsor* warned: "Off color jokes, swish routines, city humor hits the small towns and suburbs with unpleasant impact, focusing reaction upon certain entertainers—and their sponsors." A 1955 book, *Television Program Production*, by Carroll O'Meara, complained:

> What is acceptable to broad-minded night club audiences in Manhattan, Hollywood, or Las Vegas is rarely apt to be fare for admission in homes in any city or town. . . . Jaded and liquored celebrants in a night club will accept as sophisticated humor and wit what is actually nothing but smut. . . . What many entertainers fail to realize, actually, is that the areas containing the bistros, night spots and bright lights are only a minute segment of America. And yet, somehow, they insist on broadcasting to the entire nation comic and other material which is

definitely not acceptable in the average American home. . . . Our nation consists of 160 million citizens, most of whom live in small towns,
go to church on Sunday, attempt to bring up their children decently,
and do not regard burlesque shows as the ultimate in theatre.[21]

Frequent targets for early moral critics of television were the mystery
and crime anthology dramas, lead by "Lights Out," "Danger," and "Sus-
pense"; the genre's popularity reached a high point in 1950, when it
constituted approximately 50 percent of prime-time programming.
Concern over the purported violence and amorality of the programs
paralleled censorship campaigns in the comic book industry and a
general preoccupation with the threat of juvenile delinquency. Controversy over violent crime shows and other "objectionable" television
programs became more pointed, however, in 1951 when a Democratic
representative from Arkansas, Ezekial Candler Gathings, called for a
Commerce subcommittee probe of "offensive and undesirable radio
and television programs." Before the start of the subcommittee's hearings in June 1952, the television industry quickly put together a manual
of censorship called the Television Code. *Television* in November 1951
welcomed the prospective code in hopes of preempting federal intervention, and an article in *Sponsor*, entitled "TV's Hottest Problem:
Public Relations," called for a concerted public relations campaign by
the industry in its "battle for respectability."[22]

Representative Gathings said during the hearings: "There is such a
thing as leaning too heavily upon the constitutional free speech provision. . . . The radio voice and television screen and voice is [sic] a
visitor; it comes into your home." While Gathings admitted that his
original target in the House resolution was violent crime programming,
other complaints against New York network programming were also
raised during the hearings, including offensive comedy routines and
revealing necklines during variety programs. The subcommittee's report
of December 1952 commended the Television Code's effect on crime
programs and television comedy, and Gathings noted with satisfaction
during the hearings that "the necklines of dresses are higher since the
Code was put into effect."[23]

If the programming most associated with the networks in early television stirred criticism from political and social conservatives, the attacks
encouraged many television critics and writers to defend the networks
and their socially relevant, naturalistic live dramas from New York even

more strongly. Various developments—the frustrations of radio writers over sponsor censorship in 1930s' radio, the widespread caution among early television sponsors, the political panic set off by *Red Channels,* and the conservative criticism of "big city" network programs—led many writers and critics in the 1950s to look to the networks as the only guardians of program balance, artistic innovation, and social relevance in dramatic television.

Just as network leaders appropriated TV critics' aesthetic rhetoric celebrating live television for their commercial contests with program producers, the networks enlisted uneasiness over advertiser censorship in their battles with sponsors and advertising agencies. Pat Weaver, who had been in charge of advertising for the same conservative American Tobacco Company quoted in the FCC's "Blue Book," described his first actions as director of NBC television programming in 1949: "I brought in some of the top ad-agency programming men to help me at NBC and I told them, 'Look, we ruined radio. Let's not let it happen to television. Let's stage our own programs and just sell advertising time to the agencies.'" Weaver said in 1955 that while radio had been dominated by a few large sponsors and ad agencies, television was too important a sales medium to allow the same thing to happen.[24]

Weaver's career at NBC from 1949 to 1956 is identified with the network "spectacular," a large-budget, network-produced, specially scheduled live program of sixty minutes or more. The network spectaculars were generally popular with New York television critics; in 1956, Jack Gould wrote that the network spectacular "probably represents the medium's most significant single asset: its capacity to be extraordinarily good. The bookish snobs who have tried to concoct an intellectual superiority out of a righteous refusal to watch television will have to find a more persuasive dodge." Besides displaying the network's ability to assemble talent and display production values beyond those of most other television programming, the spectacular was also a network strategy to gain leverage over the television sponsor in two ways. The spectacular broke with the radio model of sponsorship by entailing a production budget few television advertisers could consider for single sponsorship. Instead, advertisers were invited as "participating" sponsors, sharing total time and production costs on a per-insertion basis, with the advertiser buying a simple insertion without direct involvement in the "editorial" content. Both the sponsor and the advertising agency were cut off from direct programming roles, leading *Sponsor* to ask in the title of a 1954 article, "Are Agencies Earning Their Fifteen Percent on Network TV Shows?" Weaver's extension of the new advertising form, which he called "magazine advertising," was resisted by many television advertisers who resented the loss of program control, sponsor identification, and the ability to reach a targeted audience and by those who feared diminished commercial effectiveness due to advertising "clutter." The case for magazine advertising was strongest at Weaver's NBC (where it was first introduced in the early-morning "Today" show) because NBC, with more affiliates and higher time charges than the other networks, feared the loss of small advertisers to ABC and DuMont networks.[25]

Few of the network spectaculars could be defended on a strict cost-per-thousand basis because they were rarely rating smashes. Instead, an NBC producer told *The New Yorker* that the spectacular operated "like a loss-leader in a chain grocery to gain traffic. Pat [Weaver] knows how to build up a network audience." Weaver told the magazine that if programming were left up to the sponsor and advertising agency, the result would be the lowest-cost programming, which would hurt the entire television industry, especially RCA's set sales. In an interview in 1955, Weaver said that although the network spectaculars were not profitable in relation to advertiser time sales, "[t]hey are paying off as far as the television industry is concerned, as far as the trade press, as far as the selling of television sets," arguing that the spectaculars convinced hesitant consumers to purchase receivers. Weaver explained his programming philosophy to the FCC's Office of Network Study in 1960: "Everyone in the country who is able to reach a television set, big enough or physically capacitated to do it, should be viewing enough to be influenced by the medium."[26]

In a 1953 staff memorandum, Weaver outlined his strategy for attracting the "light viewer" to television: "We must get the show that gets the most talk in the coming season, that wins the Peabody award, that enables me to keep carrying the fight to the intellectuals who misunderstand our mass-media development, and that can be profitably sold without affecting any of our present business." Weaver's ability to evoke the high-minded public relations value of network programming with one eye firmly set on the bottom line earned him his characterization in the industry, according to *Newsweek,* as television's "humanist huckster." A talent agent told *The New Yorker* in 1954 of Weaver: "Program-wise, the guy is terrific, longhairwise, he's great too. With Pat you can think big even about a cooking show."[27]

NBC's Weaver was the most extreme example of the networks' ability to evoke (and in Weaver's case, hyperbolize) the rhetoric of television reformers and critics in the service of network campaigns in the economy of 1950s commercial television. Max Wilk quoted Weaver on NBC's programming strategy of the early 1950s: "In that grand design, entertainment was used to get the people to watch the realism and to get caught by it, but the end would be that we would inform them, enrich them enlighten them, to liberate them from tribal primitive belief patterns."[28]

When Pat Weaver left NBC in 1956, *Sponsor* wrote that "his departure marked "the *formal period* to an *epoch of television:* The era when big ideas and big programming budgets were imperative to speeding up set sales and getting TV as an advertising medium off the ground." However, NBC was eager to reassure those concerned at Weaver's resignation that NBC's programming philosophy was unchanged. Martin Meyer, writing in *Harper's* on Weaver's departure from the network, optimistically noted that "NBC is dedicated to live broadcasting as the true benefit and unique opportunity of television."[29]

The networks frequently linked the public values of program balance and freedom of expression in the medium to the continued prosperity of the network organizations, which would permit them to support special programming and to shield the television writer from the pressures of the commercial sponsor. Pat Weaver in 1955 asserted that because of early unequal revenues of stations and networks in television: "The stations are very profitable and the networks are not. . . . it has been our plan with our affiliates from the beginning to try to . . . set up patterns whereby the networks had more strength and more prosperity in order to do things that ought to be done with special programming."[30]

In 1957, NBC executive Roger Kennedy warned of "the marks of caution's strangling hand" in television programming, but saw hope in "greater 'producer control,' insulated by purposeful network protection from agency and client interference." The key for creative freedom, Kennedy argued, was the network's commercial advantage in negotiations with sponsors: "Prosperity poured its surplus into advertising budgets; network time was sold out; and sponsors were happy to buy what they could, on the network's or station's terms."[31]

In 1955 and 1956, several observers of the industry were optimistic about the prospects for continued diversity and experimentation in television programming, especially in the field of live television drama. George Wolf, in *Advertising Agency Magazine*, called the 1955-56 season "the most heralded year in the brief history of the medium," after earlier promising that the season "would be head and shoulders above anything yet seen in the medium." Wolf wrote that critics Jack Gould and John Crosby, "astute observers of the television scene . . . see in the new programming pattern the strengthening of the entire television medium."[32]

In 1956 CBS announced the launching of television's first ninety-minute live dramatic anthology program, "Playhouse 90," voted in a 1970 *Variety* poll of television editors as the greatest network television series of all time. Gore Vidal in 1956 compared the "youth and enthusiasm" of the television medium for writers to the "bored cynicism" of Hollywood and the "rapacity and bad temper" of Broadway, and concluded: "All things considered, I suspect the golden age for the dramatist is at hand." In a similar vein, Rod Serling introduced a collection of his television plays in 1957 with this judgment of the medium: "Television today remains a study in imperfection. . . . Radio was around for twenty odd years before it . . . ultimately wrote out a finis to its potential. Television hasn't exhausted its potential or altogether found its niche. But in the area of drama it has already far surpassed that of its sister medium."[33]

The optimistic predictions by critics and writers in the mid-1950s would soon prove woefully misplaced. As CBS executive Charles Underhill told the FCC just a few years later: "The golden age of television was a golden age only in that it enabled us to learn, to experiment, to develop, to be ready to go into the golden age which 'Playhouse 90' began to tap and which was cut off, and which really marked the demise of good, live drama." In the opening pages of *The Great Time-Killer* (1962), former television writer Harold Mehling lamented: "Remember how great television used to be? Remember how television excited people, and how people *talked* about it. . . . The outstanding difference between television in the early 1950s and the early 1960s is that the young model, while light-years from perfection, showed promise of attaining decency. Today, grown-up television shows certainty of becoming a major national scandal."[34]

The behavior of the networks in the late 1950s was a bitter revelation for the partisans of live drama who had considered the networks permanent allies in "the struggle for character drama" on television. It is this disillusionment that produced the tone of betrayal and hyperbole in the rising complaints of writers and critics in the late 1950s. If the years between television's Golden Age and the "vast wasteland" are few in number, they measure a traumatic reeducation for many in the ways of commercial television.

NOTES

1. Beyond its manufacturing, network, and station operation interests in television, RCA pressed hard for the rapid exploitation of television on the VHF band in order to protect its patent position in that portion of the spectrum. In the same speech, the RCA executive urged agencies to get an early start in television and criticized those in advertising who counseled holding back until the medium attained significant circulation: "Everyone knows that to keep post-War employment at a desirable level we must increase consumer demand by fifty percent. As advertisers, it is your responsibility to create this demand. The job will be tough and you'll need the best tools you can get," Richard H. Hooper, "Television—The Post-war Sales Tool," speech to the Federated Advertising Clubs of Chicago, December 7, 1944, n.p.; U.S. Department of Commerce, *Television as an Advertising Medium* (Washington, D.C.: U.S. Government Printing Office, 1949), p. 9; Robert M. Reuschle, "Choosing the Right TV Station for Your Product," in Irving Settel and Norman Glenn, *Television Advertising and Production Handbook* (New York: Thomas Y. Crowell, 1953), p. 25.

2. Fairfax M. Cone, *With All Its Faults: A Candid Account of Forty Years in Advertising* (Boston: Little, Brown, 1969), p. 262; "Who Will Produce TV?," *Televiser*, Spring 1945, p. 9.

3. U.S. Federal Communications Commission, Office of Network Study, *Interim Report: Responsibility for Broadcast Matter*, Docket no. 12782 (Washington, D.C.: U.S. Government Printing Office, 1960), p. 164. In 1980, Richard W. Jencks, a former counsel for CBS, wrote that continuing the practice of network radio, the early years of television programming remained in the hands of advertising agencies, which negotiated with networks for specific time slots for programs that agencies brought in, Richard W. Jencks, "How Network Television Programming Decisions Are Made," in *Network Television and the Public Interest*, ed. Michael Botein and David M. Rice (Lexington, Mass.: D.C. Heath, 1980), p. 37; network-sponsor production relations are described in "TV-FM-FAX," *Sponsor*, November 1947, p. 36, and "Sponsor-Agency-Station: Who Is

Responsible for What in TV?," *Sponsor,* January 1948, p. 53; *Television,* February 1949, p. 4.

4. *Television,* November 1947, p. 6.

5. "Lining Up for TV's Big Battle," *Business Week,* March 10, 1956, p. 66; Columbia Broadcasting System, *Annual Report,* for year ending December 30, 1950 (New York: Columbia Broadcasting System, 1951), p. 5. For material on the development of packaged programs at CBS, see "Revolutionizing Radio: CBS Wants to Buy ABC and Hytron," *Business Week,* May 12, 1951, p. 21; "CBS Steals the Show," *Fortune,* July 1953, p. 82; "CBS to Build World's Largest Video Plant," *Broadcasting,* February 23, 1948, p. 14; "One Round to CBS," *Business Week,* September 3, 1949, p. 24.

6. James Whiteside. "The Communicator II: What About the Gratitude Factor?," *The New Yorker,* October 23, 1954, p. 67.

7. "Packaging Returns to the Networks," *Sponsor,* January 16, 1950, p. 58; "TV Costs: Sponsor Pays More, Gets More," *Sponsor,* April 25, 1949, p. 58; "Is the Programming Subsidy Era Over in Network TV?" *Sponsor,* September 8, 1952, p. 83; "Post-Freeze TV: What Advertisers Ask About It," *Sponsor,* June 2, 1952, p. 70.

8. John Gray Peatman, ed., *Radio and Business 1945: Proceedings of the First Annual Conference on Radio and Business* (New York: City College of New York, 1945), p. 130.

9. U.S., Federal Communications Commission, *Public Service Responsibility of Broadcast Licensees* (Washington, D.C.: U.S. Government Printing Office, 1946), p. 17.

10. On Procter and Gamble's advertising policies in network radio, see "FCC's Durr, Others Wonder Whether Radio Knows What.the People Want," *Variety,* June 20, 1945, p. 30 quoted in FCC, *Public Service Responsibility,* 1946, p. 17. The president of Procter and Gamble remarked: "Taking 100 percent as the total radio value, we give 90 percent to commercials, to what's said about the product, and we give 10 percent to the show. . . . The last thing I could afford to do is to offend the public."

11. "FCC's Durr, Others Wonder Whether Radio Knows What the People Want," p. 30 quoted in FCC, *Public Service Responsibility,* 1946, p. 17.

12. Edward Barry Roberts, "Writing for Television," in *The Best Television Plays, 1950-1951,* ed. William I. Kaufman (New York: Hastings House, 1952), p. 296; "Be Careful on the Air," *Sponsor,* September 10, 1951, p. 30.

13. "U.S. Steel Makes Friends While It Sells," *Sponsor,* April 4, 1955, pp. 39, 90, 91.

14. American Business Consultants, *Red Channels: The Report on the Communist Influence in Radio and Television* (New York: American Business Consultants, 1950), p. 2.

15. Jack Gould, *Television* interview by Donald McDonald (Santa Barbara, Calif.: Center for the Study of Democratic Institutions, 1961), p. 49; Erik Barnouw, *The Sponsor: Notes on a Modern Potentate* (New York: Oxford University Press, 1978), p. 49.

16. "The Truth About Red Channels," *Sponsor*, October 8, 1951, p. 76.

17. Max Wilk, "Writing for Television," *Theatre Arts*, February 1951, p. 49; Paddy Chayefsky, *Television Plays* (New York: Simon and Schuster, 1955), p. 131.

18. Pat Weaver, appearance on "Youth Wants to Know," NBC television, June 5, 1955, collection of the NBC Records Administration Library, New York.

19. DeForest, *Television Today and Tomorrow* (New York: Dial Press,1942), pp. 36, 355.

20. "Be Careful on the Air, Part II," *Sponsor*, September 24, 1951, p. 37.

21. Carroll O'Meara, *Television Program Production* (New York: Ronald Press, 1955), p. 328, emphasis in original.

22. Commentary on the controversies over television crime and horror programs is found in "Mysteries: They Love 'em on TV!," *Sponsor*, October 23, 1950, p. 32; Charles Winick, *Taste and the Censor in Television* (New York: Fund for the Republic, 1959), p. 4; Fred Kugel, "Thank You Senator Benton and Mr Rubicam!," *Television*, November 1951, p. 11; "TV's Hottest Problem: Public Relations," *Sponsor*, June 16, 1952, p. 27.

23. U.S. Congress, House Committee on Interstate and Foreign Commerce, *Investigation of Radio and Television Programs, Report by the Communications Subcommittee of the Committee on Interstate and Foreign Commerce*, 82nd Cong., 2d sess. (Washington, D.C.: U.S. Government Printing Office, 1952), pp. 2, 3.

24. Quoted in Stan Opotowsky, *TV: The Big Picture* (New York: E. P. Dutton, 1961), p. 41. Bernard B. Smith argued that sponsor control of 1930s radio programming stood as a warning for those who hoped television would fulfill its public service responsibilities and artistic potential. Smith called for network program control in order to shield the writer from the sponsor's narrow commercial pressures. Bernard B. Smith, "Television—There Ought to be a Law," *Harper's*, September 1948, p. 40; "Weaver Scans the Way Ahead," *Broadcasting-Telecasting*, February 28, 1955, pp. 38–39.

25. Jack Gould, "Television Today—A Critic's Appraisal," *New York Times Magazine*, April 8, 1956, p. 12; Albert J. Jaffe, "Are Agencies Earning Their Fifteen Percent on Network TV Shows?," *Sponsor*, October 18, 1954, p. 29. For Weaver's comments on the spectacular, see "The Communicator," p. 69; Richard Austin Smith, "TV: The Coming Showdown," *Fortune*, September 1954, p. 164.

26. U.S., Federal Communications Commission, Office of Network Study,

Second Interim Report:Television Program Procurement, Part II (Washington, D.C.: U.S. Government Printing Office, 1965), p. 559.

27. For a discussion of Weaver's programming philosophy, see Herman Land, "The Spectacular: An Interim Report," *Sponsor*, November 15, 1954, p. 31; Whiteside, "The Communicator," part 2, pp. 37, 67, 71; "Weaver Scans the Way Ahead," pp. 40, 42; "Stars, Spectaculars—and Uplift?," *Newsweek*, July 18, 1955, p. 49; Weaver told Martin Mayer in 1956: "I don't think any people can understand strategic thinking in television unless they are essentially broadcast-trained people.... Nowadays, going to the movies on a regular basis is actually a minority experience in American society. I think this is because of Hollywood's strategic approach in opposition to that of the advertising-trained men who look at all America as their total market, because they must do so when they deal with popular brands." Martin Meyer, "TV's Lords of Creation," *Harper's*, November 1956, p. 2.

28. Wilk, "Writing for Television," p. 241; Weaver told *Television* magazine that "the grand design of television . . . is to create an aristocracy of the people, the proletariat of privilege," cited in U.S. Congress, Committee on Interstate and Foreign Commerce, *The Television Inquiry*, vol. 4: *Network Practices, Hearings before the Committee on Interstate and Foreign Commerce*, 84th Cong., 2d sess. (Washington, D.C.: U.S. Government Printing Office, 1956), p. 40.

29. *Sponsor*, September 17, 1956, p. 1, emphasis in original; Mayer, "TV's Lords of Creation," p. 32.

30. "Weaver Scans the Way Ahead," p. 40.

31. Roger Kennedy, "Programming Content and Quality," *Law and Contemporary Problems* 22 (Autumn 1957): 542, 543.

32. George Wolf, "New TV Programming Pattern," *Advertising Agency Magazine*, June 24, 1955, p. 27; George Wolf, "TV Program Outlook Bright as New Big Season Opens," *Advertising Agency Magazine*, October 28, 1955, p. 22. Wolf concluded his article with "That tube in the living room never looked brighter than today."

33. Richard Averson and David Manning White, eds., *Electronic Drama: Television Plays of the 1960s* (Boston: Beacon Press, 1971), p.xiii; Gore Vidal, "Notes on Television," *The Writer*, March 1957, p. 34; Rod Serling, *Patterns* (New York: Simon and Schuster, 1957), p. 11.

34. FCC, *Second Interim Report*, p. 575; Harold Mehling, *The Great Time-Killer* (Cleveland: World Publishing, 1962), pp. 11–12.

PART THREE

Programs and Power:
Networks, Sponsors, and the Rise
of Film Programming

7

The Economics of Television Networking

The story of the remaking of prime-time television in the late 1950s has the networks at its center: how they acquired power over affiliates, advertisers, and program producers, and how that power was used and evidenced in prime-time programming. Changes in network position and strategy, however, did not occur in a vacuum. Long-term changes in the motion-picture industry and in American advertising altered their relationships with network television. Furthermore, changes in other aspects of the television industry—station operation, program syndication, foreign program sales, and federal regulation—presented the networks with new opportunities and hazards.

Economic concentration in the television industry is in part a product of the status of broadcasting as a quasi-public good with enormous economies of scale. Less the costs of distribution, it costs no more for a television station or network to reach (and therefore to sell to advertisers) a hundred additional viewers or a million. Thus, large-market television stations and the two dominant networks enjoyed an enormous increase in advertising revenues as television audiences multiplied in the early and mid-1950s.[1]

Unlike most other media industries or in principle any free-market business enterprise, however, there are special and formidable restraints on competition and free entry in television broadcasting. The allocation and assignment policies of the FCC precluded anything but extremely limited competition by limiting the number of valuable VHF assignments in key markets. An additional barrier to wider network competition in television was created in the structure of program distribution, specifically the tariff schedule set up by AT&T for coaxial cable service. The AT&T policies not only hurt the smaller ABC and DuMont networks, but also discouraged the entry of new competitors by discriminating against part-time and small-scale network users.[2]

Another spur to economic concentration in commercial television was the vertical integration of television networks as both station owners and network operators. Network prosperity was fueled by very high revenues and profits of owned-and-operated stations in major markets, and several analysts have argued that the situation of networks owning and operating local television stations provides a striking analogy to the vertical integration of the motion picture industry before the consent decrees that separated studios from theater ownership. The FCC's 1941 *Report on Chain Broadcasting* examined the issue of network ownership of broadcast stations in radio and concluded that if the commission were to consider the question anew without the long and firmly established practice it might well have forbidden network ownership. The Barrow Report came to the same conclusion.[3]

Potential abuses resulting from the vertical integration of station and network include artificially high clearance rates (the percentage of network programming "cleared," or broadcast, by a local station) of owned-and-operated stations, depriving audiences of worthwhile local or non-network programming and violating the licensee's responsibility to program in the public interest; the ability of networks to manipulate station compensation rates to network advantage; and the network's power to deny affiliation or otherwise retaliate against an owner of a chain of stations who refused to sell one of its stations on the network's terms. In addition, the profits from station operation may give networks an unfair subsidy in their program production activities, restraining competition and depressing program prices. Confirming some of these assertions, CBS admitted to the Senate Television Inquiry in 1956 the fact of higher clearance rates for its owned-and-operated stations than for other network affiliates, and that divestiture of its owned-and-operated stations would cause CBS to curtail its network activities due to the lost revenues.[4]

However, as the Barrow Report pointed out, by the mid-1950s the extraordinary profits of CBS and NBC were not chiefly due to their owned-and-operated stations (ABC owned and operated stations in the most lucrative markets of any of the networks, but earned only 5 percent of the total network revenues for 1955). Instead, by the mid-1950s the growing power and revenues of the networks derived from network operations themselves, built on the economic exchanges with station affiliates, program producers, and advertisers. By 1954, the rate of return on network operations exceeded that of the overall television industry. In 1955, annual profits on networking represented 116 percent of tangible investment; in 1956, with the demise of the unprofitable DuMont network, joint network profits were 141 percent.[5]

To a large extent, the postfreeze profitability of the networks reflected the lessons learned and plans made by the networks during the television freeze, particularly in network-affiliate relations. Central to these plans was network access to affiliate time in major markets, reflected in station clearance rates. In many markets the balance of power between networks and affiliates changed significantly after the freeze. Because the FCC's chain broadcasting regulations limited option time (contractually guaranteed network access to affiliate airtime) to specific segments of the broadcast day and prohibited exclusive agreements with affiliates, individual television stations were able to affiliate with more than one network. In 1952, during the freeze, only 36 percent of U.S. stations had affiliations with a single network, and at stations with multiple affiliations the overall clearance rate for programs of the primary network was only 39 percent. A congressional survey of station clearances revealed that in each case where a station rejected three or more network programs, the station was in a one- or two-station market, "where the stations enjoy a more secure position in relation to their networks and where they often have secondary affiliations with the other networks."[6]

Owners of network affiliates in one-station markets demonstrated their unique market power in several ways. A telefilm producer and syndicator complained that spot advertising rates in one-station Toledo, with 359,000 sets, were higher than those in the New York market of 4,700,000 sets. In addition, station owners in one- and two-channel markets, a majority of total stations during the freeze, were able to extract commercial advantages in their negotiations with networks over station compensation rates. According to the Barrow Report, before

1952, NBC paid a 10 percent premium on top of the customary 30 percent of gross advertising revenues to single-channel stations in important markets. ABC, in a weaker competitive position with most of its affiliates also affiliated with one of the larger networks, paid local stations up to 50 percent of gross billings in one- and two-station markets. An ABC executive told a House subcommittee in 1952 that the freeze operated to give affiliates significant power in clearance negotiations with the network.[7]

The lifting of the FCC station construction freeze in 1952 strengthened the networks in dealings with affiliates by greatly reducing the number of one- and two-station markets, bringing an end to what Pat Weaver called "a rather unusual period in terms of station arrogance." In January 1953, *Television* predicted a healthy financial future for the television industry under the new Republican administration and forecast higher profits for networks with the extinction of one- and two-station markets and the clearance problems they presented to the networks.[8]

The period 1952-54 saw the fastest growth in the number of television station licensees, which swelled from 108 to 380. The new station owners on the UHF band did not share in the prosperity, however. Despite the hopes offered by the FCC in its 1952 *Sixth Report and Order* for greater local service and wider network competition with the opening of the UHF band, UHF broadcasters were unable to compete against the VHF stations in the primarily intermixed markets the commission set up. Of the stations on the air in 1953, 68 percent were established in 1952; together the new stations received only 6 percent of total television revenues for a combined loss of $10,500,000. Sixty percent of the industry losses were incurred by the new UHF stations, and from 1953-56, more UHF stations left the air than began broadcasting. As the Barrow Report dryly concluded about the failure of the UHF allocations: "The limited development of the UHF band has certain advantages for the two leading networks because it restricts the potentialities for competition between these networks and other network and non-network sources."[9]

Revenues and profits in the television industry were distributed extremely unevenly, favoring VHF licensees over UHF operators, network-affiliated over independent stations, and large-market over small-market operators. In its professed desire to encourage localism, the FCC spread station assignments among 1,300 communities, precluding the development of four-channel local markets necessary for wider national network competition. The effect was to create a huge number of "phantom" assignments, in markets so small as to be permanently unattractive to commercial broadcasters. The Barrow study estimated that stations in markets of less than fifty thousand people were likely to be unprofitable, and by 1957, only 255 of the 1,300 assignments actually were in use.[10]

Network-affiliated stations captured a disproportionate share of television revenues, making network affiliation a requirement for station survival in all but the largest and smallest markets. Senator John W. Bricker pointed out, for example, that in the Northeast, the seventy-three CBS and NBC affiliates captured 65 percent of total revenue, leaving only 35 percent for the remaining 335 stations, including those affiliated with ABC and DuMont. In 1955, 86 percent of the profitable stations in the country were affiliated with CBS or NBC; 71 percent of the independent stations lost money. As broadcast economist Barry Litman concluded: "having a network affiliation means the difference between profits and losses, life and death." Kenneth Cox, special counsel for the Senate Commerce Committee's Television Inquiry, wrote in his 1957 committee report *Television Network Practices* that the value of network affiliation to the television station operator was so great that the network had a significant bargaining advantage with its affiliates.[11]

In every major area of negotiation with the postfreeze stations the two major networks held decisive advantages over their affiliates. The basic financial issues between network and affiliate included affiliate designation, the setting of station compensation fees (the station's share of the gross advertising revenues from the network's sale of time in the local market), the setting of the individual station's advertising rates for network and non-network (local or national spot) advertising, and the terms of option time, which mandated network access to station airtime. Subsidiary issues include the responsibility for distribution charges of the AT&T coaxial cable link and the possibility of the station's membership in the network advertiser's must-buy list, which insured inclusion of the local station in any network time purchase.

Although the networks claimed they offered broadly consistent commercial terms and policies to their affiliates, both Representative Emanuel Celler's House Judiciary investigation of 1956 and the Barrow

Report in 1957 reported wide variations in network-affiliate commercial arrangements. Likewise, a Senate Commerce Committee report in 1955 concluded: "clearly . . . the networks have no consistent affiliation policy which they apply uniformly. Nor have they proven any rational basis for past decisions to affiliate or reject affiliation with individual television stations." Both congressional investigations concluded that the television networks favored affiliations with their existing radio affiliates in the same market, and also with multiple station owners, who were sometimes able to use the power of their other holdings to negotiate more favorable terms for a particular station.[12]

In their negotiations with affiliates over the range of economic issues, the networks also had the advantage of more complete competitive information because affiliation agreements were not publicly released, even though the FCC collected the information. At hearings in 1955, Representative Celler pressed the FCC to release the terms of network affiliation agreements in order to strengthen the hand of stations in negotiations; FCC Chairman George McConnaughey refused. The Barrow Report similarly recommended disclosure of affiliation contracts to avoid network discrimination among stations.[13]

The networks' main goal in setting affiliate compensation rates and in enforcing option time provisions was ensuring maximum clearance for network programs. All three networks used sliding compensation scales that rewarded higher clearance rates; the station's share of advertising revenues increased with the number of hours cleared for the network every month. All three networks also demanded a minimum number of "free" or uncompensated hours from affiliates each month before the station received its share of gross revenues, a concession that was increasingly valuable as advertising revenues increased sharply in the 1950s.[14]

The two dominant networks also served as national spot representatives for their owned-and-operated stations and many of their large-market affiliates. In so doing, the networks had responsibility for setting the advertising rates not only for the station's network time charges, but also for network television's chief competitor, national spot advertising. The Barrow study reported network manipulation of network and spot rates to restrain competition to network advertising and to ensure high network clearances. The report concluded that the networks "have by far the major role in network rate determination" in their negotiations with affiliates. Until the FCC's chain broadcasting rules in 1941, radio networks forbade affiliates from discounting spot rates below network time charges, and the Barrow Report cited numerous cases of CBS and ABC pressure on television affiliates to keep spot rates at parity with network rates. The report also noted many examples of network pressure for higher station clearances when stations sought to raise their network rates, often pressing for explicit commitments to specific clearance levels.[15]

However, the most contentious feature of network affiliation relations in the 1950s was the option time provision, which committed a station to carry network programs a certain number of hours in each portion of the broadcast day. The original FCC chain broadcasting regulations in 1941 outlawed the practice of option time, but, under pressure from the networks and Congress, the commission relented and voted merely to restrict the number of option time hours available, and to prohibit its enforcement against the programs of another network.

Kenneth Cox objected to the use of option time in television in light of the very different market conditions reflecting channel scarcity and production costs in television as opposed to radio. Cox argued that option time usurped the local station licensee's responsibility to program in the public interest and delegated programming responsibility to the unlicensed and unregulated networks; that option time injured non-network program producers and syndicators by preempting large amounts of station time; that it restricted access of television advertisers to station time except through the network purchase; and that the practice unfairly competed against nonaffiliated stations.[16]

Emanuel Celler wrote: "That option time provisions do tend to curtail competition cannot be doubted," and argued that the practice restricted the program choices available to the public. The Cox and Barrow reports, Representative Celler, and Victor R. Hansen, assistant attorney general in charge of the Anti-Trust Division, all raised serious objections to the practice of option time on antitrust grounds. Hansen told the House Judiciary Committee in 1956: "A good beginning point, evidence thus far suggests, is the striking similarity between TV industry structure and that movie pattern condemned in Paramount." Cox concluded that option time had "sufficient similarities" with the case of block-booking in the film industry "to justify the most careful consideration by the Federal Communication Commission and the Department of Justice."[17]

The 1956 hearings of the Senate Commerce Committee's inquiry into television included testimony from some affiliates that option time served to tie the network's most popular programs to those of less appeal, which the affiliate might otherwise refuse in favor of non-network programming. The Cox Report concluded: "Since the option involves carrying the weaker programs of the network in order to get its top-rated attraction, it produces results analogous to block booking." The Barrow Report concluded in 1957: "The option time arrangement has definitely forced some programs on some affiliates that they would otherwise have not accepted. . . . If this were not the case, of course, option time would serve no useful function to the networks."[18]

The defense of option time put the networks in an awkward position. While denying it had the effect of tying weaker, less desirable network programs to the popular programs the affiliates wanted, at the same time the networks protested that any restrictions on the use of option time would be fatal to network operation. The Barrow Report pointed out that the contractual provisions of the option time clause had never been legally enforced by the networks because the networks feared a direct legal test of the practice. Arguing that the analogy with block-booking in motion picture distribution was persuasive, the report concluded: "Consequently, there is at least a reasonable possibility of a court finding that the option time practice constitutes a *per se* violation of Section 1 of the Sherman Act."[19]

NBC President Robert Sarnoff told the Senate Commerce Committee in 1956: "I think the existence of option time in the contract has a persuasive power. The fact that we may not invoke our legal rights is a matter of business judgment." In a memorandum submitted to the committee, NBC argued that "Without option time, there would be no meaning or substance to the affiliation relationship. And without affiliations, there could be no networks." In a CBS memorandum submitted to the committee, a similar stark warning was raised against restricting option time: "Either it or some equivalent tool is the keystone of network operations. Without such a tool, networks cannot operate. It would take the defection of only a few key stations in major markets to deprive a network television advertiser of so substantial a part of his circulation that the program would not continue...." CBS warned that the erosion caused by such defections by affiliates "would be fatal." The Barrow Report replied skeptically to the network claim, noting, "In many respects, this erosion is synonymous with competition."[20]

Whatever the specific contribution of the option time provision to network clearance levels in the mid-1950s, the two dominant networks were very successful in gaining access to their affiliates' prime time. Prime time from 7:00-10:30 p.m. was the chief target of the networks' efforts, because more than twice as many sets were in use in those hours, and there were also more viewers per set than at other times of the day. Network clearance was positively correlated with market size, and therefore station advertising revenue, according to the Barrow Report, which reported an average of 92 percent prime-time clearance in the top five markets. Kenneth Cox's report to the Senate Commerce Committee pointed out that in the top forty television markets that constituted 72 percent of the nation's sets, the clearance rate was more than 97 percent of prime-time half hours.[21]

The extraordinary profits of large-market television stations and of the two major networks were special subjects of congressional scrutiny in the mid-1950s, initiated by Bricker's *The Network Monopoly*. The Cox Report noted that the networks received 53-56 percent of the total television revenues from 1948-53, with CBS and NBC getting 88 percent of the total network share. Bricker's report opened with the warning: "Two networks—Columbia Broadcasting Service and the National Broadcasting Company—have an unprecedented economic stranglehold on the nation's television industry. Effective competition is stifled under this yoke of economic domination. The result is a private monopoly." In 1954, CBS, including its owned-and-operated stations and its network operations, enjoyed a 108 percent return on tangible investment; NBC received an 87 percent return. Profits from the owned-and-operated stations of CBS and NBC in 1954 were 370 percent and 297 percent, respectively, and returns from the two networks' stations in New York were between 1600 and 1800 percent. "By any standard," Bricker wrote, "such profits must be labeled *exorbitant*." The Barrow Report noted that CBS and NBC, while controlling 11 percent of total television assets, received 43 percent of industry profits in 1955.[22]

The Senate Commerce Committee under Bricker convened a lengthy series of hearings on network competition and the plight of UHF station owners in 1954, and commissioned a staff report prepared by former FCC staff counsel Harry M. Plotkin. The report called for requiring networks to affiliate in smaller, less profitable markets; restricting the amount of network-controlled time on local stations in markets of fewer than four stations; and the selective de-intermixture of VHF and UHF markets. Plotkin's report, together with minority staff counsel Robert F. Jones's *The Investigation of Television Networks and the UHF-VHF Problem* in February 1955 and Bricker's 1956 *Network Monopoly*, implicated the networks in the failure of the UHF operators and represented, according to historian Stuart Lewis Long, the "high point in Congressional criticism of networks."[23]

In its published reply to Bricker's *Network Monopoly*, CBS argued that the public was not injured by the extraordinary network profits because they did not pay television advertising costs, and that the issue of profits was irrelevant to the public interest. CBS responded sharply to Bricker's proposal to limit the service area of some large-market stations in order to counteract the disproportion of television revenues, arguing that it "is a conception at once impossible of enforcement and inconsistent with the American principle of free competitive enterprise. It would, in effect, socialize television stations, among all American businesses, by limiting their service only to an area which would permit their economic survival—and no more."[24]

An April 1956 article in *Sponsor* viewed three proposals to revise the *Sixth Report and Order's* allocation plan: de-intermixture of UHF and VHF stations, expansion of the VHF band, or a shift of television service entirely to the UHF band. CBS reportedly favored limited expansion of the VHF band and opposed the move to the uncrowded UHF band, arguing that too many stations would fragment television's audience and advertising support. The article reassured readers that the trade consensus was that the FCC would take little action, and certainly not threaten existing station operators. The same reassurance was conveyed in an April 1955 *Television* article on the release of the Plotkin and Jones reports, "The Word from Washington: Relax."[25]

The scrutiny of network practices reached a peak in 1955-57, with concurrent investigations by the Senate Commerce Committee (with two years of hearings producing seven volumes of testimony consuming 3,500 pages); the Antitrust Subcommittee of the House Judiciary Committee (3,400 pages of testimony); a Justice Department suit against

NBC in December 1956 concerning its station swap with Westinghouse; a joint Justice Department-FBI probe of "network practices relating to the sale of network time and shows"; and the investigation by the FCC's Office of Network Study under Roscoe Barrow. *Sponsor* reported in October 1957 that the Barrow Report was a "far more serious threat to the networks than the recently-completed Congressional probes and reports," and a writer in *Television* in May 1957 described the fearful mood of the industry.[26]

In retrospect, it seems some industry observers overestimated the inclination of the FCC in the 1950s to take any action contrary to the interests of the television networks. FCC commissioners George McConnaughey and John Doerfer in testimony before the Antitrust Subcommittee of the House Judiciary Committee in 1955 defended high network profits and dismissed them as a concern of the commission. Doerfer also defended the controversial network practices of option time and the must-buy provisions of sponsor contract. Doerfer's reaction to questions about network dominance and antitrust issues was: "Concentration does not bother me. . . . Somebody has to be dominant. Somebody is big."[27]

In November 1957, *Television* cited the prediction of communications lawyer Leonard Marks that the FCC would follow the Barrow Report's recommendations to ban option time and must-buy lists as well as discourage multiple ownership of television stations. *Sponsor* in January 1958 likewise predicted that a reluctant FCC would be forced to take action following the Barrow Report, at least concerning option time and must-buy practices. Two weeks later, however, the magazine reported that the FCC had announced an open-ended set of hearings on the Barrow Report in order to forestall congressional pressure for commission action in 1958.[28]

Representative John Dingle in 1957 denounced FCC Chairman Doerfer, saying the commissioner had "demonstrated a penchant for endearing himself to the networks and the big broadcasters—the people, in short, whom the FCC is supposed to regulate." In 1958, the FCC in a 4–3 vote declined to ban option time on the grounds that it was necessary for network operation. In February 1959, the Justice Department's antitrust head announced that the FCC's own evidence established the illegal status of option time under the antitrust laws, but the Justice Department deferred filing legal action pending commission action. Following the Justice Department's announcement, the networks voluntarily dropped the must-buy provisions of sponsor agreements and withdrew from affiliate representation in national spot sales, thereby relinquishing the direct power to set stations' spot rates. In 1963, under new leadership, the commission finally outlawed network option time. Bernard Schwartz, who led a short-lived House Oversight Committee investigation of the FCC in 1957-58, wrote in an analysis of FCC performance in enforcing antitrust law in the television industry: "It is largely because the Commission has not vigorously enforced antitrust policies that the networks have been able to acquire their present position of dominance in broadcasting."[29]

In fact, the attention paid to the specific issue of option time as the cause of high network clearance levels in the 1950s was largely misplaced. Despite the warnings from network leaders of the dire consequences of federal tampering with option time, most investigators concluded that the abolition of option time would have little effect on network revenues or profits, or on network negotiations with affiliates, program producers, and sponsors. The Cox Report concluded that option time was not essential for high network clearances on affiliate schedules: "It would appear that as long as network service is maintained at present levels, a network affiliation will continue to be a valuable asset, if not absolutely essential to really profitable operation in all but the largest markets." The Barrow Report concluded that option time was only one factor ensuring high network clearances, less important than basic station incentives and the power of the network in affiliate negotiations. Although the Barrow Report did call for the abolition of option time, it also cautioned: "It would be misleading to state or imply that any major changes in the structure of performance of the television industry would occur, in the foreseeable future, as a result of the elimination of option time." Schwartz concluded in 1959: "In reality, since most affiliates are utterly dependent upon their affiliations, they are completely tied to their networks, regardless of the formal terms of the affiliation agreements."[30]

With the exception of a single disgruntled station operator whose affiliation contract was terminated by NBC in a dispute over clearance levels and station advertising rates, network affiliates were publicly unanimous in defense of network practices during the congressional and regulatory hearings of the mid-1950s. Richard A. Moore, president of independent station KTTV in Los Angeles and leader of a group challenging network practices in affiliation, program procurement, and sponsorship, told the Commerce Committee in 1956 that "under the status quo, affiliated stations, program producers, and many advertisers must depend primarily upon the favor of network companies for their economic prosperity or survival. It would be understandable, therefore, if persons in that position refrained from taking a public position contrary to the position expressed by the network companies."[31]

The controversy in the mid-1950s over option time and network economic power provoked the sharpest conflict between networks and independent suppliers of television programming. Growing network control of affiliate air time constricted the non-network market available to independent producers. Because the networks were also producers and licensers of programming, the independent producers argued that practices like option time gave the networks unfair advantage in supplying television programming to local stations. The networks replied that because they viewed networks as more than mere program suppliers, the public interest permitted a competitive shield for the networks in the form of option time and similar restrictive practices. CBS President Frank Stanton told the Senate Commerce Committee:

> A network is an organic thing—that is, it is very much alive. It has to be considered as an entity. The dangers of considering it only as a set of disrelated parts to be juggled around any which way are most considerable, and not everyone has successfully avoided them, by any means.
>
> Because of the importance and complexity of the issues we are considering here, they cannot be dealt with quickly. Lunchtime gossip, tablecloth arithmetic and inexpert speculations cannot successfully deal with these issues, rooted as they are in the natural laws that govern the electron, or the economic laws that govern how an enterprise can be successfully conducted.[32]

Richard Moore called for restrictions on network option time, pointing out that the practice was reluctantly allowed by the FCC in 1941 when all network radio programming was live, therefore justifying the network's special status as purveyors of interconnected live programs. In television, however, a majority of network programs were on film, Moore noted, so the justification of special network privileges in order to support live broadcasting was weaker: "The more networks rely on film, the more they become simply competitors of other program producers and distributors, but in a favored position because, under the regulations, they have the right to force their programs upon the affiliated stations." The Barrow Report similarly concluded: "Apart from programs requiring simultaneous nationwide exposure, it is not evident that the 'need' of the network for time options on behalf of its national advertisers is significantly different in kind from that of the film producer on behalf of the national, regional, or local advertisers that purchase his program directly or through a local station."[33]

Responding to such criticism, CBS argued in a legal memorandum submitted to the committee that "a television broadcast service is much more than a miscellaneous collection of programs. . . . There must be policy direction, continuity, variety and numerous other ingredients which cannot be obtained merely by buying up the chance creations of outsiders." The leaders of NBC and CBS were eager to convince their critics within and outside Congress that tampering with network business arrangements would endanger the kind of television programming celebrated by the industry's most prominent writers and critics. The two networks' association with live anthology drama from New York provided them a handy shield from the complaints of other economic groups challenging their commanding position in the television industry.

Many of the arguments offered by the networks invoked the aesthetic privileging of live television in defense of their economic practices. NBC President Robert Sarnoff quoted the FCC's "Blue Book" to the Senate Commerce Committee in 1956 in defense of network program procurement practices. Three CBS executives argued in an article in *Law and Contemporary Problems* in 1957 that "[t]he only source of nationwide live programming is the networks. . . . While film programs may be and frequently are good, it is its live quality which is the real magic of television." In *Network Practices*, CBS's lengthy response to the congressional inquiry, the network again echoed the critics' rhetoric in defense of live programming as "the real magic of television." During the congressional investigations the dominant networks attempted to portray their critics within the industry as a group of frustrated Hollywood film producers who would do away with the programming achievements of television's Golden Age. An NBC memorandum submitted to a Senate committee argued that "If this film group should succeed in undermining the network system, the great national service provided today by three intensely competitive networks would ultimately be reduced to the lowest common Hollywood denominator. The wealth of fine education and cultural programs available in the diversified schedules of the networks would be replaced by a continuing flow of stale and stereotyped film product." Robert Sarnoff, after quoting critic Jack Gould on the aesthetic value of live over film programming, told the Senate Committee:

> Today, television broadcasting is at a crossroads: one fork has color signposts and points to programming created for the medium itself, with emphasis on live service. The other fork follows a detour to a reservoir of motion picture film, built up over the past twenty years. At NBC we have carefully weighed the alternatives for the network and our owned stations. We have decided that television's future rests along the route we now chart. We shall continue our emphasis on live television, our fresh new programs designed for the medium, and on the development of color. We believe this is the way to maintain television's momentum and vitality.[35]

Faced with regulatory challenges in the mid-1950s, the networks had strong incentives to exploit the critical privileging of live versus film programming in defense of their economic practices. This would be, however, the last time the networks so passionately allied themselves with the critical champions of television's Golden Age. Within a few years, relations between the networks and critics were utterly and irrevocably transformed, with sometimes bitter results.

NOTES

1. Barry Russell Litman, *The Vertical Structure of the Television Broadcasting Industry: The Coalescence of Power* (East Lansing: Michigan State University Press, 1979), p. 23.

2. On the role of AT&T rate policies in network competition, see Stuart Lewis Long, *The Development of the Television Network Monopoly* (Ph.D. diss., University of Illinois, 1974; New York: Arno Press, 1979), p. 85; Gary Newton Hess, *An Historical Study of the DuMont Television Network* (Ph.D.. diss., Northwestern University, 1960; New York: Arno Press, 1979), p. 69; U.S. Congress, House Committee on Interstate and Foreign Commerce, *Network Broadcasting,* House Report no. 1297, Committee on Interstate and Foreign Commerce, 85th Cong., 2d sess. (Washington, D.C.: U.S. Government Printing Office, 1958), p. 203

(hereafter referred to as the Barrow Report); also see the testimony of Victor Hanson, assistant attorney general before Representative Emanuel Celler's Subcommittee, U.S. Congress, House Committee on the Judiciary, *Monopoly Problems in the Regulated Industries, Hearings before the Antitrust Subcommittee of the Committee on the Judiciary, House of Representatives,* 84th Cong., 2d sess. (Washington, D.C.: U.S. Government Printing Office, 1956), part 2, vol. 2, p. 4132 (hereafter referred to as the Celler Hearings).

3. For a discussion of the antitrust implications of network station ownership, see Barrow Report, pp. 570-600; Bernard Schwartz, "Antitrust and the FCC: The Problem of Network Dominance," *University of Pennsylvania Law Review* 106 (April 1959): 754-95; Herbert H. Howard, *Multiple Ownership in Television Broadcasting: Historical Development and Selected Case Studies* (Ph.D. diss., Ohio University, 1973; New York: Arno Press, 1979); Barrow Report, pp. 572, 592.

4. A notorious case alleging network pressure on a chain owner involved NBC and Westinghouse in the 1950s; for a discussion of the case, see Schwartz, "Antitrust and the FCC," pp. 755-66; Barrow Report, pp. 579-92; Howard, *Multiple Ownership,* pp. 61-63. The implications of network station ownership are explored in U.S. Congress, Senate Committee on Foreign and Interstate Commerce, *Television Inquiry,* vol. 4: *Network Practices, Hearings before the Committee on Foreign and Interstate Commerce,* 84th Cong., 2d sess. (Washington, D.C.: U.S. Government Printing Office, 1956), pp. 1834-35 (hereafter referred to as Television Inquiry).

5. Barrow Report, pp. 591-92; Long, *The Development of the Television Network Monopoly,* p. 118.

6. According to the Barrow Report, "Toward the end of 1951, with the thawing of the freeze in sight and in anticipation of a flood of new stations in markets throughout the nation, NBC and CBS began to plan their future systems" (p. 210); the freeze era clearance figures are found in Long, *The Development of the Television Network Monopoly,* p. 64; U.S. Congress, Senate Committee on Interstate and Foreign Commerce, *Television Network Practices, Staff Report,* Committee Print no. 2, 85th Cong., 1st sess. (Washington, D.C.: U.S. Government Printing Office, 1957), p. 21 (hereafter referred to as the Cox Report).

7. The telefilm producer's complaint is found in Television Inquiry, p. 2692; Barrow Report, pp. 463, 464; U.S. Congress, House Committee on Interstate and Foreign Commerce, *Investigation of Radio and Television Programs, Hearings before the Communications Subcommittee of the Committee on Interstate and Foreign Commerce,* 82nd Cong., 2d sess. (Washington, D.C.: U.S. Government Printing Office, 1952), p. 213. The Barrow Report concluded regarding the disparities in network-affiliate relations dependent on the presence of local

competition: "In one-station markets . . . where the station is a primary affiliate of one of the networks, it is in fact less of a 'monopoly' of the network (less under the control of the network) than are those affiliates of the network in multi-station markets. In the one-station market the station quite frequently takes programs from all three networks and, therefore, cannot be as fully exploited as negotiable leverage by the network as can those affiliates in a three-station market, for example, where each station usually has a primary affiliation with one of the networks and takes few, if any, programs from the other networks" (p. 504).

8. Pat Weaver, "Comments on the Billy Rose Plan for Film by NBC," 1951, p. 6, collection of the NBC Records Administration Library, New York; Robert Gilbert, "Television 1953—Wall Street," *Television*, January 1953, p. 36.

9. Long, *The Development of the Television Network Monopoly*, p. 103; Barrow Report, pp. 31, 225.

10. Barrow Report, p. 226.

11. Litman, *The Vertical Structure*, p. 24; U.S. Congress, Senate Committee on Interstate and Foreign Commerce, *The Network Monopoly, Report for the Committee on Interstate and Foreign Commerce, U.S. Senate, by Senator John W. Bricker*, 84th Cong., 2d sess. (Washington, D.C.: U.S. Government Printing Office, 1955), p. 6 (hereafter referred to as the Bricker Report); the breakdown of station profits is found in Frederick Stuart, *The Effects of Television on the Motion-Picture and Radio Industries* (New York: Arno Press, 1976), p. 90; Cox Report, p. 6.

12. Barrow Report, pp. 237-41; Emanuel Celler, "Antitrust Problems in the Television Broadcasting Industry," *Law and Contemporary Problems* 22 (Autumn 1957): 565.

13. Celler Hearings, pp. 565, 3365; U.S. Congress, Senate Committee on Interstate and Foreign Commerce, *Investigation of Television Networks and the UHF-VHF Problem*, Committee Print, Committee on Interstate and Foreign Commerce, Robert F. Jones, 84th Cong., 2d sess. (Washington, D.C.: U.S. Government Printing Office, 1955), p. 21 (hereafter referred to as the Jones Report); Kenneth Cox pursued NBC President Robert Sarnoff on this point in Senate Commerce Committee testimony, Television Inquiry, p. 2438; Barrow Report, pp. 250-52; 467.

14. Barrow Report, p. 464; Television Inquiry, p. 2504.

15. Cox Report, pp. 92-93; Barrow Report, pp. 405, 422-27, 429-47.

16. Cox concurred with the original 1941 FCC ban on option time and argued that it was even more important in television given the restricted competition in the industry, Cox Report, pp. 16, 29.

17. Material on the network option time controversy can be found in Celler,

"Antitrust Problems in the Television Broadcasting Industry," p. 563; Cox Report, pp. 15-16, 98; Barrow Report, p. 389. Hansen is quoted in Cellar Hearings, p. 4130.

18. Cox Report, p. 15; Barrow Report, p. 387.

19. Barrow Report, pp. 297-99, 389.

20. Television Inquiry, pp. 2445, 2278, 1809-10; Barrow Report, p. 378.

21. Barrow Report, pp. 189, 192; Cox Report, p. 17.

22. Jones Report, p. 15; Bricker Report, pp. 1, 5, 15, emphasis in original; CBS's owned-and-operated station in New York, WCBS, earned profits of 2295 percent in 1955, Celler Hearings, p. 3351; Barrow Report, p. 194.

23. Long, *The Development of the Television Network Monopoly*, pp. 105, 106.

24. Columbia Broadcasting System, *An Analysis of Senator John W. Bricker's Report Entitled "The Network Monopoly"* (New York: Columbia Broadcasting System, 1956), pp. 10, 43.

25. "Can the FCC End the Seller's Market in TV?," *Sponsor*, April 2, 1956, pp. 26, 27, 98; "The Word from Washington: Relax," *Television*, April 1955, p. 35.

26. Testimony of Assistant Attorney General Victor Hanson, Celler Hearings, p. 4124; "Washington Talk," *Sponsor*, October 5, 1957, p. 79; Jack Adams, "Washington: The Scalpels Are Sharpened," *Television*, May 1957, p. 118.

27. Quoted in Bernard Schwartz, *The Professor and the Commissions* (New York: Alfred A. Knopf, 1959), p. 127. For Doerfer's defense of network option time and the must-buy list, see Celler Hearings, pp. 3520. 3329, 3354.

28. Marks is quoted in "Reaction to the Barrow Report," *Television*, November 1957, p. 118; "Washington Week," *Sponsor*, January 4, 1958, p. 77; "Washington Week," *Sponsor*, January 18, 1957, p. 75; Roscoe L. Barrow, "Antitrust and the Regulated Industry: Promoting Competition in Broadcasting," *Duke Law Journal*, September 1964, pp. 289-91.

29. Representative Dingel is quoted in "Washington Week," *Sponsor*, June 8, 1957, p. 85; for accounts of the FCC's actions during this period, see Barrow, "Antitrust and the Regulated Industry," pp. 290-91; Schwartz, "Antitrust and the FCC," p. 773.

30. Cox Report, p. 38; Barrow Report, pp. 326, 399-400; Schwartz, "Antitrust and the FCC," p. 785. Former CBS executive Michael Dann later maintained that the 1963 abolition of option time "had no effects on us whatsoever." See Michael Dann interview, June 14, 1979, Federal Communications Commission File, Oral History Collection, Columbia University, p. 19.

31. Television Inquiry, p. 2406. Moore told the committee that several affiliate station owners had privately encouraged his efforts (p. 1580); a Brookings Institution study in 1973, *The Economics of Television Regulation*, offered a posi-

tive reason for the acquiescence of the affiliated stations in the network practices under dispute: as three powerful consolidated sales agents for their station
chains, the networks profited from their power in the market in national television advertising, and the networks passed along some of the economic rents to
their affiliates in the form of higher time charges or compensation rates, sufficient to dissuade individual stations from dealing directly with sponsors to the
extent of threatening the networks. Roger G. Noll, Merton J. Peck, and John J.
McGowan, *Economic Aspects of Television Regulation* (Washington, D.C.:
Brookings Institution, 1973), p. 59.

32. Television Inquiry, pp. 1696-97; for similar arguments also see Columbia
Broadcasting System, *Network Practices: Memorandum Supplementing Statement of Frank Stanton, President, Columbia Broadcasting System, Inc.* (New
York: Columbia Broadcasting System, 1956), p. 4, reprinted in Television Inquiry, p. 1706.

33. Television Inquiry, p. 1532; Barrow Report, p. 354.

34. Columbia Broadcasting System, *Opinion of Counsel and Memorandum
Concerning the Applicability of Antitrust Laws to the Television Broadcast Activities of Columbia Broadcasting System, Inc.* (New York: Columbia Broadcasting System, 1956), p. 70, reprinted in Television Inquiry, p. 1986.

35. Television Inquiry, p. 2397; Richard S. Salent, Thomas K. Fisher, and
Leon R. Brooks, "The Functions and Practices of a Television Network," *Law
and Contemporary Problems* 22 (Autumn 1957): 587; National Broadcasting
Company, *Statement of Facts,* reprinted in Television Inquiry, p. 2279. CBS also
offered other rationales for network privilege, warning that remitting television
to film programming "is to destroy the only effective means of nationwide visual
communication to the entire country for national emergency purposes." CBS
President Frank Stanton warned in his congressional testimony: "To curtail or
destroy the networks' unique quality of instantaneous national interconnection
would be a colossal backward step. It would be to make to United States much
more like Europe than America. In fact, it would be a step in the Balkanization,
the fragmentation, of the United States," Television Inquiry, pp. 1715, 2129;
Sarnoff is quoted in Television Inquiry, p. 1715; for similar arguments, see "Lining Up for TV's Big Battle," *Business Week,* March 10, 1956, p. 66.

8

The Hollywood Studios Move into Prime Time

The distinct sources of network power reenforced one another in the network negotiations with affiliates, sponsors, and program producers. One of the chief issues concerning network option time, for example, was its effect on the ability of independent program producers to reach audiences with non-network syndicated programs. Likewise, network control of affiliate prime-time meant that television sponsors could reach desired markets only through network-distributed programs. The networks used their economic power in networking, derived in major part from the frequency allocation, distribution, and affiliation policies of the FCC, to alter the terms of negotiation with their suppliers (the program producers) and their customers (the television advertisers). By the mid-1950s the networks enjoyed both a buyer's market in program procurement (with monopoly power shared by three buyers of national programming), as well as a three-firm seller's market in national network advertising. Network power affected not only the terms of industry negotiations but also the forms of television programming and sponsorship in the 1950s. The manner in which the networks exercised their new power in both arenas of the network economy—program procurement and advertising sales—suggests the new outlines of the television industry in the second half of the 1950s.

In the Hollywood film industry of the 1950s, the commercial calculations regarding television were affected by the general restructuring of the motion-picture industry after World War II. It had been clear since the beginning of television that the feature film libraries of the major studios would be attractive to broadcasters. However, the timing and terms of the films' release to television depended on a number of specific factors within the industry. Reacting to a severe downturn at the national box office, the major studios slashed their fixed costs and payrolls from 1948 to 1952; especially vulnerable were middle-level performers and writers. In 1953, *Newsweek* reported somewhat hyperbolically that the only performers left on studio contract were a few big stars and the lowest-paid players.[1]

Studio austerity also encouraged a shift to independent production. In 1949, 20 percent of the features released by the eight major distributors were independently produced; in 1957, independent productions represented 57 percent of feature releases. The major studios brought in substantial revenues through leasing their stages and back lots to independent producers. The success of the CBS talent raids in radio after World War II indicated the powerful tax incentives that impelled stars and other talent to incorporate and take their income in capital gains. The stars' growing independence from the motion picture studios and the rise of independent production in Hollywood not only made the performer a producer-entrepreneur, but also increased the power of talent agents in the industry. When film stars turned to television, the long-term commitments they often demanded were difficult for advertising agencies, individual sponsors, or independent producers to offer, giving networks, the major studios, and a few large independent telefilm producers an advantage in acquiring major Hollywood performers for television.[2]

The competition from television and the other changes within the film industry affected the various sectors of the motion picture industry unevenly, reinforcing a shift of power from exhibitors to producer-distributors in the 1950s. The part of the industry faring the worst in the decade was exhibition, with thousands of motion-picture theaters going out of business. Charles Skouras, the head of Twentieth Century-Fox, in 1952 predicted that 50 percent of the theaters in the country would close, with particularly harsh effects on independent exhibitors rather than on chain owners.[3]

Television in April 1951 outlined the incentives for motion-picture studios to enter television programming, but also cautioned that the seventeen thousand theaters in the United States still constituted the producers' largest market. Motion-picture producers took seriously the threats of exhibitors to boycott any studio that sold features to television or moved too wholeheartedly into telefilm production. The threat carried weight in the industry. But in 1951, *Television* noted prophetically: "As was the case with talking pictures, Hollywood feels that once one studio makes the dash for television, all the rest will immediately follow trail."[4]

The interests and fortunes of motion-picture studios and exhibitors increasingly diverged as a result of the growing appeal of the television market and of the series of antitrust consent decrees that stripped the major studios of their movie theaters. A stock analyst's report on the motion-picture industry in November 1952 predicted a financial upturn for the studios, fueled by the appeal of color films, the promise of widescreen and 3-D formats, and more aggressive promotion of theatrical films, including the growing use of television as a marketing medium. By 1953, the national box office had improved, but by then the structure of the motion-picture industry was quite different from its pre-television and pre-divorcement days. The total number of films produced in Hollywood was much lower than in the 1940s (the number of films released fell from 488 in 1948 to 253 in 1952); and, beginning in 1953, the major studios increasingly concentrated on the big-budget spectacle film in an effort to maximize return from the relatively fixed costs of advertising, promotion, and prints.[5]

Another incentive to the studios to make fewer, more expensive films was the growing importance of the foreign box office, which encouraged the production of the more easily exported genres of adventure and spectacle with internationally established stars. The new strategy also favored adaptations of "pre-sold" material such as hit Broadway plays and popular bestsellers along with narrowly released theatrical runs at premium ticket prices. The introduction of Cinema-Scope in 1953 was very successful for some major studios: between 1953 and 1956, thirty CinemaScope films grossed more than $5 million, an amount that only a hundred films had captured before 1953. Twentieth Century-Fox, the studio with the largest commitment to widescreen, had a net revenue of $8 million from thirty-two films in 1953; in 1954, it earned $16 million from only thirteen films.[6]

It was clear, however, that motion-picture exhibitors did not share equally in the success of the big-budget Hollywood spectaculars; forced to bid more fiercely for fewer films for a dwindling audience, exhibitors saw an increasing percentage of their expenses go to film rentals. By 1954, near the bottom of the box-office slump, only 32 percent of movie theaters were profitable on box-office revenue alone. The historian Ernest Borneman summarized the effects of the consent decrees upon the structure of the film industry: "As far as the individual exhibitors, who might have been expected to be pleased now that they had at last obtained what they had asked for, the whole situation had been altered by the advent of television. Rightly, they now feared that the new production-distribution companies, unhampered by any loyalties to their one-time theaters or to any others, would now sell freely to television networks, 16mm users, and other non-theatrical buyers, leaving the theaters with a scarcity of films, an increase in competition, and an inflation of rentals."[7] Thus, one of the forces restraining the entrance of the major motion-picture studios into television, the threat of exhibitor boycotts of the studios' feature product, was weakened in the mid-1950s by changes within the motion-picture industry.

The attitude of the major studios in the early 1950s toward release of feature films to television was consistent with the pragmatic viewpoint expressed by Paramount treasurer Paul Raibourn in 1940: "When the telecasters are ready to buy films and can pay what they are worth, we will be ready to talk with them, but not for the mere glory of televison." David Selznick likewise stated the issue bluntly in February 1955: "When television is willing to pay more than the amount made in reissues, then we'll go into television." The rising fees for television programming, especially after the lifting of the FCC station freeze in 1952, increased pressure on the studios to sell off their vaults of existing features.[8]

Talent guild contracts signed with the major studios in 1947 helped delay the release of post-1948 features to television until well into the second half of the 1950s. Release of pre-1948 features was another matter, however, and was the major concern to networks, sponsors, and station operators in the mid-1950s. In June 1953, *Sponsor* argued that although the federal consent decrees had ordered production and exhibition separated, the studios still owned some of the most valuable theaters in the country and were still dependent upon theatrical exhibition as their major revenue source; television release of theatrical features was not yet in the studios' best interests, the magazine argued.[9]

Sponsor predicted that the theatrical success of widescreen and 3-D would encourage the release of feature films to television. Twentieth Century-Fox President Spyros Skouras told his stockholders in 1953 that "Up to this time, for our own sound business reasons, we have refrained from disposing of these pictures to television stations. However, with the advent of CinemaScope and other new techniques, it is anticipated that the theatrical demand for motion pictures will be generally for pictures of the new types. The demand for the older pictures will greatly decrease for theaters. Therefore, it is likely that these older pictures will be made available to television."[10]

In 1948 and 1949, the British studios Rank and Korda made television deals; foreign producers were less fearful of retaliation because their films enjoyed poor theatrical release in the United States and they had no production agreements with American talent guilds to suffer sanctions. Republic Pictures, a member of the Motion Picture Producers Association, defected from the withholding strategy when it sold its features to television and announced it was withdrawing from feature production, thus thwarting talent guild reprisals.[11]

Pressure on the major studios to release features to television increased in 1953 with the announcement of ambitious plans by a company called Vitapix to produce original telefilm and feature films for television. The company, owned by a group of television stations, was founded in 1950 to distribute features to television, primarily old Westerns and sports films from minor studios. The group announced in 1954 that they would produce television features for subsequent theatrical sales, creating a national "film network" for television. In September 1953, Vitapix President Frank Mullen told *Broadcasting-Telecasting:* "The reluctance of some leaders in the motion-picture industry to make their top quality product available to television broadcasters . . . is compelling the broadcasters to enter the field of motion-picture production for initial television release." *Sponsor* reported that the company's real purpose was less to produce films than an attempt to position itself as a distributor of features to television when the studios opened their vaults; the company hoped to package features and telefilms to individual stations. One aim of Vitapix's announcement, according to *Sponsor,* was to pressure the major studios to open up their feature libraries for television use with the threat of station operators entering film production themselves.[12]

The possibility of new film syndication and feature package deals in television obviously threatened the two dominant television networks, CBS and NBC. *Business Week* in 1956 reported a network public relations campaign against feature films on television, emphasizing the networks' commitment to live color broadcasting—a network monopoly—coupled with a refusal to clear network time for feature films. In 1956, Robert Sarnoff declared that feature films represented a "short road with a dead end," and warned of the television industry "surrendering" itself to Hollywood as feature films displaced network programming. Donald McGannon, president of Westinghouse Broadcasting, in January 1957 reported pressure from Sarnoff on NBC affiliates to boycott feature films.[13]

Network worries about feature films on television were based not only on the possibility of the non-network distribution of film programs, but also the special problems the networks faced in the television market for theatrical features. Unlike the market in series programming, for which, in the pattern established by the mid-1950s, the networks acquired licensing rights at the script or pilot stage before the program had a ratings history, theatrical features were known commodities with box-office histories and predictable ratings in television. Moreover, buyers of theatrical films for television, including the networks, often were forced to bid for feature film packages that tied less attractive titles to desirable films. Finally, acquiring feature films for television meant negotiating with a few major studios in a relatively concentrated seller's market, very different from the buyer's market for original series programs for television.

The cooling of the studios' hopes for subscription television after 1955, given the repeated refusal of the FCC to license its commercial use, also encouraged the release of features to television. In February 1956, *Sponsor* reported that Paramount, with continued major investments in pay television, was the only studio still holding out hopes for the service. The widespread prediction that the diffusion of color television sets was imminent and the fear that it would weaken television's demand for the stockpile of primarily black and white films spurred the major studios in the mid-1950s to reevaluate the television market for feature films. The timing of the release of film libraries to television also may have been affected by other internal changes in the motion-picture industry. One analyst argued in 1957: "Hollywood's change of policy on marketing its films to television was accompanied by shifts in financial control of the movie producing industry . . . new entrepreneurs have entered the business with an eye on its television as well as its theatrical market."[14]

The trigger for the flood of feature films to television in the mid-1950s was Howard Hughes's sale of the RKO film library. *Business Week* in 1953 reported a Hollywood rumor that Hughes was preparing to sell eight hundred prewar RKO films for television, although the article concluded that any major Hollywood-television feature deals were at least two years off. In July 1955, Hughes sold RKO to General Tire and Rubber Company for $25 million; in December 1955, General Tire sold the RKO library of 740 features to C&C Television Corporation for $15 million. C&C renegotiated agreements with the Screen Actors Guild concerning residuals and release dates (SAG had no sanctions concerning continuing production in its agreements with the new owner), and, beginning in June 1956, began a series of single-market television sales, bartering features for local advertising slots, up to ten each day. In mid-1957 C&C estimated its revenues from the RKO library to date at $25 million. By June 1956, four other major studios joined RKO in releasing features to television; by 1958, the final three major studios had joined them. In July 1956, *Television* reported that 2,500 feature films had been released to television in the previous thirteen months as studios scrambled to license their feature libraries in order to avoid a feared buyer's market. In 1956, Columbia reported an income of $9,700,000 on its feature sales to television; Warner Brothers earned $15 million in television sales that year.[15]

The release of features to television in the mid-1950s at first seemed to promise an alternative to network program distribution and sponsorship in television. In addition to the Vitapix plan to broker station time and distribute feature film programming, National Telefilm Associates and Twentieth Century-Fox organized a feature film network, selling one-hour blocks of programming to national sponsors on 128 stations. Twentieth Century-Fox sold its library to National Telefilm Associates for a 50 percent interest in NTA Film Network, which syndicated feature films to 110 noninterconnected stations with ninety minutes of cleared time a week for sale to national sponsors. In November 1956, *Business Week* speculated on the possibility of a studio-syndicator programming service rivaling the networks. Barter deals were arranged between the studios and individual stations in some film packages: MGM acquired 25 percent of the *Los Angeles Times*'s KTTV in exchange for a seven-year lease of 725 pre-1949 features. According to *Sponsor*, it was a model for other studios looking for television deals. The next month the magazine reported the largest spot advertising transaction in television history by Colgate for the KTTV feature slots. MGM, in its stock-ownership swaps for television stations, made a twelve-market deal in a single day worth $20 million, and arranged $37 million in sales by March 1957. By September 1956, MGM had gained stock ownership in seven stations. In 1956 alone, 2,700 features were released to television, two-thirds the total number of films made available in all the previous years.[16]

An October 1956 article in *Sponsor* discussed the effects of the release of more than three thousand features by that date. Feature films, contrary to some trade predictions, did very well in the ratings, boosting the number of sets in use and occasionally winning independent stations higher ratings than their network affiliate competitors. However, the new film programming did not, despite network warnings, bring about either affiliate defections or permanent national networks for distributing feature films. Likewise, despite the eagerness of national sponsors to support feature films in network prime time, networks refused to program prime-time feature films in the 1950s, with the exception of *The Wizard of Oz* as a CBS spectacular and some feature film programs offered as specials on ABC. If the CBS-MGM *Wizard of Oz* deal was not, as some predicted, a signal for the opening of the network prime-time market for feature films, neither was the release of Hollywood features the beginning of the end of network televison, as some of the apocalyptic network presentations had suggested.[17]

In 1957, *Television* reported that the flood of features had not displaced thirty-minute telefilms as some in the industry had feared. The biggest impact of feature films in 1950s' television was not felt in network-controlled prime time but in the affiliate-controlled afternoon and late-night fringe periods, and the largest casualty was locally produced programs, especially children's programming. Ralph M. Cohen, the vice president of Columbia's telefilm subsidiary Screen Gems (distributor of Columbia's newly released feature product), wrote in 1957 that although the rating success of feature films had surprised and frightened some in the television industry, feature films would settle down into merely one other source of television programming.[18]

In the debates of the mid-1950s, the words *film programming* were often used equivocally to refer both to feature films on television and original television programming on film. The word *Hollywood* acquired a similar generic meaning in the trade and critical debates over television programming, blurring the distinct interests within the motion picture industry and their relation to television. Although many observers at the time linked the two, the release of theatrical films to television was distinct from the production by major studios of original programming for the medium. Motion-picture exhibitors, for example, were less concerned with the major studios' production of telefilm because the low-budget thirty-minute telefilms cast with largely unknown talent did not compete directly with theatrical product in movie theaters. In 1944, when RKO set up its telefilm subsidiary, RKO Television Corporation, N. Peter Rathvon, the studio president, took pains to reassure the company's exhibitors:

> Motion-picture exhibitors are the customers and the only customers of the major distributing companies. Exhibitor interests come first . . . but this cannot be done simply by simply ignoring this new medium of entertainment. . . .
>
> We believe that the most suitable types of television programs . . . will be far different in character from the feature motion pictures created in Hollywood for theatical exhibition. . . .
>
> Rather than stand aside while others preempt the field, it would seem to be in the best interests of the entire motion-picture industry that production-distribution companies should participate in television, not only to protect themselves but the exhibitors as well, by directing television programming into fields which would be far removed from feature films created for the theater. . . .[19]

Despite such protestations of industry solidarity, the studios pursued an increasingly independent path regarding the production of original material for television, similar to their actions regarding the release of feature films to television. The period 1952-56 has been called the golden age of telefilm syndication for original programming, and attitudes toward telefilm among studio and network leaders altered with the growing profits for film programming. The period was one of growth and consolidation in the telefilm industry, marking the growing involvement of both the major studios in telefilm production and of the networks in filmed series licensing. The increasing appeal of film programming in the mid-1950s resulted from several factors: 1) the recognition of audience acceptability of telefilm reruns; 2) the growing value of afternoon and late-night periods of both independent and network-affiliated stations; and 3) the growing markets for telefilm programming outside the United States.

Arguments over the reuse of film programs in television had been perennial in the trade press since the beginnings of commercial television. Frequent analogies to theatrical films suggested that few viewers would be interested in seeing even a popular film program more than once, and therefore the practical value of television films would be limited to a single transmission. In 1952, *Sponsor* warned that estimates of the future value of telefilm programming might be exaggerated. The magazine argued that consumers and dealers of advertised goods would object to reruns, and cited sponsor Blatz Beer's cancellation of "Amos 'n Andy" reruns because of viewer protests. The issue of reruns was not merely one of ratings, *Sponsor* wrote, but of audience attitudes, pointing to an industry consensus that reruns were perceived as unwelcome and unacceptable by audiences and might provoke a powerful if intangible negative response against the television advertiser.[20]

By 1954, however, *Sponsor* noted that summer rerun ratings could in fact exceed those of the originally aired episode; Nielsen reported that only 2 percent of the average television audience saw sixteen of twenty-one episodes a season, and that 64 percent saw fewer than three shows. A telefilm producer argued in *Television* in 1955 that a telefilm series could be reused endlessly in rerun cycles of three years, reflecting vastly revised industry expectations about the commercial life of popular telefilm programming.[21]

Following the lifting of the freeze on station construction by the FCC in the spring of 1952, the expanding television audience attracted new sponsors, many of whom looked to film programming and to fringe time for exploitation. In July 1952, *Sponsor* reported the decisive move of Procter and Gamble, network radio's largest sponsor, into filmed television. *Television* noted a large increase in the scheduling of reruns on weekday afternoon (stripping a single program at the same hour five days a week) as daytime audiences increased and became more attractive to sponsors. In January 1956, *Sponsor* pointed to a large increase in such afternoon strip program sales, especially by CBS and NBC film syndication arms.[22]

The same article in *Sponsor* pointed to another reason for the increasing attractiveness of film programs: the rapid growth of the international market for telefilms. George Shupert, head of ABC film syndication, told the magazine that by 1957 the firm could expect from 20-25 percent of its income from foreign sales. Foreign syndication was particularly attractive to telefilm producers because, with a majority of production costs already recouped through network licensing, such subsidiary revenues represented mostly clear profit. Although F. W. Ziv set up an international sales unit as early as 1953, it was in the late 1950s and early 1960s that foreign program sales exploded, and by then the networks and large telefilm producers dominated a huge international market for American television programming.[23]

The growth of the international market in telefilms both followed and fueled a larger postwar shift by U.S.-based multinational corporations and their advertising agencies into new foreign markets. For example, the campaign in 1955 to establish commercial television in Great Britain, although led by members of the British Conservative party, received substantial assistance from the American advertising agency J. Walter Thompson. As the historian Herbert Schiller points out, the expansion of the American communications industry abroad in the 1950s and 1960s was also encouraged by policies of the U.S. government. Foreign sales of American programs were accompanied by major direct investments in foreign companies and markets by U.S. television networks, equipment manufacturers, and program distributors. The international TV market was also spurred by flattening growth rates in the domestic markets for consumer goods and television receivers in the late 1950s and early 1960s; by 1962, for the first time a majority of the world's television sets were located outside the United States.[24]

The opening of the network market for telefilm in the United States, with its promise of immediate capture of most or all program production costs, together with the growing domestic and foreign syndication markets and the increasing value of reruns, encouraged new telefilm production in the mid-1950s. Subsidiary profits for successful telefilm programs were also growing: George Bauer estimated the merchandising revenues in 1953 from products associated with just two programs, "Hopalong Cassidy" and "Howdy Doody," at $1,750,000,000. In 1955,

Sponsor reported that Ziv's telefilm revenues were up 250 percent since 1953, and expected to rise 100 percent in 1955; Guild Films reported a rise in revenues in 1954 from $500,000 to $1,700,000. In 1955, *Sponsor* reported that Screen Gems almost doubled its sales in that year and predicted a 25 percent increase in overall sales for 1956 resulting from increased network commitments, the use of syndicated film on daytime strips, and the beginning of substantial export earnings. By the fall of 1955, the telefilm industry was consuming ten times the amount of raw stock used by all theatrical film producers.[25]

The growing market for telefilms did not go unnoticed by the major Hollywood studios. The studios were involved in television as far back as the 1930s, although in his dissertation on television and the motion-picture industry, Alan Larson concludes that most of the major studios were merely "dabbling" in telefilm production until 1949, awaiting larger television audiences and program fees. By 1952, Columbia (Screen Gems), Universal (United World Films), Republic (Hollywood Telefilms), and Monogram (Interstate Television) studios were telefilm producers. Universal Pictures bought Decca Records, in part to acquire a distributor for its telefilm programs. *Business Week* in 1952 reported a number of studio-television links, but described the general mood among the major studios as "watchful waiting." Nicholas Schenck, the head of Loews, Inc., told the magazine that his attitude toward telefilm production was to let others make mistakes first. The basic constraint on the major studios was economic: *Business Week* reported that the major studios "probably can't make shorts for commercial sponsorship profitable now. . . . They will have to slash costs first," the magazine argued.[26]

By the mid-1950s, however, the growing market for film programming provoked a rapid consolidation of the telefilm industry. The major studios, after seeing independent telefilm producers F. W. Ziv, Desilu, and Hal Roach, Jr., buy up studio lots for television production, quickly moved into the market for original film programming. By 1955, MGM, Warner Brothers (Sunset Productions), Twentieth Century-Fox, and Paramount had joined Columbia in telefilm production. In September 1955, two large telefilm companies, Screen Gems and Television Programs of America, together responsible for ten network shows and nine syndicated programs, announced a merger. A January 1955 *Sponsor* article predicted that while the large telefilm producers would get larger, the smaller firms would be bought out or go out of business, noting the purchase of United Television Programs by the Music Corporation of America (MCA) for $1 million. According to *Variety,* the rush of the major studios into telefilm production after the success in 1955 of "Disneyland," the first studio-produced major film series, caused "awe and fear" among independent telefilm producers who worried about the majors' impact in syndication markets. *Television Age* reported in 1955 that the top twenty telefilm producers did 90 percent of the industry's business, with the remaining thirty firms "struggling for survival." By 1956, according to the historian Barbara Moore, "few small syndicator firms were left."[27]

There is a tendency in the literature on 1950s television to cast ABC as the engineer of the move from live anthology drama to the Hollywood-produced telefilm series in the late 1950s. Many accounts cite ABC's merger with United Paramount Theaters (UPT) in 1953, and the ascension of UPT executive Leonard Goldenson to the presidency of the network as responsible for bringing a new "Hollywood" mentality into television. However, this personalist account may obscure the more telling economic motives for ABC's special interest in telefilm and overestimate the distinctions among the three networks by the end of the 1950s. Whether measured by program schedules, programming philosophies, or corporate personnel, basic differences among the three networks since the mid-1950s are not substantial. The economic incentives at ABC for turning to new program forms and sources in the mid-1950s merely anticipated wider trends in network programming in the 1950s.

Martin Mayer, after describing ABC in 1961 as "the industry leader in matters of programming, selling and dealing with affiliate stations," wrote that "The rival networks, most of the advertising agencies, and the staff of the FCC believe, rightly or wrongly, that the ABC influence has tended to destroy what integrity the network business had." Mayer argued that "The other networks live with the tattered remnants of the idealism that characterized the early days of broadcasting, while ABC— certainly from the time of its purchase by Paramount Theaters in 1953— has been strictly a business enterprise."[28] The distinction between a profit-maximizing ABC and the high-minded CBS and NBC leadership, a commonplace in the contemporary and subsequent literature, becomes increasingly untenable in the second half of the 1950s.

The programming "innovations" at ABC are attributable more to specific conditions in the economics of network affiliation and program production in the 1950s than to Goldenson's background or tastes. ABC and DuMont in the early 1950s lagged far behind the two dominant networks in affiliate clearance rates, audience circulation, and advertising revenues. Both networks faced difficulties in gaining adequate station clearances given the small number of three- and four-channel markets. Even after the lifting of the licensing freeze, ABC often had to settle for a UHF affiliate with small audiences or a split affiliation with one of the stronger networks. At the end of the 1950s, 80 percent of ABC's affiliates were stations established after the lifting of the television freeze. Their financial and audience position as a group was far inferior to the 108 stations established before the freeze. In 1953, ABC had a live clearance rate (the proportion of affiliates airing a network-supplied program live) of only 34 percent. In 1955, ABC still had only eighty-four affiliates, far fewer than CBS and NBC, and the network only had a 58 percent live clearance rate, significantly below those of the two dominant networks. In contrast, CBS had 121 stations with 87 percent live clearance, and NBC 104 stations with 90 percent live clearance.[29]

ABC's dependence on delayed broadcast by its affiliates made film programs more attractive because they required neither simultaneous clearances nor the use of visually degraded kinescope transcriptions. The FCC Office of Network Study summarized the effect of the network's weakness in station affiliation: "[B]ecause of this 'comparative disadvantage,' ABC initiated two policies which have had far-reaching effects on the television programming process": seeking new program sources and new sponsorship strategies.[30]

ABC gained the financial resources to acquire new programming only through its merger with United Paramount Theaters, initiated in 1951 and approved by the FCC in 1953. Under the terms of the Paramount consent decree signed with the Justice Department in 1949, Paramount's former exhibition arm, UPT, was ordered to reduce its number of theaters from 1,400 to 650 within five years, and UPT brought ABC the promise of $30 million in program development money for the network. UPT also brought television station operating experience through its ownership of WBKB, the Balaban and Katz station in Chicago, one of the earliest commercial stations. The FCC, in its approval of the merger, voted to reverse the recommendation of its hearing officer, an unusual step, and to wipe out UPT's former parent Paramount's substantial record of antitrust violations before 1948.[31]

In its weaker competitive position, ABC was forced to grant greater sponsor concessions and rate discounts than did the two dominant networks. Moreover, when ABC did acquire a popular program from a sponsor, it often watched helplessly as the advertiser or agency moved the program to a stronger network. ABC Network President Oliver Treyz told the FCC in 1960 that "In February 1953, when you approved the merger, our network programming structure . . . did not represent any central network thinking, philosophy or point of view. It was, rather, a structure of programs scheduled by advertisers who bought ABC time periods in which they placed their own programs. . . ." Goldenson described the same subordinate relationship with television sponsors: "They brought us only their poor programming. They took their best ones to the other two networks, and when a good one developed at ABC they took that away, too. So we simply took control of the programs."[32]

In 1953, Goldenson announced a five-year plan for parity with NBC and CBS, building the prime-time schedule night by night. Goldenson argued that with the two dominant networks in control of major broadcast talent through long-term contracts, ABC needed to seek out new program sources. In turning to Hollywood for new programming, the network also hoped to avoid the high-priced bidding contest for star-filled live spectacular programs of the other two networks. The network's telefilm strategy was built not upon network production, but rather upon the licensing of independently produced programs by the network instead of the sponsor. In this way, ABC could ensure that successful programs would remain on the network. ABC made an early Hollywood telefilm deal in 1953, when the network signed an exclusive agreement with producer Hal Roach, Jr. In exchange for ABC funds for the pilot and a portion of the episodes' production costs, the network acquired syndication rights and a profit share in the series.[33]

Although ABC's "Warner Brothers Presents" is often cited as initiating the involvement of the major studios in television production, their presence in network prime-time programming goes back at least to a 1952 Ed Sullivan tribute to MGM on CBS in 1952. Following Disney's successful CBS Christmas special, the studio had invited all three networks to develop telefilm projects, but only ABC was willing to put up

$500,000 for the proposed Disneyland amusement park as part of a production package.[34]

A *Television* article argued that Disney turned to television as much for exploitation and promotion as for programming; one-third to one-fifth of the weekly sixty-minute "Disneyland" was devoted to direct studio promotion. The promotional segments were in part designed to placate theater owners by advertising current theatrical product, and were also used by Disney to promote the company's new amusement park. One episode of "Disneyland" presented a sixty-minute promotional film for the forthcoming theatrical feature *20,000 Leagues under the Sea,* and many in the industry credited the telefilm with the box-office success of the film. As a prime-time network series, "Disneyland" was also unprecedented in the number of reruns it employed, with only twenty original episodes per season.[35]

In 1955, ABC and Disney announced plans for "The Mickey Mouse Club" as the network's first afternoon program; meanwhile, Disney reported that 80 percent of its employees were working in television. In its first season the sixty-minute "Mickey Mouse Club" followed the "Disneyland" formula of twenty original episodes, twenty reruns and twelve repeated reruns, and an unprecedented number of commercial minutes in each program, with twelve advertising minutes per hour from four different sponsors. The program featured heavy promotion of Disney films, comic books, and amusement park operations; *Television* reported widespread objections to the program's twenty-two advertisements per episode, warning of overcommercialization in the program.[36]

The importance of ABC's telefilm deal with Disney, which was not a major Hollywood studio, was the model it provided for the entrance of the major studios into telefilm production for the networks. In 1954, ABC contracted with Warner Brothers for a sixty-minute telefilm series, and the next year MGM and Twentieth Century-Fox launched film series. The format of the new studio shows varied from TV spin-offs of existing studio properties (the rotating series of "Casablanca," "Kings Row," and "Cheyenne" from Warner Brothers) to extended "looks behind the scenes" at studio feature activities, and direct recyclings of existing studio footage. "MGM Parade," a thirty-minute compilation and promotional program, was produced directly by the studio's trailer department.[37]

All the new studio programs devoted from nine to fifteen minutes each week to straight promotion of forthcoming theatrical releases or re-releases. A 1955 *Sponsor* article objected to the heavy promotional quality of the new studio series, and the following year the magazine warned sponsors that the major studios often demanded promotional time above their production fee for telefilm programming. At the end of 1955, *Television* attributed the rating weakness of most of the new studio series to the persistent overcommercialization. The major studios generally favored the sixty-minute format, not only because it permitted extended theatrical promotions, but also because the sixty-minute length gave an advantage to the major studios as telefilm producers over their independent competitors: the studios were better able to handle the higher budgets of the longer programs. Erik Barnouw argues that the ABC deal was a bonanza for Warner Brothers, which collected substantial syndication and foreign sales revenues with very small talent residuals based on its strategy of casting relative unknowns; such profits attracted the other studios to telefilm production.[38]

There was no doubt of the appeal of the new programming at ABC. "Disneyland" was ABC's first show in television's top ten. *Television* estimated that "The Mickey Mouse Club" alone contributed almost half of the network's 1954 earnings, and almost a fourth of its earnings in 1955. The two Disney telefilm programs were responsible for making 1955 ABC's first profitable year as a network and station owner. By 1959, Warner Brothers was single-handedly responsible for supplying one-third of ABC's prime-time schedule. By the 1958-59 season, ABC had achieved ratings parity with CBS and NBC in markets where the three networks had equal affiliation status. However, although its network billings increased 500 percent from 1953 to 1958, ABC remained handicapped by fewer affiliates and inferior clearances, and its advertising revenues were less than half of those of CBS or NBC. In his master's thesis on the rise of ABC, Fred Silverman noted that at the end of the 1950s the network was still locked out of between 10 percent and 18 percent of the U. S. population because of its weaker affiliate roster.[39]

ABC's move into Hollywood telefilms was only one marker of a fundamental recalculation in the mid-1950s of network strategies regarding program procurement, programming form, and advertising practices, and it is misleading to see ABC's experience as aberrant to the strategies of the two dominant networks. ABC's rise in program ratings to genuine competition with CBS and NBC was a signal of the changing opportunities and strategies of all three networks. ABC's programming philosophy included a rejection of the network spectacular, the irregularly scheduled lavish entertainment specials produced live by the networks and associated most commonly with NBC President Pat Weaver. ABC executive Donald Coyle argued that "People are creatures of habit—they want the same entertainment every week. That's when NBC made its big mistake, when it went so heavily on spectaculars." Martin Mayer reported a possibly apocryphal boast by Goldenson that he wanted ABC to become the Universal Studios of the television industry; "MGM and Twentieth Century always got the publicity, but Universal made the money," Goldenson said. In a profile of Goldenson in 1957, *Sponsor* quoted him on the aims of ABC: "We're in the Woolworth business, not in Tiffany's. Last year Tiffany made only $30,000." *Sponsor* cited what Goldenson considered unsuccessful or "bad" programming: "Fantasy, the type of fantasy where a person dreams. Otherwordly fantasies. People basically want programs with which they can identify. This is why he feels anthology to have a limited TV future." In the place of network spectaculars and live anthology dramas, ABC pursued what Goldenson called the "bread and butter" programming of the telefilm action series. As *Forbes* explained: "Unlike the other networks, who claim to supply something for everybody, Goldenson and Treyz don't even pretend to that goal."[40]

As *Forbes* implied, the differences between ABC and the other networks by the end of the 1950s was one more of public relations than of substance. Former NBC and CBS executive Michael Dann in 1979 responded to the charge that ABC's 1950s programming policies had a negative influence on the other networks: "I don't think so at all. The advent of ABC had an adverse impact in the sense of making it a three-network economy under a monopoly set up instead of a two-network economy...."[41] Although ABC had been a leader in seeking new program sources and sharply redefining the aims and responsibilities of a television network, by 1960 the program philosophies and prime-time schedules of the other networks were nearly identical.

NOTES

1. "How Hollywood Hopes to Hit the Comeback Trail," *Newsweek*, January 12, 1953, p. 108; "Movies—End of an Era?," *Fortune*, April 1949, p. 140; Tino

Balio, ed., *The American Film Industry* (Madison: University of Wisconsin Press, 1976), pp. 316-20. Balio (p. 316) reports a 50 percent drop in contract employees at Hollywood studios from 1946 to 1956. Also see Janet Staiger, "Individualism versus Collectivism," *Screen*, July-August 1983, pp. 68-79.

2. Discussion of the role of independent film production is found in Amy Schnapper, "The Distribution of Theatrical Feature Films to Television," Ph.D. diss., University of Wisconsin, 1975, p. 33. In 1953, half of the feature films distributed by Warner Brothers were independent productions; by 1957 the proportion was 70 percent. Alan David Larson, "Integration and Attempted Integration Between the Motion-Picture and Television Industries Through 1956," Ph.D., diss., Ohio University, 1976, p. 204. On the rise of the talent agency in 1950s television, see Ben Bodic and Alfred J. Jaffe, "Talent Agents: Have They Won Control Over TV Costs?," *Sponsor*, January 24, 1955, pp. 35-37; and Bodic and Jaffe, "Talent Agents: What's the Alternative to Paying Their Price?," *Sponsor*, February 7, 1955, p. 36; U.S. Federal Communication Commission, Office of Network Study, *Second Interim Report: Television Network Program Procurement*, part 2, Docket no. 12782 (Washington, D.C.: U.S. Government Printing Office, 1965), pp. 680-720; John Bartlow Martin, "Television USA: Wasteland or Wonderland?," part 3: "The Master Planner," *The Saturday Evening Post*, November 4, 1961, p. 37; "MCA—Putting the Business in Show Business," *Forbes*, November 15, 1965, pp. 20-25.

3. Milton MacKaye, "The Big Brawl: Hollywood Versus Television," Part 1 *The Saturday Evening Post*, January 19, 1952, p. 19.

4. "California as a Program Source," *Television*, April 1951, p. 37; Larson, "Integration and Attempted Integration," p. 141. In February 1952, *Life* magazine wrote: "Although theater owners are being legally divorced from Hollywood, they still exert a deadening influence on its behavior. They have banded together and threatened any production company that furnishes feature films—old or new—to TV." "Hollywood and TV," *Life*, February 25, 1952, quoted in Morleen Getz Rouse, "A History of the F. W. Ziv Radio and Television Syndication Companies 1930-1960," Ph.D. diss., University of Michigan, 1976, p. 135.

5. Material on the changes in the feature film industry is found in George Bauer, *Government Regulation of Television* (New York: New York University Graduate School of Public Administration, 1956), p. 407; Freeman Lincoln, "Comeback of the Movies," *Fortune*, February 1955, pp. 130, 155.

6. Lincoln, "Comeback of the Movies," pp. 130, 155; Frederick Stuart, *The Effects of Television on the Motion-Picture and Radio Industries* (New York: Arno Press, 1976), p. 55; Lawrence L. Murray, "Complacency, Competition and Cooperation: The Film Industry Responds to the Challenge of Television," *Jour-*

nal of Popular Film 6 (1977): 56; Lincoln estimated that 50 percent of Hollywood's box office revenues came from abroad (p. 155).

7. Lincoln, "Comeback of the Movies," pp. 130; also see Michael Conant, *Antitrust in the Motion-Picture Industry: Economic and Legal Analysis* (Berkeley: University of California Press, 1960), p. 172; Murray, "Complacency, Competition and Cooperation," p. 51; Ernest Borneman, "United States versus Hollywood: The Case Study of an Antitrust Suit," in *The American Film Industry*, ed. Balio, p. 343.

8. Raibourne is quoted in "Radio and Filmdom Both Keep Eye on Television," *New York Times*, July 28 1940, sec. 2, p. 10, cited in Larson, "Integration and Attempted Integration," p. 38; Sarnoff in Robert Cuniff, "Selznick Talks About Television," *Television*, February 1955, p. 32.

9. "TV Feature Films: 1953," *Sponsor*, June 15, 1953, p. 48.

10. Ibid.; "Speed of Switch to CinemaScope Will Key 20th's Pix Flow to Video," *Variety*, April 15, 1953, p. 3.

11. The British studios' strategy is discussed in Schnapper, "The Distribution of Theatrical Feature Films," pp. 50, 59; the case of Republic in Milton MacKaye, "The Big Brawl: Hollywood vs. Television," *The Saturday Evening Post*, January 26, 1952, part 2, p. 121; Irving Bernstein, *The Economics of Television Film Production and Distribution* (Los Angeles: Screen Actors Guild, 1960), p. 81.

12. The plans of Vitapix are discussed in "Will Vitapix Create TV Film Revolution?," *Sponsor*, January 11, 1954, pp. 42, 92, 94; "Vitapix, Princess Plan First Runs Made for TV," *Broadcasting-Telecasting*, September 7, 1953, p. 34.

13. "Will Feature Films Reshape TV?," *Business Week*, November 24, 1956, p. 131; Sarnoff is quoted in "Sponsor Scope," *Sponsor*, December 15, 1956, p. 12; Donald McGannon, "There's Room for Features, Network Too," *Television*, January 1957, p. 41.

14. "The Movie Makers Look for Gold in the TV Screen," *Business Week*, April 23, 1955, p. 156; "You Can Crack the Hollywood Dam but You Have to Know How," *Sponsor*, February 6, 1956, p. 68; Larson, "Integration and Attempted Integration," p. 277; Helen B. Schaffer, "Movie-TV Competition," *Editorial Research Reports*, January 18, 1953, p. 51.

15. The RKO deal is discussed in "TV and Film: Marriage of Necessity," *Business Week*, August 15, 1953, p. 109; Schnapper, "The Distribution of Theatrical Feature Films," pp. 85-89; Abby Rand, "2500 Films—How Will They Change TV?," *Television*, July 1956, pp. 64; "Report to Sponsors," *Sponsor*, July 25, 1955, p. 1; "That Tom . . . He Makes Money!," *Television*, September 1955, pp. 25-26. General Tire put up only $5 million in cash for the RKO library.

16. The various feature deals are descibed in "Will Feature Films Reshape

TV?," p. 136; "Report to Sponsors," *Sponsor,* July 25, 1955, p. 1; "Report to Sponsors," *Sponsor,* August 20, 1956, p. 1, September 3, 1956, p. 1, September 17, 1956, p. 1; Schnapper, "The Distribution of Theatrical Feature Films," pp. 90-93; U.S. Congress, Senate Committee on Interstate and Foreign Commerce, *Television Network Practices, Staff Report,* Committee Print no. 2, 85th Cong., 1st sess. (Washington, D.C.: Government Printing Office, 1957), p. 2; Schaffer, "Movie-TV Competition," pp. 52-54.

17. "Feature Film's Spectacular Impact," *Sponsor,* October 15, 1956, pp. 27-28, 118, 120; Abby Rand, "Feature Film Goes Bigtime," *Television,* April 1956, p. 52.

18. Abby Rand, "The Outlook for Film," *Television,* July 1957, p. 63; Schaffer, "Movie-TV Competition," pp. 48-49; Ralph M. Cohen, "Cycles Pass, Quality Stays," *Television,* January 1957, p. 45. For a report on the MGM-CBS *Wizard of Oz* deal, see "Report to Sponsors," *Sponsor,* August 6, 1956, p. 2.

19. *Radio Daily-Television Daily,* June 15, 1944, pp. 5, 7, quoted in Larson, "Integration and Attempted Integration," pp. 60-61.

20. "Is the Rush to Film Shows Economically Sound?," *Sponsor,* July 28, 1952, pp. 69-70.

21. "Film Basics," *Sponsor,* July 12, 1954, p. 186; Don Sharpe, "TV Film: Will Economics Stifle Creativity?," *Television,* April 1955, p. 81.

22. "Is the Rush to Film," p. 69; "As the Film Men See It," *Television,* July 1956, p. 51; "Film's $100,000,000 Year," *Sponsor,* January 23, 1956, p. 31.

23. "Film's $100,000,000 Year," p. 133; John Tebbel, "U.S. Television Abroad: Big New Business," *Saturday Review,* July 14, 1962, p. 44.

24. For discussion of the growth of the foreign telefilm market and its context, see "U.S. Television Abroad: Big New Business," pp. 44-45; Erik Barnouw, *The History of Broadcasting in the United States,* vol. 3: *The Image Empire* (New York: Oxford University Press, 1970), pp. 108-17; Barnouw, *The Sponsor: Notes on a Modern Potentate* (New York: Oxford University Press, 1978), pp. 107-19; Norman Horowitz, "Syndication," in *Inside the TV Business,* ed. Steve Morganstein (New York: Sterling Publishing, 1979), pp. 71-94, 144. Regarding J. Walter Thompson's role in Great Britain, see H. H. Wilson, *Pressure Group: The Campaign for Commercial Television in England* (New Brunswick: Rutgers University Press, 1961). For a discussion of the political and economic context of U.S. media expansion, see Herbert I. Schiller, *Mass Communications and American Empire* (Boston: Beacon Press, 1971); Schiller, "The U.S. Hard Sell," *Nation,* December 5, 1966, pp. 609-12; William H. Read, *America's Mass Media's Merchants* (Baltimore: Johns Hopkins University Press, 1976); Chin-Chuan Lee, *Media Imperialism Reconsidered* (Beverly Hills: Sage Publications, 1980).

25. Bauer, "Government Regulation of Television," p. 360; "Ad Men Pose

Top Radio-TV Questions for 1955," *Sponsor,* January 10, 1955, p. 38; "TV 1955: Big Spending, Big Programs," *Sponsor,* December 26, 1955, p. 96; "TV Film's $100,000,000 Year," pp. 29, 132; Jack Gould, "TV Films Boom Hollywood into Its Greatest Prosperity," *New York Times,* July 3, 1955, p. 1.

26. Larson, "Integration and Attempted Integration," p. 100; "Hollywood Learns to Live with TV," *Business Week,* August 9, 1952, pp. 43-48.

27. *Sponsor,* September 19, 1955, p. 2; "Ad Men Pose Top Radio-TV Questions," p. 38; "Majors Worry Syndicators," *Variety,* May 11, 1955, p. 39, quoted in Larson, "Integration and Attempted Integration," p. 237; "Fall Film Outlook," *Television Age,* August 1955, p. 46; Barbara Ann Moore, "Syndication of First-Run Television Programming: Its Development and Current Status," Ph.D. diss., Ohio University, 1979, p. 39.

28. Martin Mayer, "ABC: Portrait of a Network," *Show,* September 1961, p. 59.

29. Mayer, "ABC," p. 61; Fred Silverman, "An Analysis of ABC Television Network Programming from February 1953 to October 1959," master's thesis, Ohio State University, 1959, p. 8; FCC, *Second Interim Report,* p. 178.

30. FCC, *Second Interim Report,* p. 178.

31. "AB-PT's 'Full Speed Ahead' Sets in Motion '$30,000,000 Agenda'," *Variety,* February 11, 1953, p. 1; Bauer, "Government Regulation of Television," p. 44; Bauer reports a record of 180 antitrust complaints against Paramount; also see Jean Bergerman, "One Party Television Too?," *New Republic,* February 23, 1953, pp. 17-18.

32. FCC, *Second Interim Report,* p. 179; Silverman claims that ABC's schedule reflected no concern with audience flow, adjacencies, counterprogramming, that the network did little program research or promotion, "An Analysis of ABC," p. 10; Goldenson is quoted in Stan Opotowsky, *TV: The Big Picture* (New York: E. P. Dutton, 1961), p. 48.

33. Silverman, "An Analysis of ABC," pp. 62, 142; FCC, *Second Interim Report,* p. 181; Goldenson denounced ABC's pre-merger program schedule as "vaudeville" to Martin Mayer, "ABC," p. 60.

34. Silverman, "An Analysis of ABC," pp. 64, 104; Charles Sinclair, "Should Hollywood Get It for Free?," *Sponsor,* August 8, 1955, p. 32.

35. For a discussion of the Disney strategy, see Cuniff, "Selznick Talks About Television," pp. 67, 144; Silverman, "An Analysis of ABC," p. 105; Larson, "Integration and Attempted Integration," p. 231.

36. *Television,* October 1954, p. 11; "Disney: How Old Is a Child?," *Television,* December 1954, p. 72; Silverman, "An Analysis of ABC," p. 155; Frank Orme, "TV's Most Important Show," *Television,* June 1955, pp. 34, 85; "The Critics' Viewpoint," *Television,* November 1955, p. 64.

37. Silverman, "An Analysis of ABC," p. 154.

38. Sinclair, "Should Hollywood Get It for Free?," p. 31, "You Can Crack the Hollywood Dam," p. 65; "The Critics' Viewpoint," p. 64; Jack Gould, "TV: One Long Plug," *New York Times*, July 25, 1955, p. 41; "The Movie Makers Look for Gold in the TV Screen," p. 155; Barnouw, *The Image Empire*, p. 63.

39. Silverman, "An Analysis of ABC," pp. 106, 154, 236, 372; Orme, "TV's Most Important Show," p. 32; "ABC Crowds Out the Other TV Networks," *Business Week*, May 9, 1959, p. 46; "The abc of ABC," *Forbes*, June 15, 1959, p. 17; Goldenson told the magazine that it would take two years to translate the ratings into advertising revenue.

40. Mayer, "ABC," p. 61; "The TV Fan Who Runs a Network," *Sponsor*, June 8, 1957, pp. 45, 46; Silverman, "An Analysis of ABC," p. 325; "abc of ABC," p. 17.

41. Michael Dann interview, Federal Communications File, Oral History Collection, Columbia University, p. 8.

9

The New Structure
of Television Sponsorship

The shifts in television program sources and formats in the mid-1950s were inseparable from a new appreciation by network executives and others of the changing nature of the postwar American consumer economy and the role of television as a sales agent in it. ABC's programming strategy was linked to a new marketing strategy among television advertisers. As Fred Silverman concluded: "Synonymous with the development of 'bread and butter' programming was the network's recognition of the young post-war families with small children.... In fact, practically all of the programs developed and/or acquired by ABC between 1954 and 1956 were geared to these families." Leonard Goldenson told *Forbes:* "We're after a specific audience, the young housewife—one cut above the teenager—with two to four kids, who has to buy the clothing, the food, the soaps, the home remedies."[1]

The composition and strategies of television advertisers clearly changed through the 1950s with the growth of the TV industry. An NBC Research Department report cited the growth of television as an advertising medium (overtaking radio in 1952; passing magazines and newspapers in national advertising in 1955) and connected it to a long-term trend in marketing: "In virtually all industries, the emphasis in the battle for profits has shifted from the factory to the marketplace ... marketing activities are the single most important influence on profits." The report described manufacturers increasingly reaching out to the final consumer directly in order to gain greater control of the market for their goods, using advertising as "pincers on both dealer and consumer." The final marketing stage would be "supermarketing," that is, pre-selling to the consumer, a task to which television was uniquely suited.[2]

NBC President Pat Weaver, a former advertising executive, proved a tireless promoter of the mission of television advertising in the modern American economy. In speeches to manufacturers and trade groups in the early years of television Weaver argued home the point: "Advertising is to mass production what individual selling was to craft production." In 1955, Weaver warned a group of advertising executives that the increasingly impersonal retailing style of drugstores and supermarkets had made the personal sales pitch obsolete, while automation made it more difficult for factories to cut back production when demand slackened.[3]

Advertising agency McCann-Erikson's 1951 forecast of American advertising and television twenty years into the future predicted that "The "The next twenty years will see the re-emergence of the family unit as the core of our social system. . . . The implications of this trend for advertising are several. More persons will be involved in buying decisions— thus requiring family appeal both in media and copy." Seconding Weaver, the report argued that in the next two decades: "Advertising will bear a bigger burden of building consumer franchise because of the increased impersonal nature of the retail outlet."[4]

August Premier, director of marketing services for Johnson Wax Company, wrote later of the special appeal of television for producers of small-ticket consumer goods: "The medium is extremely suited to low interest products because it is an intrusive medium. Products can be injected where they are not wanted—which doesn't sound very moral but which is a fact of life with television. . . . Television is the medium which depends least on consumer cooperation to develop a rich response to symbolic stimulation." NBC's Research Department cited a 1960 audience research report which it said demonstrated that "The viewer watches commercials in the same way that he watches programs—in fact he looks for the same things in commercials that he seeks in programming. He does *not* think of commercials as something different and apart from programs. The viewer not only watches commercials and is influenced by them, but he feels *obligated* to watch and be influenced."[5]

Along with the heightened, perhaps inflated, estimates of the role of advertising in domestic prosperity and the power of television advertising as a marketing tool, the composition of television advertisers also changed in the early 1950s, achieving a structure that has remained relatively stable since. In 1950, NBC television counted among its top ten advertisers Ford, General Motors, RCA, Philco, and Mohawk Carpet Company, as well as two cigarette manufacturers. General Mills was number twenty-nine in the list of television sponsors, and Procter and Gamble was number twenty-four. Beginning in 1952, however, Procter and Gamble and other giant manufacturers of small-ticket consumer goods made major moves into television sponsorship. Procter and Gamble's television advertising budget grew from $7,200,000 in 1951 and $14,200,000 in 1952 to $23,700,000 in 1954, when it became the nation's largest network advertiser.[6]

In 1952, NBC reported that one-third of all food purchases, 40 percent of drugstore sales, and 50 percent of non-food supermarket purchases were a result of impulse buying, arguing: "Most impulse buying is actually 'reflex' buying—the buying of brands which have been pre-sold by advertising." The report offered television as the advertising medium best suited for this task of consumer pre-selling. Another NBC research report noted a 14 to 22 percent rise in 1953 in television's share of the advertising budget of drug and home-remedy products. Regarding the level of taste and acceptability of drug and home-remedy product advertisements, the network reassured manufacturers that Stockton Helfrick, chief NBC censor, "advises that *very* few products would be turned down (or out) on this basis. He says we are following an 'open door' policy."[7]

Along with the shift toward makers of small-ticket consumer goods, economic concentration among television sponsors and advertising agencies accelerated through the 1950s. By 1955, NBC reported that the product mix and share of network television sponsors matched the top six product categories of network radio in the 1930s. The top six product groups (food products, toiletries, automobiles, household equipment, tobacco products, and soaps) constituted 78 percent of 1954 network billings. In addition, the top twenty-five advertising agencies accounted for 78 percent of network advertising revenues. In 1955, the number of television advertisers actually fell, despite network billings up 27 percent. In 1956, NBC reported that nine advertising agencies were responsible for more than 50 percent of network television billings. In 1957, the number of network television sponsors again fell by about 10 percent with product type and advertiser concentration continuing. The top six product categories now accounted for more than 80 percent of network television revenues, and Procter and Gamble alone was responsible for $1 of each $11 spent on network television.[8]

The trend toward concentration continued through the decade; in 1958, NBC, which had by far the largest number of small network sponsors due to participating sponsorships in programs like "Today" and "Tonight," noted that one-third of its sponsors contributed less than 1 percent of total billings, while another group constituting 37 percent of network advertisers contributed 92 percent of overall revenues. By 1958, the top twenty advertisers contributed 57 percent of total network advertising revenues (compared to 53 percent in 1957, with Procter and Gamble, Colgate-Palmolive, and Lever Brothers in the top three slots). In 1959, NBC reported that 10 percent of television's advertisers—thirty-two companies—contributed 65 percent of total network advertising revenues.[9]

In 1958 NBC noted that corporate image advertising on television was down sharply (that year both General Motors and U.S. Rubber dropped corporate image campaigns), and warned that "in the near future agencies which have been promoting the corporate angle (particularly in television) will have to change their thinking." The national economic recession in 1958-59 also affected the composition of network advertisers, with the billings of electrical appliance manufacturers dropping 62 percent in 1958. One of the motivations for the network's encouragement of multiple sponsorship forms at the end of the 1950s was a desire to avoid the volatile swings of recession-sensitive durable goods manufacturers, who often sponsored entire programs, in favor of a less volatile combination of makers of low-priced products of consumer goods.[10]

The shift in the composition of television sponsors and the dispersal of advertisements over several different programs in "participating" sponsorships altered the relation of the sponsor to television programming. The FCC's Office of Network Study in 1960 noted the appeal of television for manufacturers of low-cost consumer goods with little product differentiation, and its 1965 report argued that such advertisers adopted a different attitude toward the medium. The small-ticket consumer goods manufacturers like Procter and Gamble and General Foods were less interested in corporate image advertising than in individual product advertising; they tended to choose well-tested programs with maximum popular appeal and to make program purchase decisions almost completely on the basis of ratings. The Office of Network Study reported that such sponsors bought participations in programs on the basis of pilots or established ratings histories, which handicapped anthology programs and live programs and generally favored formulaic program styles.[11]

The changing nature of television advertising supported the new network programming strategies articulated by ABC in the mid-1950s. While a few years earlier NBC was heaping scorn on ABC's "get age" strategy of programming aimed exclusively at housewives and families with its prime-time Western and adventure programs, by 1960 NBC's *Research Bulletin* repeatedly underlined the importance of the same demographic group, arguing "homes with housewives 35 to 49 are the major consumer group."[12]

The new sponsorship format of multiple advertising participations quickly spread through the three networks in the late 1950s. The Office of Network Study underscored the sponsorship shift in noting the number of prime-time programs on the three networks according to sponsorship type (Table 1).[13]

The shift in television advertising from single to multiple sponsorship in the late 1950s had important implications for program producers and

Table 1. Changing Sponsorship Forms, 1955-65

Season	Single Sponsor	Alternating	Multiple
1955-56	75	30	10
1956-57	57	2	17
1957-58	61	46	1
1958-59	55	43	13
1959-60	40	50	25
1960-61	31	51	24
1961-62	26	27	47
1962-63	24	18	52
1963-64	15	18	54
1964-65	12	22	57

networks, and for the nature of prime-time entertainment. Connected to both the move to Hollywood telefilm programming and the changes in television advertising were efforts by the networks to assert program control in the medium. As important to the networks as dominating program procurement was their desire to assert control over the television schedule. The chief obstacle to network control of the program schedule was the sponsor "time franchise," the control of a specific scheduling slot by a single advertiser. In the first years of television the networks encouraged sponsors and agencies to enter the still-unprofitable medium in part by offering such "newcomer" rights to the network schedule, but by the early 1950s the networks were struggling to wrest schedule control away from advertisers and abolish the time franchise.

The networks faced sponsor opposition in their attempts to gain control of the program schedule. One industry executive explained in 1953: "A good time spot is a property to protect and hold. Some advertisers have spent years getting outstanding spots on the air, changing from relatively poor positions to better ones as they become available." As time went on, however, the networks enjoyed a surplus of buyers for prime-time program slots, and they increasingly chaffed at the restrictions of sponsor scheduling control. All three networks voiced growing concern over the effects of a single weak program upon the entire network schedule, reflecting heightened network sensitivity to audience flow, program adjacencies, and counterprogramming. A 1954 *Sponsor* article reported the unilateral shift by NBC of two advertiser-supplied programs that had occupied their network time slots since 1949. *Sponsor* noted that although it was doubtful that sponsors had any legal right to a time franchise, the networks' new policy disrupted advertisers' programming plans and their point-of-sale promotions tied to the specific schedule position.[14]

Sponsor's 1954 year-end report on the industry noted network attempts to gain scheduling control and abolish the time franchise, and saw in the displacements of established program slots a signal of network power in a new seller's market of advertising time. The networks enjoyed their strongest year ever (ABC revenues were up 67 percent to $26 million; NBC's up 30 percent to $100 million; and CBS's up 44 percent to $117 million, making it the nation's largest advertising medium), with prime-time advertising sold out on all three networks and the cost of the network sponsor's "must buy" list of mandatory stations up 25 percent. *Sponsor* pointed to the "white-knuckled grip the TV webs are keeping on programming control, especially at NBC and CBS," and reported a growing network tendency to discard any program that didn't meet the network's ratings expectations. In 1954, *Sponsor* warned that regardless of escalating program and time charges, sponsors could not afford to do without television. By 1956, *Sponsor* reported that there was no longer much power in a network time franchise. In 1957, the magazine wrote that the networks were narrowing the thirty-minute separation traditionally placed between programs of competing sponsors of similar products. All these incidents pointed to an increasingly uninhibited exercise of network scheduling power.[15]

An example of the shift of power between sponsor and network were the fortunes of "The Voice of Firestone," a popular-music program that began on radio in 1927 and was broadcast on NBC television until 1954, when NBC told Firestone that it wanted the time period for another program. The Firestone program was produced directly by the sponsor —the opening and closing musical numbers were composed by the wife of the company's president—and the format of the show had remained unchanged over thirty years, according to a 1957 *Television* profile of the program. Pat Weaver's pleas to Firestone to move the program out of prime time were unavailing, and an NBC executive warned his superiors that a preemptive move by the network would involve "losing a client of 25 years standing, sacrificing a substantial piece of needed radio business and possibly assuming a law suit." In 1954, when NBC *did* unilaterally move "Firestone" into fringe time with poor affiliate clearances, the sponsor publicly blasted the network and moved the show to ABC. NBC's displacement of Firestone focussed rising sponsor complaints over network repudiation of the time franchise and the inability of sponsors to reach a targeted audience, if not always the highest ratings. In 1959, "Firestone" was cancelled again, this time by the newly competitive ABC network, again for unsatisfactory ratings in its time slot. In a *Television* editorial, "L'Affaire Firestone," Frederick Kugel raised the public relations importance of preserving low-rated quality programs and overall program balance in the context of increased public criticism of the networks.[16]

The networks' new scheduling attitudes provoked opposition from other groups in the television industry. An advertising executive complained to a trade group in 1954: "A nasty word has sprung up in this business of ours. It is 'bumping' the advertiser. I'm sure the networks do not intend to cavalierly bump the advertisers whose support helps build them, but I want to tell you that some of us think it looks that way."[17]

The extinction of the network time franchise was only part of a larger effort by the networks to assert program control, bringing new roles for sponsors, advertising agencies, and program producers. The sponsor abandoned single sponsorship of a series in favor of a participating sponsorship with three, four, or as many as ten sponsors for a single series. Along with the move came a fundamental shift in advertising strategy from the idea of corporate goodwill association with a given program and the ability to tailor point-of-sale promotions and other marketing efforts with a specific program and audience, in favor of participations in several programs across the broadcast schedule. Pat Weaver led the attempt to discredit the traditional importance attached to sponsor goodwill in television advertising. In his 1952 "Memorandum on Planning," Weaver noted that "sponsor identification must be dealt with as an ineffective means of measuring sales effectiveness," and in a 1952 presentation to General Foods he argued that "Sponsor identification is a man-made device for measuring audience awareness of who presents a program. It has no provable relationship with sales effectiveness. The highest sponsor identification ratings are frequently for clients with bad sales records. The gratitude factor in selling is a minor sales weapon. It its more blatant form, it is an admission that product selling on its merits has failed." In 1954, Weaver chided a panel of advertising executives: "In selling a product, a good product, to the American public, with good advertising, you should not have to ask for something free, which is what you do when you overdo the gratitude factor."[18]

As "The Voice of Firestone" demonstrated, some network sponsors were not exclusively interested in circulation or ratings. This was especially true of many of the sponsors of prestige drama, such as U.S. Steel, Alcoa, and Philco, who often pursued corporate image advertising aimed at a smaller audiences of higher-income groups. One television advertiser complained to *Sponsor:* "I want a program to be identified with my product. I want people to know that I'm paying for what they see. But what do I get for my $70,000? A minute and a half announcement in the middle of a big thing that's got no connection with me or my product." Other sponsors complained that the networks refused to tolerate anything other than a strategy of maximum ratings. An advertising agency executive told *Sponsor:* "It's a fight for supremacy between the networks. All they want is to kill the ratings of the other fellow. It makes no difference if we and our client like a program. If the other network gets a better rating, we know we're on our way out." A network representative replied to the complaints of television advertisers with the dubious reassurance that "[o]nly sponsors who are unwilling to see the necessity of protecting our lineup will ever face a refusal to renew a franchise."[19] Television advertisers interested in minority programming probably took little comfort from network reassurances that only when a sponsor found itself in disagreement with the network need it fear unilateral network action. The economic position of the three networks made it difficult for the television advertiser to resist network pressure to alter, shift, or scrap programs that failed to meet network ratings expectations.

For advertising agencies working in television, network control of program procurement and scheduling overturned roles the agencies had played in programming in the first half of the 1950s. As one agency executive complained to *Sponsor* in 1955: "It's supposed to be our function to kick around ideas with our clients. To come up with something that we feel will help his product and then to develop it and try it out. It used to be like that, but no more. Today all we can do is look at the lists of what the networks have to offer, and if we're lucky, we can find a participating position somewhere." Pat Weaver responded to critics by pointing out that when NBC bumped four sponsor-controlled programs, it offered the advertisers other time periods: "The times offered might or might not have been quite as good as the other times were, but in all cases there were excellent reasons why that advertiser was harming the value of the advertisements adjacent to him on both sides and affecting the over-all circulation pattern of all the advertisers who were buying time on our facilities . . . we felt these changes had to be done, because, after all, who is going to run the network for you? Who is going to run the schedule and keep the circulation up?"[20]

One major controversy arising from the new assertion of network power in programming accompanied the introduction in 1956 of the ninety-minute CBS-produced "Playhouse 90." The show displaced three thirty-minute programs, "Four Star Playhouse," "The Johnny Carson Show," and "Quiz Kids." Two of the three bumped programs were produced by independent producers, and all three were sponsored on a single or alternating-sponsor basis. A CBS submission to the Senate Television Inquiry suggests the network's stiffened attitude toward the sponsor regarding scheduling control:

> Despite the fact that in the opinion of CBS program executives "Four Star Playhouse" was not an outstanding program, at no time were sponsors of that program told that the program was not acceptable. On the contrary, the advertising agency for Bristol-Myers and Singer was advised in February of 1956 that if those clients did not desire to participate in the sponsorship of "Playhouse 90" but wished to continue to sponsor "Four Star Playhouse," CBS television would endeavor to find another suitable time period. At the same time the advertising agency was informed frankly that CBS television could give no assurance that a suitable time period would be available.[21]

A letter from Robert P. Mountain, the account representative at Young and Rubicam for the sponsors of the cancelled programs, disputed the network's account of the negotiations over the introduction of "Playhouse 90":

> This all boils down to the fact that Bristol-Meyers, Singer, and General Foods have now been told by CBS that CBS is not taking their time away from them provided they buy the program that Columbia has arbitrarily put in their time. Also, the fact that no other time is available to them.
>
> It is our position that Columbia is asking us to take another gamble on a wholly-owned and exclusive CBS package, and, worse than that, we are not being asked—we're being told.[22]

Thus "Playhouse 90," traditionally represented as a high point in the aesthetic achievement of live anthology drama and a jewel in the networks' public relations crown during a time of public scrutiny, also stands as a marker of the new hard-nosed network attitudes about control of television's prime-time schedule. The growing network power in the 1950s television economy was being felt in other ways as well.

NOTES

1. Fred Silverman, "An Analysis of ABC Television Network Programming from February 1953 to October 1959," master's thesis, Ohio State University,

1959, p. 389; "abc of ABC," *Forbes,* June 15, 1959, p. 17.

2. National Broadcasting Company, *Television and Modern Marketing* (New York: National Broadcasting Company, 1960), pp. 1, 3, 5, collection of the NBC Records Administration Library, New York.

3. Pat Weaver, "Memorandum to Executive Group: NBC Television: Principles, Objectives, Policies," November 1949, p. 2; Weaver, "Selling in a New Era," speech to the Advertising Club of New Jersey, May 24, 1955, pp. 3, 9, 11, emphasis in original, collection of NBC Research Department, New York.

4. "Advertising in 1972," National Broadcasting Company, *Sales Facts Bulletin,* March 26, 1951, n.p., collection of NBC Research Department, New York.

5. August Premier, "The Advertiser in Television," in *The Meaning of Commercial Television,* ed. Stanley T. Donner (Austin: University of Texas Press, 1967), p. 27; National Broadcasting Company, *Research Bulletin,* June 20, 1961, p. 2, emphasis in original, collection of NBC Research Department, New York.

6. National Broadcasting Company, *Research Bulletin,* no. 8, 1950, n.p.; National Broadcasting Company, *Research and Planning Bulletin,* April 3, 1953, n.p., collection of NBC Research Department, New York.

7. National Broadcasting Company, *Sales Facts Bulletin,* March 12, 1952, n.p.; NBC, *Research and Planning Bulletin,* July 15, 1955, pp. 2-3, collection of NBC Research Department, New York.

8. NBC, *Research and Planning Bulletin,* November 8, 1955, pp. 4, 6; NBC, *Research and Planning Bulletin,* September 24, 1956, p. 1; NBC, *Research and Planning Bulletin,* April 26, 1957, p. 6; NBC, *Research Bulletin,* April 30, 1958, pp. 1, 4, collection of NBC Research Department, New York.

9. National Broadcasting Company, *Research Bulletin,* May 4, 1959, pp. 1, 2; National Broadcasting Company, "National Television Advertising in 1958," *Research Bulletin,* April 13, 1959, n.p.; National Broadcasting Company, "National Television Advertising in 1959," *Research Bulletin,* April 22, 1960, p. 1, collection of NBC Research Department, New York.

10. National Broadcasting Company, "Advertising and Marketing Highlights," *Research Bulletin,* July 14, 1958, n.p.; National Broadcasting Company, *Research Bulletin,* April 30, 1958, p. 3, collection of NBC Research Department, New York; Barry R. Litman, *The Vertical Structure of the Television Broadcast Industry: The Coalescence of Power* (East Lansing: Michigan State University Press 1979), p. 32.

11. U.S. Federal Communications Commission, Office of Network Study, *Interim Report: Responsibility for Broadcast Matter,* Docket no. 12782 (Washington, D.C.: U.S. Government Printing Office, 1960), p. 139; U.S., Federal Communications Commission, Office of Network Study, *Second Interim Report:*

Television Network Program Procurement, part 2, Docket no. 12782 (Washington, D.C.: U.S. Government Printing Office, 1965), pp. 497-528, 527.

12. National Broadcasting Company, "An Analysis of ABC's 'Get Age' Campaign," *Research Bulletin,* May 16, 1958, p. 5; National Broadcasting Company, *Research Bulletin,* September 4, 1960, n.p., collection of NBC Research Department, New York.

13. FCC, *Second Interim Report,* p. 736.

14. Robert M. Reuschle, "Choosing the Right TV Station for Your Product," in *Television Advertising and Production Handbook,* ed. Irving Settel and Norman Glenn (New York: Thomas Y. Crowell, 1953), p. 25; "What Are Your 'Rights' to a Time-slot?," *Sponsor,* April 5, 1954, pp. 29, 110; for a discussion of the exploitation of point-of-sale and other merchandising opportunities of sole-sponsorship, see George J. Abrams, "TV Advertising for the National Sponsor," in *Television Production Problems,* ed. John F. Royal (New York: McGraw-Hill, 1948), p. 80.

15. "Year End Report," *Sponsor,* December 27, 1954, pp. 29, 90, 110; "TV Show Costs: Why They Went Through the Roof," *Sponsor,* September 6, 1954, p. 40; "Network TV Lineup: Tear It Down, Build It Up," *Sponsor,* May 14, 1956, p. 28; *Sponsor,* February 2, 1957, p. 9.

16. "We Don't Care What Our Rating Is," *Television,* September 1957, pp. 55, 115; Pat Weaver complained of the scheduling roadblock that the program represented to the network in a speech to the Television Affiliates Meeting, Chicago, November 18, 1953 (p. 3); J. K. Herbert, memorandum to Frank White, April 11, 1953, p. 6, collection of the NBC Records Administration Library, New York; Frederick Kugel, "L'Affaire Firestone," *Television,* May 1959, p. 112.

17. Association of National Advertisers, "Planning TV's Tomorrow," panel discussion, New York City, November 9, 1954, n.p., collection of the NBC Records Administration Library, New York.

18. Pat Weaver, "Memorandum for Planning," 1952, p. 16; Weaver, "Presentation to General Foods," 1952, p. 4, collection of the NBC Records Administration Library, New York; "Planning TV's Tomorrow," n.p.

19. "The Great Debate on Network Show Control," *Sponsor,* October 31, 1955, p. 38.

20. Ibid.; "Planning TV's Tomorrow," n.p.

21. U.S. Congress, Senate Committee on Foreign and Interstate Commerce, *Television Inquiry,* vol. 4: *Network Practices, Hearings before the Committee on Foreign and Interstate Commerce,* 84th Cong., 2d sess. (Washington, D.C.: U.S. Government Printing Office, 1956), p. 2232 (hereafter referred to as Television Inquiry); another much-discussed case involved CBS's treatment of the shows "Joe and Mabel" and "You Can't Take It With You"; see U.S. Congress, House

Committee on the Judiciary, *Monopoly Problems in the Regulated Industries, Hearings before the Antitrust Subcommittee of the Committee on the Judiciary, House of Representatives,* 84th Cong., 2d sess. (Washington, D.C.: U.S. Government Printing Office, 1956), part 2, vol. 2, p. 4000ff; Television Inquiry, p. 681ff.

22. Television Inquiry, p. 2241.

10

Network Control of the
Program Procurement Process

The demise of the sponsor time franchise and the decline of single sponsorship were two elements of the new network strategies of program procurement and scheduling. Ironically, the networks succeeded in gaining control of the procurement and scheduling of prime-time programming at the same time they abandoned earlier efforts to produce a majority of their programs themselves. In-house network production was less important, even less desirable, than the power the networks could exercise in negotiations with outside program producers and network advertisers. Like the changing patterns of television sponsorship, the new program procurement policies of the networks represented a sharp break with previous industry practices.

In the late 1940s and early 1950s, the networks delegated television program production and scheduling to sponsors and advertising agencies, despite the networks' proclaimed wishes to avoid the pattern of 1930s radio when sponsors and agencies dominated network program production. In 1950 and 1951, both CBS and NBC moved to take program production from the outside groups through large investments in network production facilities; the key to network program and schedule control, the networks reasoned, was in-house production of programming. It was this assumption that was repudiated with the network programming and sponsorship policies of the mid-1950s.

In 1950 CBS acquired three new New York production studios and began construction of large studio facilities in Hollywood; in 1951, the network expanded to fifteen New York production spaces and began construction of Television City in Hollywood, which was finished in October 1952. Stock analyst Robert Gilbert called CBS's Television City "a factory to produce lower cost shows." *Television* in 1951 reported a projected CBS investment of $35 million in Television City and noted the network's contract control of several major Hollywood stars in long-term contracts, including Bing Crosby and Jack Benny. NBC followed a similar strategy in the early 1950s, opening its Burbank studios a day after CBS's Television City; in 1952, NBC told a House subcommittee that the network itself produced 59 percent of its entire schedule. A *Sponsor* article in January 1950 reported network moves to in-house production, led by CBS, designed to keep successful programs on the network and to assert control over the program schedule.[1]

The success of "I Love Lucy" and other network-licensed film programs in 1952, however, pointed to new methods of maintaining network control despite program production by outside packagers and independent producers. "Packagers (Not Nets) Lead in Building New Shows," declared a 1952 *Sponsor* article, noting that contrary to previous network plans, independent packagers were now the leaders in program development. The move to independent production reflected new network confidence in their continued domination of affiliates and national sponsors despite the increased use of film programming. The networks' confidence, according to *Television*, stemmed from their recognition that film programming could indeed strengthen network control if the network secured licensing rights for telefilms in exchange for development money.[2] This was precisely the arrangement ABC and the other networks used as telefilms increasingly dominated network prime-time schedules in the second half of the 1950s.

A memorandum submitted to the Senate Television Inquiry in 1956 by CBS's legal counsel offered a rationale for the network's shift from its earlier policy of self-production: "[I]n the early years of television the networks arranged for time on affiliated stations and produced almost all the programs which were used at that time. Because the job of producing programs has become too great even for the networks and the stations to handle themselves and because the production of programs by outsiders has become a profitable business, others have begun to help in providing that part of the programming business."[3]

A series of *Sponsor* articles document the changing attitudes of the networks. In 1952, *Sponsor* reported a trend away from advertising agency-packaged programs, predicting that such programming would dwindle to almost nothing within a few years. A few months later an article noted that due to rising program costs, many sponsors were more interested in joining an established show than in developing new programs themselves. In January 1953, *Sponsor* predicted that the end of the FCC station freeze, bringing more affiliates and "firmer" networks with fewer split affiliations, would push program and time charges sharply higher. The rising costs and risks of program production, it argued, would accelerate program development by networks and independent packagers in the place of sponsors and advertising agencies. In March 1953, the magazine identified growing trends both to film programming and to network packaging, led by CBS's aggressive moves as packager. *Sponsor* noted in September 1953 that CBS packaged twenty-four sponsored programs, sixteen of twenty-two prime-time hours, and reported that advertising agencies were complaining of a network monopoly in program packaging.[4]

In the mid-1950s, CBS and NBC began to cut back from these high levels of in-house production. Many in the industry saw such moves as not only a product of the increasing shift to film programming, but also as a network response to congressional and public criticism of network practices regarding UHF and network affiliation agreements. In 1956, F. W. Ziv made its first network telefilm sale, and *Sponsor* pointed to pressure on the networks to make more outside production deals stemming from the increased federal scrutiny of network practices. In 1957, *Sponsor* announced: "The era of domination by network staff produced shows is over." Only five of the twenty new shows announced for the forthcoming network prime-time schedule were network produced, it reported. At the same time, however, CBS President Hubbell Robinson noted that more than half of the top CBS shows were either network co-productions or programs in which the networks had profit participations or subsidiary rights, and *Sponsor* reported that the decline in direct network production did not signify a loss of network control over programming or scheduling.[5]

The paradoxical result of the retreat of the networks from their earlier policy of in-house production in favor of licensing independently packaged programs was even tighter network control of prime-time programming. By 1955, *Television* noted that the networks, not the advertising agencies, had the decisive voice in programming matters, reversing the pattern of network radio. With exceptions like J. Walter Thompson's control of "Kraft Television Theatre," McCann-Erikson's control of "Death Valley Days," and advertising agency production of many afternoon serials, agencies were increasingly concentrating on the production of commercials, not programs. In the second half of the 1950s the positions of sponsor and network as licensee of independently produced programming were reversed. From 1957 to 1964, the proportion of advertiser-licensed prime-time programming on all three networks declined from 36 percent to 8 percent (on ABC the decline was from 33 percent to 2 percent), and the proportion of network-produced or licensed programming increased from 64 percent to 92 percent.[6]

The networks' new negotiating strength over program producers and television advertisers gave the networks the power and prosperity they had argued earlier was necessary to protect live drama, program balance, and free expression, all shielded from the deleterious influences of both Hollywood filmmaking and the broadcast sponsor. Yet the new network power effected a programming crisis in the eyes of many television critics, a virtual extinction of the program values advocated by defenders of live drama, and an exodus of some of television's most prominent dramatic writers.

The withdrawal from direct program development of most television advertisers and agencies, the decline of the network time franchise, and the move from single to multiple sponsorship meant that in order to sell a series for network release, the telefilm producer had to sell directly to a network. The market for independently produced telefilms was progressively reduced to virtually three firms—the three networks. Their monopsony power as buyers largely determined the outcomes of negotiations with program suppliers. Testifying before the FCC's Office of Network Study, independent producer and packager David Susskind denounced the "'death grip' on programming by the television networks." Susskind recalled that in the first half of the 1950s the independent producer had a market composed of fifty advertising agencies, and a hundred to a thousand sponsors in addition to the networks; "Today," he told the panel in 1960, "you must sell to the network or you don't get on the air."[7]

The monopsony power of the television networks in their dealings with program producers enabled the networks to acquire significant stakes in program production revenues, syndication profits, and foreign and subsidiary revenues. Unlike the entrenched and highly profitable oligopoly of three network firms virtually constituting the market for big-budget film series programming, the telefilm production industry was characterized by uneven profits, easy entry, and high turnover of firms. The earlier network strategy of in-house production was replaced by a network appreciation of the power of their negotiating position with independent producers who would assume the major risks of program production and still be forced to share profit and subsidiary rights with the networks. An independent program producer told *Sponsor* in 1955: "We used to have a large number of potential buyers. Now we have three, the networks. And most of the time, even if we should come up with a show they want, they'll cut themselves in and try to take over control."[8]

The effect of network control of prime-time affiliate schedules was to foreclose non-network programming from most of the nation's television markets in prime time and to reduce the telefilm market to the three networks or to a national sponsor who could itself arrange time on a network. An executive of Screen Gems told the Celler Committee that the only other potential buyers besides the three networks of network-distributed telefilms were large television advertisers with an existing time franchise on one of the networks: "[w]e can only secure sponsors who have time or who can buy time. In that sense, our general national sales effort is somewhat circumscribed to sponsors whom we know have time franchises. There is very little point to our interesting a sponsor who has no time." Unfortunately for such independent telefilm producers, the time franchise in network prime time was vanishing under pressure from the networks. In addition to the cases of the "Voice of Firestone" and "Four Star Playhouse," the committee heard reports from several other sponsors whose programs or time periods were unilaterally preempted by the networks.[9]

The FCC's Office of Network Study reported that in the 1955-56 season half of CBS and NBC prime-time programming was still produced by outside sources and licensed directly to sponsors. Sponsors and advertising agencies were attractive as buyers of telefilm programs to the telefilm producer because they were generally interested only in the original network run of the program, not in profit participations, domestic or foreign syndication, or merchandising rights in the program. The telefilm producers, most of whom also had extensive syndication arms, and many of whom also managed their own merchandising operations, could either reserve the highly profitable syndication activities for their own organizations or sell such rights to others in separate transactions.[10]

A larger issue stirred in the "Playhouse 90" scheduling controversy was the charge that in their procurement, scheduling, and promotion decisions, networks favored programs that they produced or in which they had an ownership interest. In apparent recognition of network sensitivity to such issues, CBS told the Television Inquiry that its plans for "Playhouse 90" were suspended while it sought legal counsel on possible antitrust problems: "Only after CBS television received an oral opinion from its counsel that no violation of the antitrust laws was involved did CBS television go forward with its plans."[11]

Victor R. Hansen, assistant attorney general in charge of antitrust enforcement, told the Celler Committee in 1956 that the Justice Department had initiated a probe of charges of network coercion of sponsors to purchase network-produced shows; that by March 1956 the investigation had grown too large for Justice Department investigators, and the FBI had been called in to assist a larger inquiry into "network practices relating to the sale of network time and shows." A 1956 *Sponsor* article reported that the Justice Department was investigating charges that the networks pressured sponsors to participate in network-produced programs against those controlled by advertisers.[12]

A group of telefilm producers and syndicators, the Association of Television Film Distributors, argued in a memorandum to the Senate Commerce Committee in 1956 that because network prime-time advertising slots were so valuable to sponsors, the network-sponsor negotiations over program selection and scheduling were extremely lopsided. The group argued that the seller's market in network advertising time sales allowed networks to tell television sponsors to take it or leave it. Even if a telefilm producer succeeded in committing a sponsor to a series sale, the deal would be contingent on network approval, and "if a network has a program of its own in mind, the approval is most difficult to obtain, nay, frequently impossible."[13]

Kenneth Cox, who led the Senate Commerce Committee's Television Inquiry, noted that "There can be no doubt, for example, that the networks occupy such a key position, by virtue of their control over the best time in the key markets, that they have the power either to exclude independently produced programs from their schedules, thus making way for their own programs, or to give such programs access to network time only in return for the granting of an interest in the independent programs. The power exists—it is only a question of whether it is exercised." Cox concluded: "[T]here appears to be a strong possibility that, on occasion, the network executives involved in these program choices have not acted with complete impartiality, with consequent injury to competing program producers."[14]

A 1954 *Sponsor* article noted that even if a program was developed outside of the network organization, most independent producers and sponsors shared profit interests with the network in order to achieve favorable network scheduling and promotion. The effect, the magazine reported, was to make most independently packaged shows captives of the networks. ABC President Oliver Treyz told the Office of Network Study that his network desired "whenever possible to be the licensee so that we can count on having it on our schedule if we determine it should be there." "It is a factor" in deciding whether the network would accept the program, Treyz admitted.[15]

The networks publicly denied coercion of either advertisers to purchase time on programs in which the networks had a propriety interest, or of program producers to share profits or subsidiary rights as a condition for network exhibition. However, in a 1954 internal memorandum NBC President Pat Weaver outlined the network's attitude:

> When we build a work to create a hit and then build around it, we are of course continuously aware of that show's arrangement with us. From bitter experience it has become obvious that we cannot expect a client realistically in most cases to overlook the blandishments of our competition and that when one has a great smash hit one is continually losing it unless it is under contract to the network itself. . . . If, on the other hand, the show can leave and go to another facility and therefore be built to destroy what we are trying to build competitively, it must be considered in the less-favored group.[16]

The Office of Network Study was skeptical of network assurances that the networks' proprietary interests in prime-time programs had no effect on their procurement or scheduling decisions, concluding that "there is considerable evidence, information and data in the record which indicates that network managers, by somewhat more sophisticated business practices, have since about 1956 progressively assumed control of the economics of television program production and procurement." Furthermore, argued the FCC, "there is also strong evidence to indicate that those policies and practices have tended to restrict the market for television programs and to impose competitive burdens on independent producers which have tended to 'dry up' the sources of television programs."[17]

The "more sophisticated" instruments of network program control identified by the Office of Network Study included network "co-production" of series programming from the early stages of story idea, outline, script, or pilot; in exchange for such "development" money, the networks would acquire profit participation, syndication rights, and merchandising rights. The independent producer and packager Mark Goodson told the Office of Network Study that the networks usually "insist" on financing the television pilots and in return demand profit shares, syndication, and foreign sales rights. The networks, according to Goodson, also demanded the same concessions in cases when the networks were not involved in financing of pilot episodes, in exchange for the "risk" of scheduling the series with the advertising time unsold. Finally, Goodson said, the networks demanded the same concessions without pilot participation and in cases when the producer or packager had already made a sale to a network sponsor. Dick Powell, president of Four Star Productions, told the FCC that even in the absence of network pilot financing, the independent producer was forced to grant or share syndication rights to a network "in order to sell at all." Pilots are perishable commodities, and it was difficult to find buyers among television sponsors, Powell told the Office of Network Study, so producers were forced to take the network's best offer.[18]

The Office of Network Study, examining the nature of network financial contributions at the script and pilot stage, concluded that "It appeared possible that the so-called 'tie-in' practice had evolved into a more sophisticated method of operation in which the network created a 'facade' of necessity for its proprietary control through an alleged relation between such control and the ability of network managers to provide appropriate advertising 'forms' for sponsors to ensure that the programs appearing in their schedules would meet a 'high standard' of 'quality' and subject matter." This last justification was discounted by the FCC, which argued that nearly all in the industry agreed that there was no necessary relationship between a network's proprietary interest and its creative control over the program schedule.[19]

Independent station operator Richard Moore pointed out to the Senate Television Inquiry that "many independent program producers are solvent companies, with adequate resources, who do not need financial assistance to complete a pilot film or to bring a prospective film to completion. Regardless of financial resources, however, one thing an independent producer does need is an acceptable network time period." Kenneth Cox was also skeptical of the justification of network profit participation on the grounds of its investment in pilot development:

> It is possible that in some cases the independent producers concerned do not really need the assistance of the networks and that this is given simply to provide some justification for the network's acquisition of an interest in the program. Thus some of the producers of programs in which the networks have acquired participations are substantial concerns with ample capital, so that it would not appear that they needed the financing arranged for by the networks. That is, they did not need the network's money, but they did need access to broadcast time which only the networks can give.[20]

NBC President Robert Sarnoff told the Senate Television Inquiry in 1956 that NBC sometimes made a profit on its program procurement practices, in addition to its sale of advertising time, by purchasing a program from an independent producer and selling the same program to national sponsors at a higher price. Moore told the committee: "Under these circumstances, it would be understandable why a network might prefer to purchase a program itself, and then sell it to a sponsor as a compulsory package of time and program, rather than sell its time alone for a program owned by a sponsor."[21]

The second network rationale for their profit participation in independently produced programs was the risk a network assumed when it purchased a pilot which might not result in a series commitment, or when it scheduled a series for network release without assurance of commercial sponsors for the scheduled time period. The Office of Network Study pointed out, however, that if the networks wished to avoid such programming risks they could offer discounts or other incentives to advertisers who licensed their own programs and therefore assumed the risks of audience support, something the networks refused to do. The

Office of Network Study, noting network claims of risk-taking, commented dryly: "It should be pointed out, however, that these claims of network managers that present advertising practices require them to assume heavy financial burdens and 'enormous risks' have not been reflected in network earnings and profits."[22]

The FCC noted that in the period between the start of hearings in 1960 and the Office of Network Study's *Second Interim Report* in 1965, the combined income from network operations (exclusive of the networks' owned-and-operated stations) had more than doubled. Thus, the *Report* argued, network claims of increased programming risks and expenses under the new procurement practices "seem highly forced and tenuous, if not absurd. . . . Indeed, overall it appears that the ratings-circulation time rate 'formula' of program production and procurement has resulted in greater economic stability and financial success for network managers." Network profits from syndication increased from $1,947,000 in 1960 to $7,738,000 in 1964. Network revenues from foreign telefilm sales alone grew from $1,700,000 in 1957 to $15,800,000 in 1964.[23]

Network control of the program procurement process not only affected the terms of entry into the network telefilm market, but also had profound effects on the market for syndicated, non-network programming. Despite the much larger number of stations on the air after 1952, the television market was still concentrated in a relatively small number of large markets; an 1954 article in *Broadcasting-Telecasting* pointed out that "If a series was sold in every TV market in 1954, the 20 major markets would have provided 40 percent of the syndicator's revenue. Unless the program was sold in those major markets, it had little chance of earning back its cost."[24]

It was these same few major television markets where network control of affiliate prime time was most pronounced. The Office of Network Study described the effects of the new network program procurement practices on the television syndication market. Formerly, independent program producers sold programs in a market of many competing buyers made up of networks, advertising agencies, and sponsors; however, "[m]ore recently, due largely to the program activities and practices of network managers in collaboration with 'independent' producers, such an alternate program source is no longer available. Under modern program procurement . . . production of first run quality syndicated programs as an alternative source of station program service competition in 'quality' with current network offerings has 'virtually disappeared.'"[25]

Network licensing of film programming for network use often gave the networks control of subsequent syndication rights. The Association of Television Film Distributors told the Celler Committee in 1956 that "When a network asks that we give it the subsequent syndication rights to a program which we produce, in order to find time for that program on the network, it is in essence using the power granted to it by the FCC and its affiliated stations and using it to destroy competition in another field, unrelated to its network function." The Staff Report of the Senate Television Inquiry noted the networks' control of most prime-time hours in the nation: "As a result, the only way a film producer can be sure of sufficient circulation to support his program is to sell it to a network or to an advertiser who can arrange to broadcast it over a network."[26]

The telefilm syndication business was very competitive, with widespread price cutting by desperate producers selling films below production costs in order to recoup some portion of their investment. By 1956, because of increased network programming of fringe time, the increasing availability of large numbers of feature films and off-network series programs (series previously licensed for network exhibition), and overproduction in the telefilm industry, distributors of original syndicated programming faced a serious oversupply of programs on the syndication market. *Television* estimated that there was room for perhaps six of the twenty-nine first-run syndicated series offered in 1956. *Broadcasting-Telecasting* at the end of 1955 estimated that supply exceeded demand of first-run syndicated programming by a factor of four. The result was a shakedown of the industry; survivors included the networks, the major studios, and some of the large independent producers generally distributing off-network programs and feature films.[27]

The Television Inquiry heard testimony from the major telefilm producers that revealed the sharp decline in the production of telefilm programs for original syndication. Screen Gems, Official Films, Motion Pictures for Television, Inc., Guild Films, Television Programs of America, Ziv, and MCA all had drastically cut back or ended production for original syndication while at the same time making their first network telefilm deals or expanding their network-licensed business. A questionnaire sent by Television Inquiry Chair Warren Magnuson to twenty telefilm producers and syndicators elicited the following response from Reuben R. Kaufman, president of Guild Films:

> Our company has been fairly successful in the field of syndication, but the problems which face all syndicators have compelled us to change somewhat the character of our operation and to diversify the sources of our income. . . . While not completely giving up the producing and distribution of films for television syndication, we are now following a policy of producing the finest quality film series for primary offering to network sponsors under the theory that if a program is really good enough it cannot be kept off the networks. Under present conditions syndication business is indeed in a sad plight. Fortunately for us, we have the resources to do something about the situation, but this does not apply to some of the other syndicators who should have had an opportunity to help develop this industry.[28]

Telefilm producers who wished to remain in the syndication market were faced with a cost-price squeeze; as a result of the inability to clear significant portions of prime time for syndicated programing against network competition, telefilm producers were unable to cover rising production costs in the static or shrinking market. The only alternative was the attempt to make network telefilm sales, either directly to one of the three networks or to a national sponsor who could place the program on the network. As independent telefilm producer Bernard L. Schubert explained to the committee: "we are not planning any first-run film series to be offered for syndication because, economically, it is impossible for us to gross enough money on local or syndicated sales to justify such a venture. Our average budget for a first-run network, half-hour TV picture runs around $32,000. In our opinion, in order to make any money from a first-run syndicated film, the budget for each film should not exceed a maximum of $25,000 per subject. Based on current costs, this is almost impossible."[29]

Michael M. Sillerman, president of Television Programs of America, explained the growing financial straits of independent syndication for telefilm producers: "[T]he budgets for national network shows are higher than those offered for syndication. This follows from the shortage of prime viewing time available for syndication and the greater risks involved in satisfying local and regional advertisers within this narrow framework." Sillerman offered as example the forty television markets in which both CBS and NBC had basic affiliates (comprising the networks' must-buy lists for national sponsors), which reached more than 70 percent of the nation's television sets; of the annual 3,360 half-hour prime-time slots on the two networks' affiliates in the forty markets, 94 percent were occupied by programs of the networks. Sillerman continued: "there are only seven markets in the entire United States which have four or more VHF outlets. Since all three networks employ option time (with its preemption powers), there are only seven important markets where non-network advertisers can be assured of continuity in sponsoring a program during prime evening time." Both Hal Roach, Jr., and Ralph M. Cohn of Screen Gems reported that their firms were forced to cut production of syndicated programs due to the difficulty of access to sufficient station time.[30]

Telefilm producers still producing programs for original syndication reported that production budgets had to be kept 25-40 percent below the levels of programs for network sales. The result of the contraction of the market for original syndicated programming was not only the concentration of telefilm production on the network market, but also the dominance in the syndication market by off-network programs, reruns of programs previously produced by, or sold to, the three networks. Official Films told the Senate Committee: "As a result of the difficulties that we encounter due to the problems in the industry, the only plans we have for syndication products will be rerun films after the network sponsors have already telecast them." Guild Films wrote the committee that although it had never made a network telefilm sale, it was raising its per-episode budgets from $25,000 to $50,000 in an effort to make such network sales; "it is our experience that it is practically impossible to recoup the cost of such a high-budget series from syndication alone, and if we fail to obtain network sponsors of this type of series, we shall be compelled to stop making them."[31]

The Office of Network Study reported the declining number of first-run syndicated series offered from 1956 to 1964: twenty-nine in 1956; twenty in 1957; sixteen in 1958; fifteen in 1959; ten in 1960; seven in 1961; three in 1962; three in 1963; and one in 1964. Conversely, the number of half-hours of new off-network programs released for syndication rose from 484 in 1957 to 2,474 in 1964. The Office of Network Study concluded that the syndication market by 1960 was dominated by network reruns, deflating the independent producer's market for original syndication material and boosting the value of the networks' profit shares and syndication rights in off-network programs. The report concluded: "The inability of independent entrepreneurs successfully to compete in the so-called network television program market except upon terms dictated by network managers seems obvious from the above history." "By 1959," *Sponsor* reported, "Ziv and CBS together accounted for a third of the revenues from syndication, almost as much as the next five or six companies combined." A distributor told *Television* in 1961: "Today, with regionals pulling out of syndication like there's no tomorrow, with time periods as tight as A-bomb security in Siberia, with . . . bankruptcies, this business plain stinks."[32]

The dominance of network reruns over original syndicated material likewise restricted the programming choices for individual station operators to a pool of programs primarily created under the procurement policies of the three television networks. The choice for station managers became, as the Office of Network Study put it, "between programs designed and chosen—perhaps on the basis of financial interest—by the managers of the three national networks for program exhibition in the current season or similar programs similarly designed and chosen in past seasons."[33]

In summary, the economic and regulatory forces within the television industry of the 1950s combined to give the networks unprecedented power in relation to affiliates, advertisers, and program suppliers. Within a few years, the sources and forms of television programming and advertising support underwent tremendous change in large part under the direction of, and to the benefit of, the three networks. Although it is true that the ABC network, acting from its special economic circumstances, moved somewhat more quickly to the new procurement, sponsorship, and audience strategies, by the early 1960s all three networks directly licensed approximately 90 percent of their prime-time entertainment programming in pursuit of the same mass audiences and advertisers. In 1960, *Broadcasting* estimated the proportion of programs which included network profit participations at 58 percent for ABC, 60 percent for NBC, and 68 percent for CBS. Indeed, by the early 1960s ABC's schedule contained *fewer* film Westerns than either of the other networks.[34]

The consequences of these changes in the commercial practices of television were apparent to audiences witnessing the transformation of prime-time program forms and genres. Especially sensitive were the critical partisans of television's Golden Age, and the writers of live television drama. For many of these observers, the economic and programming changes represented not merely a succession of program cycles and economic practices, but the end of their careers in, and hopes for, the medium.

NOTES

1. U.S. Federal Communications Commission, Office of Network Study, *Second Interim Report: Television Network Program Procurement*, part 2, Docket no. 12782 (Washington, D.C.: U.S. Government Printing Office, 1965), pp. 173-74; Robert Gilbert, "Television 1953—Wall Street," *Television*, January 1953, p. 36; "California as a Program Source," *Television*, April 1951, p. 40; U.S. Congress, House Committee on Interstate and Foreign Commerce, *Investigation of Radio and Television Programs, Report by the Communications Subcommittee of the Committee on Interstate and Foreign Commerce*, 82nd Cong., 2d sess. (Washington, D.C.: U.S. Government Printing Office, 1952), p. 268; "Packaging Returns to the Networks," *Sponsor*, January 16, 1950, pp. 21, 58.

2. "Packagers (Not Nets) Lead in Building New Shows," *Sponsor*, January 28, 1952, pp. 31, 45; *Television* reported in 1951 that the networks had become very active in film production and syndication, notwithstanding earlier fears that film programs would loosen the network's hold on affiliates and sponsors, and that independent program suppliers would weaken network control of program schedules. Frederick Kugel, "The Economics of Film," *Television*, July 1951, p. 45.

3. Columbia Broadcasting System, *Opinion of Counsel and Memorandum Concerning the Applicability of Antitrust Laws to the Television Broadcast Activities of Columbia Broadcasting System, Inc.* (New York: Columbia Broadcasting System, 1956), p. 71, reprinted in U.S. Congress, Senate Committee on Foreign and Interstate Commerce, *Television Inquiry*, vol. 4: *Network Practices, Hearings Before the Committee on Foreign and Interstate Commerce*, 84th Cong., 2d sess. (Washington, D.C.: U.S. Government Printing Office, 1956), p. 1987.

4. "Is the Programming Subsidy Era Over in Network TV?," *Sponsor*, September 8, 1952, p. 83; "Have Sponsors Stopped Taking Program Risks in TV?," *Sponsor*, December 1, 1952, pp. 24, 25; "500 TV Stations: How Major Agencies See

the Picture," *Sponsor*, January 12, 1953, p. 23; "Have TV Show Costs Reached Their Ceiling?," *Sponsor*, September 21, 1953, pp. 29, 106.

5. "Network TV Lineup: Tear It Down, Build It Up," *Sponsor*, May 14, 1956, pp. 28, 102; Evelyn Konrad, "Will 'Outside' Packagers Reshape TV?," *Sponsor*, April 20, 1957, pp. 27-28.

6. "The Agencies Still Have the Final Say in Programming," *Television*, June 1955, pp. 39, 41; FCC, *Second Interim Report*, p. 214.

7. Ibid., pp. 550, 552; Susskind told *Broadcasting* that in order to place "Way Out" on CBS he was forced to give the network a 50 percent interest in the program, "Creators Turn on the Created," *Broadcasting*, June 26, 1961, p. 32.

8. "The Great Debate on Network Show Control," *Sponsor*, October 31, 1955, p. 38.

9. U.S. Congress, House Committee on the Judiciary, *Monopoly Problems in the Regulated Industries, Hearings Before the Antitrust Subcommittee of the Committee on the Judiciary, House of Representatives*, 84th Cong., 2d sess. (Washington, D.C.: U.S. Government Printing Office, 1956), part 2, vol. 2, pp. 4025, 4036-39 (hereafter referred to as the Celler Hearings).

10. FCC, *Second Interim Report*, pp. 209, 687; Senate Commerce Committee staff counsel Kenneth Cox also raised the issue of network ownership and personnel ties to several independent producers, including a CBS interest in Desilu, the network's purchase of Terrytoons, and an NBC interest in Barry-Enright Productions, producers of several television quiz shows, soon to be in the public eye for other reasons. U.S. Congress, Senate Committee on Interstate and Foreign Commerce, *Television Network Practices, Staff Report*, Committee Print no. 2, 85th Cong., 1st sess. (Washington, D.C.: U.S. Government Printing Office, 1957), p. 75 (hereafter referred to as the Cox Report).

11. Television Inquiry, p. 2233

12. Celler Hearings, p. 4124; "What Are Admen Telling the FBI About 'Divorcement'?," *Sponsor*, May 28, 1956, p. 32.

13. Celler Hearings, p. 4066; see also "How Film Distributors Would Change Network Television," *Sponsor*, June 11, 1956, pp. 30-31.

14. Cox Report, pp. 65-66; Michael M. Silverman of Television Programs of America told the Celler Committee that Whitehall Pharmaceuticals was told by CBS that it would have to pick up a CBS-produced program if it wished to sponsor a TPA-produced show on the network; Celler Hearings, pp. 4016-17.

15. Alfred J. Jaffe, "Are Agencies Earning Their 15% on Network TV Shows?," *Sponsor*, October 18, 1954, p. 109; FCC, *Second Interim Report*, p. 326.

16. Pat Weaver, "Memorandum on the Spectaculars," March 8, 1954, p. 9, collection of the NBC Records Administration Library, New York.

17. FCC, *Second Interim Report*, pp. 211-12.

18. Ibid., pp. 658, 687.

19. Ibid., p. 367.

20. Television Inquiry, p. 2907; Cox Report, p. 75.

21. Television Inquiry, pp. 2435, 1583.

22. FCC, *Second Interim Report*, pp. 17, 362, 738; see also Ashbrook P. Bryant, "Historical and Social Aspects of Concentration of Program Control in Television," *Law and Contemporary Problems* 34 (Summer 1969): 627 for a later endorsement of the Network Study Group position by its director.

23. FCC, *Second Interim Report*, p. 739; Arthur D. Little, Inc., *Television Program Production, Procurement and Syndication* (Cambridge: Arthur D. Little, 1966), pp. 50, 73.

24. Leslie Harris, "The Thorny Side of Syndicated Film," *Broadcasting-Telecasting*, November 8, 1954, p. 94.

25. FCC, *Second Interim Report*, p. 758.

26. Celler Hearings, p. 4069; Cox Report, p. 29.

27. Barbara Ann Moore, "Syndication of First-Run Television Programming: Its Development and Current Status," Ph.D. diss., Ohio University, 1979, pp. 33-34, 38; Albert R. Kroeger, "Programming: Short Supply, Big Demand," *Television*, April 1964, p. 72; "Film: Its Supply and Demand," *Broadcasting-Telecasting*, November 21, 1955, p. 28.

28. Television Inquiry, pp. 2911-13, 3066.

29. Ibid., p. 3067.

30. Ibid., pp. 3087, 3081-82, 3089, 3111.

31. See the testimony of representatives of Bernard L. Schubert Productions, Official Films, Inc., Television Programs of America, Hal Roach Studios, and Four Star Films, Inc. in Television Inquiry, pp. 3065-112, 3444-47; "The Great Debate," p. 38.

32. FCC, *Second Interim Report*, pp. 16, 19, 762; also see "First-run Film Series: Its Heyday Is Past," *Broadcasting*, May 8, 1961, p. 84; Little, *Television Program Production*, p. 82; "Syndicators' New Programming for '59," *Sponsor*, November 8, 1958, p. 44; Albert R. Kroeger, "Dark Days in Syndication," *Television*, October 1961, p. 36.

33. FCC, *Second Interim Report*, p. 767.

34. Ibid., p. 725; *Broadcasting*, May 1960; quoted in Erik Barnouw, *The History of Broadcasting in the United States*, vol. 3: *The Image Empire* (New York: Oxford University Press, 1970), pp. 150-51; Martin Mayer, "ABC: Portrait of a Network," *Show*, September 1961, p. 63.

PART FOUR

Crisis and Counterattack, 1958-60

11

"The Honeymoon Is Over":
The End of Live Drama

The late 1950s marks the period of greatest instability and change in prime-time programming in television history. Two historical studies of prime-time programming support the complaints of contemporary television critics about declining program diversity in the mid-1950s. The economist Stuart Long concludes that two measures of program variety—the range of simultaneous program choices at quarter-hour intervals in prime time and the total available daily program choices—both peaked in 1953, fell sharply through 1956, and continued to decline through the rest of the decade. Joseph Dominick and Millard Pearce examine prime-time schedules from 1954-74 and note a nearly continuous decline in program diversity over two decades, with the steepest fall from 1955-60. Dominick and Pearce also conclude that differences in program types among the three networks likewise declined over two decades, with the sharpest decline again in the second half of the 1950s. Their study notes an increase of one-third in the homogeneity of the three networks' prime-time schedules from 1955-59. These studies support contemporary observers, including *Sponsor*'s 1957 survey that called the 1956-57 television season the "shakiest season on record for network TV programs," with a casualty rate of 34 percent for network prime-time programs.[1]

The growing homogeneity within and across the program schedules of the three networks reflects the shift from live anthology drama to filmed action adventure in the late 1950s. ABC embraced the new programming most emphatically, canceling all of its prestige drama shows in the 1955-56 season in favor of new Hollywood telefilm series. ABC did not act alone, however; the proportion of prime-time programming produced live on all three networks declined from 50 percent in 1955 to 31 percent the following year. The number of live dramatic programs on all networks declined from fourteen in 1955-56, to seven in 1957-58, and to only one by 1959-60. NBC noted that the number of prime-time half-hours of sixty-minute dramatic programs fell from eleven in 1956 to only four in 1959, while the number of prime-time half-hours of telefilm Westerns rose from seven to thirty in the same three-year period. In the 1957-58 season, four of the top five programs were Westerns, and in July 1958, *Television* reported that Westerns constituted 26 percent of total network prime-time hours. A 1960 *Variety* article reported that the three networks planned not one regularly scheduled live prime-time program for the new season.[2]

The programming changes of the late 1950s repudiated the programming values championed by the major television critics. In his 1960 dissertation on TV critics, Frank Henry Jakes argued that "The 1957-58 television season was one of significance for television criticism. It marked the outbreak of an open feud between representatives of the television industry and many of the critics—a feud that was to continue for many seasons."[3] Three issues dominated complaints of television writers and critics in the late 1950s: changes within dramatic anthology programs, the shift to continuing character filmed series, and increasing censorship pressures upon TV writers. The ensuing debates over program balance and freedom of expression inevitably became inflected by the regulatory and business scandals within the television industry of the late 1950s.

The repudiation of the aesthetic tenets of the Golden Age was evident within several of the long-running dramatic anthology series in the mid-1950s. Observers noted a decline in the power of the anthology drama producer in favor of a system of alternating producers, a dilution of responsibility that weakened protection for the writer of controversial material. For example, *Time* magazine wrote that veteran "Philco Playhouse" producer Fred Coe lost editorial control over the program after sponsor complaints of downbeat stories in 1954. Vance Bourjaily reported that beginning in 1955, Philco began to demand to see story outlines and put pressure on the program's producers to use established stars and avoid unhappy endings.[4]

Many anthology programs in the mid-1950s also began to move away from the psychological naturalism championed by defenders of live television drama in favor of melodrama and spectacle. In April 1957, *Sponsor* noted: "As the TV season proceeds, more and more dramatic anthology shows are relying on straight melodrama. Behind this trend is the conviction among Madison Avenue program experts . . . that big audiences no longer are attracted by finely and soberly developed themes." Roger Bolin, director of advertising for Westinghouse, the sponsor of "Studio One" from 1949 to 1958, testified that by 1957 "a run of psychological dramas" on the program caused the sponsor to fear "getting a reputation for a downbeat type of show." Fearful of "being typed as a sponsor that showed mainly studies of abnormalities," Westinghouse moved the series to Hollywood with new producers and directors for what was to be its final season. In November 1957, *Sponsor* reported that "Kraft Television Theatre," the longest running network prime-time dramatic program and the only remaining sixty-minute weekly prime-time program produced in New York, would change its format. The revised format included new opening and closing sequences, bigger production budgets, more youth-oriented appeal, and greater use of Hollywood stars. It was to be the final season for the program.[5]

In his 1960 dissertation on live television drama, William Hawes argues that "in earlier anthologies controversy and experimental dramas played a significant part. Today such dramas have practically disappeared from the few remaining anthology programs." After 1952-56, when the networks offered approximately a dozen anthology dramas each season, anthology dramas were replaced by network specials, star-built dramatic programs, and action-adventure telefilms on the networks. In addition, several anthology programs shifted from live to film formats, including "Ford Theatre," "Lux Video Theatre," and "Studio One." According to Hawes, "Once they were in Hollywood and once the television industry had embraced a desire for scope, the intimate drama and the live anthologies were doomed, because spectacular dramas could more easily be produced on film."[6]

Some observers attributed the decline of live anthology drama in part to a growing disenchantment with the genre among television critics. Dramatic anthology programs had always received disproportionate critical scrutiny compared to other programming; *Sponsor* reported in 1957 that although the typical network film series was reviewed once or twice a season, a live drama series might get forty national newspaper reviews, usually at least twenty-five per season. Beginning in 1955, a number of television reviewers sharply criticized several anthology drama programs for their subject matter and tone. Initiated by Jack Gould at the *New York Times,* the criticism was echoed by others in the trade press. Typical of the new critical antipathy toward psychological drama in television was an essay by Robert Kass in the *Catholic World* in 1956 on the work of some prominent TV writers:

> In looking over the body of work of these well-paid scriptwriters, I am struck by the fact that, in several instances, they have labored so resolutely in the name of the "sick" school of drama . . . almost exclusively concerned with psychoneurotics and deviants who suffer from assorted maladies of the soul and spirit. The popularity of the misfits both in the theatre and TV is a mystifying one and represents an unhealthy preoccupation with sex and psychoanalytic misbehavior. . . . Apparently there is no drama in sane, ordinary people any more. Mr. Chayefsky's "little" people, the misfits who inhabit the lower depths of the Bronx, Mr. Serling's twisted introverts, Mr. Rose's rebellious outcasts are all crowding the TV dials week after week.[7]

The new critical attacks on the television psychodrama probably had an effect on sponsors. As Frank Henry Jakes explains: "Some sponsors, reportedly smarting from harsh criticism of the dramatic shows they had sponsored, decided to play it safe and buy filmed series, which it was said the critics seldom reviewed." Bourjaily placed much of the blame for the demise of live drama at the hands of unsympathetic critics.[8]

However, it seems unlikely that hostile reviews did more than reinforce more powerful influences in the industry unfavorable to live drama. Despite public reservations about television psychodrama, for most critical defenders of live drama "the danger was not that TV drama would become small and delicate and melancholy; the danger was that it might cease to exist," according to critic Gilbert Seldes in 1956.[9] It was the cancellation of anthology dramas in favor of continuing character programs that received the harshest critical condemnation. Defenders of live anthology drama were particularly disturbed because the new episodic form fundamentally altered the functions of playwright and critic. For many of the most prominent writers and critics in television, the move to the continuing character series was more than merely a shift in program forms or commercial practices; it meant an end to their careers in the medium.

Parallel to the new generation of television playwrights, television critics had enjoyed heightened visibility and power with the flourishing of live television drama in the mid-1950s. An NBC survey reported that newspaper space devoted to television rose 500 percent between 1953 and 1955. A 1957 *Newsweek* article on television critics, "Big Men on the Paper," called television critics "the new elite of the editorial room." *Newsweek* singled out Gould and John Crosby as especially influential "because of the respect for their opinions in the upper echelons of the network." Television critics and writers were frequent allies in defense of live television in the mid-1950s, and writers enlisted critics in their creative battles with sponsors and networks. As Rod Serling explained in the foreword to a collection of television plays, "My own feeling is that the television critic has one primary purpose. He's there to needle and prod the industry into quality. . . . " David Susskind told *TV Guide* in 1959: "I have never been a critic lover, but in the low condition television has been in the past year, the most potent voice has been the critic. He is against the shoddy and the cheap. Without the critic, I believe we would have more mediocrity than we have now."[10]

Seldes in 1956 described the programming shifts in terms of Hollywood versus New York and the aesthetic specificity of the television medium. "[W]hile the tradition of intelligent hour-long drama persisted in New York," Seldes wrote, "dozens of producers in Hollywood were working on series of their own." Decrying the influence of what he called the "oil slick of Hollywood" on the medium, Seldes warned that "the economics of the situation are favorable to the spread of the filmed play, and the only hope for a reasonably intelligent TV drama lies in the hour-long play done live—and (so far) chiefly in New York."[11]

Television critics grew more pessimistic about the future of live drama around 1954, in part in reaction to a flood of thirty-minute telefilms modeled after the successful "I Love Lucy" and "Dragnet." Many critics found the new program format of the continuing character filmed series, where main characters, themes, and plot ideas for the entire series are established in the pilot episode—to be intrinsically resistant to thoughtful criticism. After lamenting the decline of live anthology programming, Crosby concluded in a 1958 essay: "I remember when there were ten or twelve hour-long drama shows on the air a week, and you could write a little essay, pointing out trends in dramatic themes, styles in acting and all sorts of other reasonably creative efforts. . . . Today you'll find gossip, or interviews, or personalities, or chit-chat or most everything except criticism." In another 1958 essay Crosby admitted: "After the first show, I don't know what to say about a western or quiz show, and I don't know anybody else who does either."[12]

The reaction of some prominent television writers to the shift from anthology to continuing character programming was even more hostile than that of the television critics. In sharp contrast to the earlier editions of *The Best Television Plays*, the third volume, published in 1954, contained a sharp denunciation of the medium by TV writer Manny Rubin:

> There is no resilience in television anymore, no dilation, no profession of idea. By this time the firmly entrenched TV programs with ratings higher than last year's skits have developed a style from which they seldom stray. Thanks to Hooper, Nielsen, and other sponsor watchdogs, likes and dislikes are charted and certified: the TV mold hardens and becomes uniform. . . .
>
> Television is not the best medium to start if one is a beginning writer. The standards are uniform and there is little room for experimentation. . . . There will be no F. Scott Fitzgeralds in TV, no Faulkners, no Hemingways. For TV writing has become a hack job. It has conformed too readily to commercial restrictions, and of all the giants who bow before the magniloquent power of the camera, I believe the writer's loss is the greatest of all.[13]

By the end of the decade many of television's most prominent writers shared Rubin's bitterness toward the medium in which earlier they had invested great hope. In *The Television Writer* (1962) Erik Barnouw described the market for the television writer in the mid-1950s: "Diversity was vanishing; series after series was a carbon copy. Crime formula dominated almost all schedules. . . . It was especially catastrophic for the future of the medium that the 'anthology series' seemed in danger of disappearing." Ernest Kinoy, president of the Writers Guild of America-

East, described the work of the television writer on continuing character film series programs: approached by a producer with a story idea, the
writer worked on a pilot script, and if the pilot was sold to a network for
series production, the producer invited ten or twelve writers to view the
pilot, read a sample script, and contribute in conformance to guidelines
of the series' characters and plot premises. As Kinoy explained: "You are
asked to bring him an idea, which will duplicate the product he has
shown you in the pilot and the form that he has given you. If it does not
do what he wants, if it does not duplicate this problem, in essence, then
he will not buy it. And why should he be expected to? This is what he has
contracted to deliver to a customer...."[14]

Financial rewards for writers of filmed television were considerable if
they developed a concept for a continuing series and thereby acquired a
share in its syndication and subsidiary revenues; such revenues were
potentially much greater than those from straight sales of scripts. Barnouw worried about the larger consequences of the shift to telefilm programming: "the long run risk to television was incalculable. Suddenly
there was no reason for any new writer to turn to television. To writers of
substance, new or established, the invitation to write variations on a
formula was an invitation to go elsewhere. Chayefsky, Vidal, Aurthur,
Foote, and Wishengrad turned elsewhere. Many writers who stayed did so
because they had nowhere else to go. Required to write formula or nothing, their talents were tragically wasted and misused. After citing the
earlier accomplishments of live television drama, Barnouw described
the state of the television writer in 1961 to the Office of Network Study:
"Today television itself no longer has a place for such work. The writers
who did this work have gone away or been whittled down. The author of
'Requiem for a Heavyweight' now writes formula mysteries of the super-
natural and even wins prizes for them: a symptom of the low estate to
which television drama has fallen, in just a few short years." The object
of Barnouw's scorn, Rod Serling, presents an unusual case of a prominent and often controversial writer of live television drama who remained active in the transition to filmed series programming through his
role as creator (and 50 percent owner) and frequent writer of the thirty-
minute telefilm series the "Twilight Zone" from 1959-64. In the third
volume of his *History of Broadcasting in the United States*, Barnouw
elaborated upon the creative implications of the shift to the filmed
series: "The episodic series was conceived for rigid control. It invited

writers to compose, to a defined formula, scripts for specified actors and often for a particular sponsor, who was inclined to think of a play as a setting for commercials . . . too often, the formula invitation attracted the hack, and turned talented writers into journeymen."[15]

In a 1957 article, "The TV Pattern: Signs of Revolt," Marya Mannes wrote that many television critics saw the medium "set in a rigid pattern from which it either cannot or will not break free. . . . Television has reached a plateau of accomplishment where growth seems arrested, aspiration suspended," measured against the ambitions and achievements of the medium three to five years earlier, she argued.[16]

The FCC's Office of Network Study heard testimony in New York in June 1961 from a number of prominent writers and producers from the era of live television. The FCC's Report noted that the witnesses were "in virtual agreement that at about the 1957-8 television season, due to a number of factors, much of the diversity in entertainment programs disappeared from network schedules and that such schedules tended to become disproportionately loaded with action-adventure type film programs and other film series programs of a 'stereotyped' nature." Susskind told the panel that 1954 was "the last year of freedom and the last year of intelligent, unfettered expression" in television, "before the costs became astronomical, before the meddlers and inhibitors became infinite, it was before the whole structure of television and the temper of television underwent a complete transformation."[17]

Television producer Worthington Miner described the new market for television writers in the production of continuing character series, where "there is a formula; there is a character that is already created; they must write to those characters. There must be so many people shot or killed in a half-hour. The whole thing is laid out. Anybody can fill in. And the dialogue isn't even very literate. So that it really doesn't take much writer to do it, and no self-respecting writer will do it, certainly won't do over his own name. . . . The creative writer has no place in such a situation," he concluded. Barnouw told the Office of Network Study that the story of the decline of the writer in television was "tragic and sobering," and noted that "There is no opportunity for the writer . . . to demonstrate anything at all; there's hardly any reason for him to go into television at the present time. I don't remember any time in the last twenty-five years when writers in general in the broadcast field have been as bitter or as disillusioned as they are at the present moment in regard to the opportunities that exist in the form of the program structure."[18]

Writer-producer Robert Alan Aurthur told the Office of Network Study that the only opportunities for writers to work in television were in telefilm series, and argued: "It's possible by this method to turn out good stock, entertaining films, but I think it is quite impossible to turn out anything that has any real intrinsic value." Unlike the anthology programs, writing for film series provided no rehearsal period for rewrites, and the writer was excluded from the set during production. Of the television writer, Aurthur said simply, "he doesn't exist in films."[19]

A Warner Brothers executive told the Office of Network Study that as a telefilm series began "to get into the mould, certain writers we rehire quite often because they prove to have a good grasp of the series." Kinoy noted the change from a few years earlier, when the industry seemed eager to develop writing talent; now, he argued, there was "virtually no opportunity for writers in the television medium who have not already attained some reputation to attain it. You cannot build a reputation either in the trade or in the public eye as a writer of episodes of a crime show or a Western when your product is indistinguishable from the week before or the week after."[20]

High on the list of complaints of television writers in the second half of the 1950s was the growing commercial censorship of their work. Barnouw saw 1954 as the year when the climate for dramatic writers shifted, as sponsors and networks grew more cautious and censorship pressures increased. "The result," he wrote, "was a fascinating series of disputes and explosions. Most were settled behind closed doors. A writer who brought a script quarrel to public attention risked his livelihood." The new commercial pressures brought more intrusive sponsor involvement in dramatic programs; according to Barnouw, "Such harassment inevitably doomed the anthology series, which in 1954-55 began a rapid decline." Producer Robert Montgomery told the Office of Network Study at its 1961 New York hearings that he admired the "courage" of those television writers who criticized network practices, "in being willing to speak out, . . . because whether those who are here or not realize it, in my opinion they have taken their livelihoods in their hands when they come down here."[21]

Aurthur in 1958 described the perception of writers of anthology drama: "We were driven off television; we did not abandon television.

Television left us." He also denounced what he called "the new stone age" in network leadership, signaled by the move of a number of ABC executives to NBC in the late 1950s: "People have come over from ABC to show them how ABC did it. A vice-president named Robert Stone is in charge—really is a powerful man at the network. There have been mass firings from secretaries right up to the entire—almost the entire creative staff. [Stone] is on record as saying about people like me: 'Those bums come a dime a dozen. I can buy them for a dime a dozen.' That's a terrible thing to say, because we bums are much more expensive than that. And it is a clear case of deciding that television has only one function: that function is to be a profit medium." Aurthur recalled his unsuccessful battle as a producer to limit the number of commercial breaks per program; eventually the network told him flatly: "The Crest story is very important." Aurthur continued: "The strange thing about television is that the Crest story is really more important, and the drama is something that goes in between the commercials and will be sacrificed at any given time for that purpose."[22]

The new constraints upon and management attitudes toward the writers and producers of live drama led to an exodus of creative talent from the medium and to a new cynicism about the status of working in television. Fred Coe quit NBC after the first year of a three-year contract, telling *Time:* "Plans and ideas I have submitted have either been ignored or have drawn no interest. A silent telephone on your desk is a terrible thing." David Davidson, national chairman of the Writers Guild of America, told the FCC in 1961: "Never in history have so many writers been paid so much for writing so badly." Davidson described the Hollywood telefilm production companies as "assembly line" operations, "sausage factories," where writers prepare a script, turn it in and are told to "get lost." As Davidson confessed to the Office of Network Study, "I'm afraid that we writers of American television today are, for the most part, being paid extremely well to do our absolutely worst work. Such writers as once took pride in their work would like nothing better than to be made honest again."[23]

Part of the writers' disillusionment with television reflected their perceptions of the medium's diminished cultural status. In 1961, Paddy Chayefsky described recent offers that he had received to work in television, all to develop filmed series:

Those offers, however, required an idea man more than they required a writer. The sort of thing I was asked to do was to conceive a television series, and generally supervise the remaining scripts in the series. The thing here, you see, is that no writer who takes himself seriously wants to write the sort of thing that passes for a television series. I fault television, not for ignoring writers, but for failing to provide them with the sensation of stature that writers require if they are to think of themselves as artists. No writer wants to be known as the creator of a television series. The thing that a writer aspires to is to recognition as a poet, or at the very least, as a social commentator. Television has offered writers notoriety, even money under new patterns of profit participation, but it has never offered pride. To this day, I resent being known as a TV writer, and I should not think of again writing for television until the epitaph "TV writer" did not bear a frightful connotation of lesser artist or apprentice artistry.[24]

Serling told *Playboy* in 1961 that he didn't blame television writers who had left the medium for Broadway or the motion pictures. "Television at its best is a kind of finger exercise for the more important things later on," he confided. The diminished status of the television writer by the end of the 1950s is also suggested by the profile of the successful TV writer offered by Ross Davidson, director of Program Services at NBC, in 1961: "Our candidate is a healthy, and probably young, realist who has . . . discarded *for the moment* any idea of revolutionizing television so that it works for *him*. He is an adaptable artist. . . ." The same year ABC executive Daniel Melnick put matters even more starkly, explaining that the new action-adventure programs required "a different type of television writer, one who doesn't have a burning desire to make an original statement."[25]

Abundant evidence was offered in the 1959-61 FCC hearings that advertising agencies, sponsors, and networks had all grown more sensitive to controversial material in the second half of the 1950s. As one advertising executive told the panel: "We just don't like letters of criticism. . . . Even if there are five letters we find our clients become very sensitive to them and would rather not have any. . . ." Another advertising executive told the Office of Network Study that the typical agency has "one, two, three, four people reading scripts on each show." The FCC report noted that most agencies read scripts, had an on-set pro-

ducer, and screened rushes on behalf of their clients. A widely publicized 1959 "Playhouse 90" incident underscored what such scrutiny
could mean. An advertising executive described his agency's role in a
"Playhouse 90" drama about the Nuremburg war crime trials, sponsored
by the American Gas Association:

> [W]e get paid for going through the script. In going through the
> scripts, we noticed gas referred to in half a dozen places that had to do
> with death chambers. This was just an oversight on somebody's part.
> We deal with a lot of artistic people on the creative end, and some-
> times they do not have the commercial judgement or see things as we
> are paid to see, and we raised the point with CBS and they said they
> would remove the word "gas," and we thought they would, and they
> did in some cases, and at the last minute, we found that there were
> some still left in. As a result—and this was just, I think, stupidity—the
> show went on the air where the word "gas" was deleted by the en-
> gineer rather than rehearsing the talent.[26]

The Office of Network Study's 1965 report, summarizing two months
of testimony from network advertisers in 1959-60, concluded: "As a
general proposition, sponsor aversion to controversy, thought-provok-
ing material, 'downbeat' material, etc., permeates and shapes the production of 'formula type' program series from start to finish." Charles
Winick, in *Taste and the Censor in Television* (1959), reported that sex-
ual topics were more strictly censored in television than in radio, film, or
on the stage; that irony and satire were severely restricted; that expression of antisocial ideas largely prohibited, political issues proscribed,
and labor and the workplace banished as dramatic topics.[27]

One television advertiser summarized the sponsor's attitude toward
television programming to the FCC: "a large corporation is expending a
lot of dollars to bring entertainment to the viewer, and this corporation
does not desire to bring such entertainment that, when it's all over, the
viewer is pretty sad and depressed about the state of the world—in
other words, where the script might be built around one-tenth of one
percent of the misery and desolation of the country—and we call that, I
would say, a company policy to try and provide entertainment for this
company that is good and has depth, but does not go the extreme of misery of the very small minority of people."[28]

Several sponsors told the Office of Network Study of prohibitions on
television subject matter. In 1955 Westinghouse objected to a "Studio

One" program dealing with an A-bomb test because the company was promoting its "Atoms for Peace" program and "was beginning to build peacetime atomic plants for General Electric." A General Electric executive told the Office of Network Study that GE was opposed to downbeat programs in general because such programs were incompatible with the company's advertising slogan, "Progress Is Our Most Important Product," a slogan delivered weekly by GE's television spokesman Ronald Reagan.[29]

Gail Smith, director of advertising for General Motors, told the Office of Network Study that his company "has elected to avoid being concerned with matters that are controversial and we endeavor to see that programs with which we are associated do not become associated with controversial matters." As Smith elaborated, "Generally speaking, it would certainly be desirable not to have commercial placement in a program where the first act or second act might end at a very high emotional pitch, or a show that is constantly one of a highly emotional nature."[30]

By the mid-1950s, the large manufacturers of mass-market consumer goods, the dominant television sponsors, had similar program prohibitions. For example, the advertising vice president for General Foods explained to the Office of Network Study that "as it is a seller of food products and has a 'feeling that eating is a pleasant experience,'" the company has "definitely gone in for the light entertainment shows." According to the General Foods executive, a program "must be light, it must be pleasant." Another sponsor, a coffee manufacturer, forbade "the mention of tea" on any of the programs it sponsored. General Foods killed an episode of "Richard Diamond, Private Detective" that concerned a poisonous snake loose on a passenger ship. Edwin W. Ebel, General Foods' vice president for advertising, explained to the FCC panel that "What was supposed to be a whodunit was actually a horror story. Women don't like snakes, especially when they're running around loose and when the story is followed by a baby Jello commercial." In still another example, as an alternating sponsor of "Alfred Hitchcock Presents," Revlon was able to prevent the network airing of an episode (where a magician's deranged apprentice attempts to saw a woman in half) despite the fact that the episode was already completed and scheduled for broadcast.[31]

Albert N. Halverstadt, general advertising manager of Procter and Gamble, television's largest advertiser, told the FCC group:

The writers should be guided by the fact that any scene that contributes negatively to the public morale is not acceptable. Men in uniform shall not be cast as heavy villains or portrayed as engaging in any criminal activity. There will be no material in any of our programs which could in any way further the concept of business as cold, ruthless and lacking in all sentiment or spiritual motivation. If a businessman is cast in the role of villain, it must be made clear that he is not typical but is as much despised by his fellow businessmen as he is by other members of society. Special attention shall be given to any mention, however innocuous, of the grocery and drug business as well as any other group of customers of the company.[32]

The company distributed a twenty-one-point "Editorial Policy" to advertising agencies supervising Procter and Gamble shows and applied it to all its broadcast programs. Beyond the flat prohibition, "There will be no materials for or against sharply drawn national or regional controversial issues," the sponsor's "strict rules" specified that:

In general, the moral code of the characters in our dramas will be more or less synonymous with the moral code of the bulk of the American people. The usual taboos on sex subjects will be observed. Material dealing with sex perversion, miscegenation, and rape is banned, as are scenes of excessive passion and suggestive dialogue. Suggestive situations covered by innocuous dialogue will not be used.... Care will be exercised that lines in scripts with double meanings or unconscious ambiguities are not used for broadcasts.

If it is necessary in the development of conflict for a character to attack some basic conception of the American way of life ... answer must be completely and convincingly made some place in the same broadcast.

There will be no material that may give offense either directly or by inference, to any organized minority group, lodge, or other organizations, institutions, residents of any state or section of the country, or a commercial organization of any sort.[33]

Television sponsors maintained a tight grip on program content. Robert E. Gorman, an advertising executive of Allstate Insurance, which sponsored "Playhouse 90" in a multiple sponsorship format from 1957-60, told the Office of Network Study that of seventy-eight scripts involved, the company had demanded 175 changes, 95 percent of them for "reasons of taste" as opposed to business reasons. A memorandum from Miles Laboratories to Screen Gems included a prohibition on headaches and upset stomachs in its programs, and a memorandum from Liggett and Myers to the producer of "The Ed Wynn Show" banned pipe and cigar smoking by guests and ordered cigarette vending machines and advertising posters in the background of dramatic sets to highlight Chesterfield cigarettes. The memorandum also noted that "'natural' smoking action is a requisite by the cast," of the Chesterfield brand only, of course. Serling identified the first run-through of a live program like "Playhouse 90" as the time when advertising agency representatives demanded multiple script changes. He told *Broadcasting* in 1960 that "They automatically and arbitrarily delete from the English language any word that suggests a competitive product. You can't 'ford' a river if it's sponsored by Chevy; you can't offer someone a 'match' if it's sponsored by Ronson lighters." Serling told *Newsweek* in 1959 that "In some cases, you can't even use the word *American*. It might be the name of a rival tobacco company."[34]

In writing the script for "Noon on Doomsday" (a fictionalization of the Emmett Till lynching case) for "The U.S. Steel Hour," Serling was subjected to such sponsor, agency, and network pressures that he complained that he attended "at least two meetings a day for over a week, taking down notes as to what had to be changed." As Serling described the changes: "A victim was changed from a Negro to Jew, then to an unnamed foreigner. The locale was shifted from the South to an unnamed place in New England. . . . I finally suggested Alaska and Eskimos as a way out." Serling's play was finally set in a New England town, with no suggestion of racial issues; even references to Coca-Cola—associated with southern settings—were proscribed. Serling told the Fund for the Republic that "The result was that I was destroyed by this show professionally, I think, for about eleven or twelve months. People kept referring to me as 'that guy who wrote that thing.' It also stuck to me that I was now a controversial writer, so-called."[35]

J. Edward Dean, director of advertising for DuPont, told the FCC that the well-done serious drama was not as "well liked as other shows which were less stressful, and that the message that was taught through our commercials was not as well learned as in those shows which were . . . lighter, happier—had more entertainment value." He told the panel that his company was not interested in "controversial" programs, which he defined as programs where "there is one group in conflict with another." Max Banzhof, advertising director of the Armstrong Cork Company, cited American race relations as an example of an issue unsuitable for dramatic presentation on television, telling the FCC group that his firm was not afraid of controversy, "but it must be remembered that a controversial subject is best handled by objective, factual, and calm presentation of the two or more points of view. . . . The race issue, for example, is emotionally charged and a dramatic show cannot clearly, dispassionately and objectively reflect opposing views with equality. It's usually one-sided and subjective in order to be dramatic."[36]

Harold A. Carlborg, head of censorship for CBS, offered a similar rationale for banishing race as a subject of television drama: "In the matter of segregation, it would be difficult to present a dramatization dealing with some aspects of this problem on a sponsored program, particularly at a time when the subject is considered highly inflammatory. . . . It would be impossible to maintain any balance of dramatizations highlighting one side of such a currently explosive issue as segregation in a sponsored *entertainment* program." The only major dramatic anthology program with a black lead in the 1950s, "Philco Playhouse"'s "A Man Is Ten Feet Tall," with Sidney Poitier, was cast by associate producer Robert Alan Aurthur only after the sponsor and network announced the series was to be canceled at the end of the 1955 season, reasoning he would be beyond the reach of reprisals.[37]

Not surprisingly, the television writer and producer were at the center of most disputes over program controversy in the late 1950s. Herbert Brodkin, producer of several dramatic anthology programs, told the Office of Network Study in 1960: "I never produced a quality series with which there was not a great deal of attempted advice, interference, suggestion, etc.," from sponsors. Brodkin testified that the kind of dramatic program the sponsor objected to most vigorously was "the kind of play which dealt with life, the world around us and its problems. . . . Generally, the closer we came to life the more trouble we had in getting such a script approved and on," Brodkin told the panel, and John Frankenheimer told David Susskind that "It used to be difficult to do anything controversial in television: now it's impossible." Congressman Emanuel Celler told the Association of National Advertisers in 1957 that: "The artist is being pummeled into conformity, the singer, the actor, the writer, the composer are compelled to strip themselves of their God-given individuality and imitate. The goal is not the integrity of performance, but the clink of coin into the sponsor's coffers, the smell of the green bill."[38]

Perhaps even more telling was the conclusion of the FCC Office of Network Study in its *First Interim Report* in 1960 that explicit censorship was in fact less significant than the widespread self-censorship practiced by television writers and producers. C. Terence Clyne of McCann-Erickson explained that the degree of continuous self-censorship by most television writers kept the need for explicit sponsor intervention to a minimum by the late 1950s: "Actually there have been very few cases where it has been necessary to exercise a veto, because the producers ... and the writers involved are normally pretty well aware of what might not be acceptable." Winick concluded that the most important constraint to the television writer's free expression was self-censorship; the average number of censorship changes for a thirty-minute teleplay was in fact only between one and ten, he reported. Shelby Gordon, a former CBS script editor and producer, wrote bitterly in 1959: "Today there's no censorship problem to speak of. New writers who are attracted to television generally have nothing to say. The rest of us have forgotten how to say it. . . . We're businessmen, we fill a need. We supply a commodity, even Westerns. We shudder when our kids see them, just like anyone else, but we continue to write them just the same because they pay as well as any other kind of drama on television and because they're just as valid. Black hat, white hat; the law vs. crime; there's not much more idea than that in the biggest productions on television."[39]

Rod Serling told the Fund for the Republic that sponsors and advertising agency representatives reserved the right to demand changes on their sets during rehearsals, and that as a writer he had never challenged their demands. In a 1958 profile, Serling discussed self-censorship: "I have pre-censored myself in the sense that I know that I'm not going to write those things that are socially sticky and unacceptable in terms of the mass medium. The alternative is bucking your head against a stone wall. In television, the writer is the last guy on the team, in terms of policy, in terms of basic concept of his show. . . . It's best I write those things that can be shown. The only alternative is to try another medium—theatre or novel-writing—where you can say what you please."[40]

As Jack Gould described the revised image of the television writer in

1961: "Those who are still around are trained in the taboos of the business: they anticipate them and keep them out of their scripts right from the beginning. The agency people testified to this at the FCC hearings. They said, 'We don't have any trouble with the writers any more. They know what we don't want and they leave it out.' So you have this terrible sterility." Barnouw told the Office of Network Study in 1960 that young writers viewed television "as an artistic dead end, a mere appendage of advertising. . . . How different this is from the situation of a few years ago. Already that period, in retrospect, looks like a golden age," he told the panel.[41]

The complaints from television writers and critics of growing conservatism and mediocrity in prime-time programming were occasionally echoed by industry leaders in the late 1950s. The intermittent self-criticism within the trade provided a faint counterpoint to the dominant chorus from the industry of hostile rejection of any criticism. One advertising executive admitted pessimism about the direction of network prime-time programming to the FCC's Office of Network Study:

> I think the honeymoon is over—ten years of television. A good deal of the novelty has worn off, and unless a continuing vitality is injected into the program schedule, television can be hurt as an advertising medium. . . . I do not think that the advertiser or his agent can have this uppermost in mind when he selects a program. He is, after all, and we are by the same token, businessmen buying television for business reasons. The tendency is to select a program which you are pretty sure can succeed because you're riding 2,500,000 or 5,000,000 dollars on it. This results in a certain sameness of program as witness the fact that in the upcoming year [1959-60] forty-five percent of the network programs will be either Westerns or suspense dramas, because they have been successful forms.[42]

Growing criticism of network prime-time programming was noted in the trade press in the 1956 television season. A 1956 *Sponsor* article reported that for the first time, no new network program made the top ten most popular shows list, and the magazine blamed a new conservatism in networks, agencies, and sponsors. In October 1957, *Variety* discussed the new television season under the page one headline "New Season a Dud." A February 1957 *Television* article noted: "Seldom has there been such a savage critical slashing at new program offerings as there has been this season, from within as well as outside the industry."[43]

Part of the new sponsorship and programming strategies in the mid-1950s was an increased reliance on audience ratings. The shift from single sponsorship to participating sponsorship in the late 1950s represented a change in the tactics of television advertising, away from the association of an advertiser with a specific program and time slot, and toward the purchase of independent slots across several different programs and time periods. Networks grew increasingly intolerant of low-rated sponsor vehicles for goodwill or specialized audiences, and the advertising model shifted to so-called "formula buying" based on specified targets of cost per thousand viewers and program ratings. The Office of Network Study hearings revealed widespread formula buying in the late 1950s by large television advertisers, using cost-per-thousand targets and thresholds; Scott Paper, for example, demanded a minimum one-third share of the prime-time audience for any program it sponsored.[44]

A 1957 editorial in *Sponsor* attributed the new emphasis on ratings to the entrance of large sponsors, especially Procter and Gamble, into prime time and to the use of formula buying. The editorial noted: "One day (soon we hope) broadcast historians will look upon the rating madness of the mid-1950s as one of the oddest chapters in the development of a dynamic industry," and the magazine blamed the rating services, sponsors, and advertising agencies for overemphasizing the importance of ratings. "On the network level rating worship has reached peak absurdity," the editorial complained. In 1957, recently ousted NBC President Pat Weaver blamed cost-per-thousand formula buying for the narrowing of program formats and the concentration on regularly scheduled, continuing series programming which, he argued, risked the loss of television's light viewer. Weaver denounced the new ratings consciousness at the networks, arguing that the television industry should not "degrade everything to win ratings that count as equals moppets, morons and that fragment of our population that looks at anything."[45]

Richard W. Jencks, former counsel for CBS, wrote later that in the second half of the 1950s, rating information became more instantaneous and detailed, in part a consequence of advertisers moving away from the strategy of buying viewer gratitude to that of buying circulation and demographics. In 1957, the rating firm American Research Bureau announced the start of Arbitron, an instantaneous rating service providing minute-by-minute ratings from seven cities; *Sponsor* magazine noted at the time: "There is no disagreement that if Arbitron catches on, the ratings business will never be the same." In 1958, Nielsen announced it too would provide an instant rating service. The enhanced rating services both responded to and encouraged a more volatile, ratings-conscious program philosophy at the networks.[46]

A handful of industry executives echoed the complaints of television critics in the 1956-58 period. In July 1957, Hubbell Robinson cited heightened public and critical dissatisfaction with network programming and pointed to industry fears that program quality would continue to decline. "It is obvious to anyone with eyes to see and ears to hear that in television's programming a considerable amount of soft underbelly exists," Robinson declared, and he scored the industry's "willingness to settle for drama whose synonym is pap," led by "carbon-copy westerns." A 1957 *Sponsor* article observed: "there are no daring and expensive programming experiments in the offing," as it noted the shift to film formats in prime time and the continued decline in both sixty-minute and thirty-minute dramatic programs. In January 1959, *Television* reported: "In 1958, the industry was subjected to a mounting stream of criticism ranging from the charge of mediocrity to allegations of over-commercialization and rate instability." The president of Crosley Broadcasting, Robert E. Dunville, in an article in the same issue of the magazine, wrote: "There is not much disagreement with the opinion that imitation, sameness and an oversupply of Westerns are things to be concerned with."[47]

In a speech to the Association of National Advertisers in December 1957, the advertising executive John P. Cunningham warned that "There is a possibility that a most important advertising tool is in danger of being blunted and dulled. We should alert ourselves to it." Cunningham noted that viewer surveys in "Videotown," the sample community of New Brunswick, New Jersey, showed increasing viewer boredom with network programming, leading, according to adman Cunningham, to "less penetration per skull per dollar." Cunningham noted that television had always had its detractors, "but lately the criticism of programming has been rising to a crescendo. And this is very much our business, because pallid programming can rob the best commercials of much of their power.... Our agency's Videotown research shows clearly that the grumbling is not confined to the professional critics. The

Index of Boredom has been rising steadily. But people are long-suffering—they will watch programs that bore them—but they tend to tune out their minds—which is bad for advertisers."[48]

A December 1957 research report prepared for CBS warned: "Perhaps the most serious long-term problem in the environment of nighttime viewing is viewers could get overall 'television fatigue' leading to gradual erosion of interest and attention (even though sets in use would not decline until a competitive evening entertainment media appears on the scene)." A December 1957 *Sponsor* article reexamined the sample television market of New Brunswick, New Jersey revealing set penetration at the saturation level of 93 percent (unless color sets became less expensive, the article warned, there was little prospect of significant new set sales), a level of viewership flat since 1954, and growing viewer complaints of boredom and "creeping mediocrity." In 1958, *Sponsor* noted that the charges of mediocrity raised by some within the industry, including Edward R. Murrow, David Susskind, Pat Weaver, and Hubbell Robinson, echoed the "elitist" television critics. In a October 1958 speech Murrow denounced network prime-time schedules as evidence of "decadence, escapism and insulation from the realities of the world," and accused network leaders of underestimating the intelligence of viewers. Widely reported and commented upon, Murrow's speech was reprinted in *The Reporter* and *TV Guide*.[49]

Rising complaints about network programming from within and without the industry came at a time of some unsettling economic prospects for commercial television during the national economic recession of 1957-59. The growth in television receiver sales slipped after 1957, reflecting what some in the industry feared was a saturated market. Television's share of total advertising expenditures for all media also slowed its growth after 1956. The national economic recession weakened the networks' seller's market in advertising time; the sponsors' new power in negotiations with the networks and the surprising success of the quiz show programs in 1955-57, often licensed directly by their sponsors, suggested to some a long-term trend of declining network economic power. The crucial question, according to *Sponsor* in 1958, was whether the unprecedented soft market in network prime-time advertising slots was due simply to the general economic recession, or instead to sponsor reaction to the "routine fare" of network programming. Some advertising agencies were cutting back on television budgets in favor of other media, according to the magazine.[50]

The pessimistic vision that resonated most deeply in the trade in this uncertain period was "TV: The Light That Failed," by Richard Austin Smith, in the December 1958 issue of *Fortune*. Most troubling was the way in which Smith connected the critics' charges of growing program mediocrity to the new economic pinch the industry was experiencing in 1958. Smith argued:

> Whatever remained of radio's old willingness to risk new formats and get along on modest ratings has all but vanished from TV. The mounting pressure of costs on sponsors and networks alike has weakened the will to experiment. . . . Yet as the medium loses its capacity to excite, to create and to lead, its audiences will inevitably shrink. And as audiences shrink, more pressure to stick to "successful" formats and eschew the unknown may well follow, resulting in the disastrous cycle of economic pressure making for shoddy programs, shoddy programs reducing the television audience, smaller audiences increasing the economic pressure. . . .[51]

Smith reported an unprecedented decline in network revenues in 1958, increased pressure on network advertising rates with the rise of ABC to full competition, and a new buyer's market in network advertising time in the soft national economy. In addition, Smith foresaw possible FCC curtailment of network option time, which the networks had warned would destroy the network system, noted the near-saturation level of set ownership, and argued that many viewers and advertisers were becoming disenchanted with the medium. According to Smith, the economic pressure of the cost-price squeeze in network television increased the power of ratings and outside packagers in programming and would lead to the exodus of creative talent from the industry. Smith pointed to the effects of these economic pressures in the medium: "television has reached a kind of ceiling, . . . mediocrity is increasing, and . . . only through some drastic change in the medium's evolution will the excitement and aspiration of, say, 1954 return to our TV screens."[52] To the critical and economic problems that Smith outlined would soon be added the most serious business and regulatory scandals in the medium's history.

NOTES

1. Stuart Lewis Long, *The Development of the Television Network Oligopoly* (Ph.D. diss., University of Illinois, 1974; New York: Arno Press, 1979), p. 120; Joseph R. Dominick and Millard C. Pearce, "Trends in Network Prime-Time Programming, 1953-74," *Journal of Communication* 26 (Winter 1976): 76-77; "Sponsor Scope," *Sponsor,* April 6, 1957, p. 9.

2. Martin Mayer, "ABC: Portrait of a Network," *Show,* September 1961, p. 61; "Sponsor Scope," *Sponsor,* April 27, 1957, p. 10; Frank Henry Jakes, "A Study of Standards Imposed by Four Leading Television Critics with Respect to Live Television Drama," Ph.D. diss., Ohio State University, 1960, p. 9; National Broadcasting Company, "Television Trends," *Research Bulletin,* November 25, 1959, p. 5, collection of the NBC Records Administration Library, New York; Richard Ozersky, "Television and Imitations of Life: Social and Thematic Patterns in Top-Rated Television Dramatic Programs During the Period 1950-1970, a Descriptive Study," Ph.D. diss., New York University, 1976, p. 31; Herman Land, "After the Western—What?," *Television,* July 1958, p. 55; "'Live' TV: It Went Thataway," *Variety,* May 4, 1960, p. 23.

3. Jakes, "A Study of Standards," p. 11.

4. William Kenneth Hawes, Jr., "A History of Anthology Drama Through 1958," Ph.D. diss., University of Michigan, 1960, p. 55; "The Busy Air," *Time,* December 9, 1957, p. 79; Vance Bourjaily, "The Lost Art of Writing for Video," *Harper's,* October 1959, p. 155.

5. "Sponsor Scope," *Sponsor,* November 27, 1959, p. 10; U.S. Federal Communications Commission, Office of Network Study, *Second Interim Report: Television Network Program Procurement,* part 2, Docket no. 12782 (Washington D.C.: U.S. Government Printing Office, 1965), pp. 405-6; "Sponsor Scope," *Sponsor,* November 16, 1957, p. 11.

6. Hawes, "A History of Anthology Drama," pp. 8, 32, 35, 51. For commentary from CBS television executive Perry Lafferty on the changes, see Max Wilk, *The Golden Age of Television: Notes from the Survivors* (New York: Delacorte Press, 1976), p. 260.

7. "Sponsor Scope," *Sponsor,* April 27, 1957, p. 10; Bourjaily, "Lost Art of Writing for Video," p. 156; Robert Kass, "Radio and TV," *Catholic World,* June 1956, p. 225.

8. Jakes, "A Study of Standards," p. 9; Bourjaily, "Lost Art of Writing for Video," p. 156.

9. Gilbert Seldes, *The Public Arts* (New York: Simon and Schuster, 1956), p. 183.

10. "Big Men on the Paper," *Newsweek,* April 15, 1957, p. 104; Rod Serling,

Patterns (New York: Simon and Schuster, 1957), p. 10; Bob Stahl, "What Good Are Television Critics?," *TV Guide*, January 24, 1959, pp. 8, 11.

11. Seldes, *The Public Arts*, pp. 183-84, 190.

12. John Crosby, *Detroit Free Press*, August 21, 1958, p. 33, cited in Jakes, "A Study of Standards," p. 73; Crosby, *New York Herald-Tribune*, July 6, 1958, cited in Jakes, "A Study of Standards," p. 72; for a reaction to the rise of the thirty-minute telefilm, see Gilbert Seldes, "A Clinical Analysis of TV," *New York Times Magazine*, November 23, 1954, pp. 56, 59.

13. Manny Rubin, "The Beginning Writer in Television," in *The Best Television Plays*, vol. 3, ed. William I. Kaufman (New York: Merlin Press, 1954), pp. 355, 357.

14. Erik Barnouw, *The Television Writer* (New York: Hill and Wang, 1962), p. 35; FCC, *Second Interim Report*, pp. 631-32.

15. Stan Optowsky, *TV: The Big Picture* (New York: E. P. Dutton, 1961), p. 127; Barnouw, *The Television Writer*, 1962, p. 36; FCC, *Second Interim Report*, p. 542; Erik Barnouw, *The History of Broadcasting in the United States*, vol. 3: *The Image Empire* (New York: Oxford University Press, 1970), p. 26. For a discussion of Serling's career in the 1950s, see William Boddy, "Entering the 'Twilight Zone,'" *Screen* 25 (July-October 1984): 98-108.

16. Marya Mannes, "The TV Pattern: Signs of Revolt," *Reporter*, May 2, 1957, p. 19.

17. FCC, *Second Interim Report*, pp. 535, 549.

18. Ibid., pp. 587, 542, 544, 546.

19. Ibid., p. 583.

20. Ibid., pp. 671, 632.

21. Barnouw, *The Image Empire*, pp. 34, 36; FCC, *Second Interim Report*, p. 541.

22. "What's Wrong with Television Drama?" *Film Culture*, no. 19 (1959): 19; FCC, *Second Interim Report*, pp. 585-86.

23. "The Busy Air," p. 79; Davidson is quoted in Bill Greeley, "Writers Blast Dearth of Quality TV, Blame 'Controls' and 'Cost-Per-M,'" *Variety*, June 21, 1961, p. 45; FCC, *Second Interim Report*, p. 629; also see "Creators Turn on the Created," *Broadcasting*, June 26, 1961, pp. 28, 32.

24. FCC, *Second Interim Report*, p. 638.

25. "Interview with Rod Serling," *Playboy*, November 1961, p. 35; Ross Davidson, "The New Television Playwright and His Markets," *Writer*, April, 1962, p. 61, emphasis in original; "Disillusion Between the Lines," *Television*, June 6, 1961, p. 92.

26. U.S. Federal Communications Commission, Office of Network Study, *Interim Report: Responsibility for Broadcast Matter*, Docket no. 12782 (Washing-

ton, D.C.: U.S. Government Printing Office, 1960), pp. 142-43, 170, 149; Mayra Mannes, ed., *The Relation of the Writer to Television* (Santa Barbara: Center for the Study of Democratic Institutions, 1960), p. 7.

27. FCC, *Second Interim Report*, p. 371; Charles Winick, *Taste and the Censor in Television* (New York: Fund for the Republic, 1959), p. 18.

28. FCC, *Interim Report*, p. 169.

29. FCC, *Second Interim Report*, pp. 406, 483. The GE executive also told the Office of Network Study that the company rejected a science fiction story because "it was too far out" in light of the company's "'science-oriented commercials.'"

30. Ibid., pp. 472, 471.

31. Ibid., pp. 457, 458, 31; "Sponsors Spell Out Their Do's, Don'ts," *Broadcasting*, October 9, 1961, p. 34.

32. "Sponsors Spell Out Their Do's, Don'ts," p. 23; "Two Views on Sponsor Control," *Broadcasting*, October 2, 1961, p. 24.

33. Ibid.

34. "Sponsors Spell Out Their Do's, Don'ts," p. 35; FCC, *Second Interim Report*, p. 711; "Who Controls What in TV Films," *Broadcasting*, October 17, 1960, pp. 30, 34; Mannes, *The Relation of the Writer*, p. 12; "TV Writer Sizes Up His Craft," *Broadcasting*, January 4, 1960, p. 42; "The Weary Young Man," *Newsweek*, September 28, 1959, p. 81, emphasis in original. *Time* reported that the Ford auto company forbade the use of skyline shot of New York City because it included the Chrysler building. "The Tarnished Image," *Time*, November 16, 1959, p. 80.

35. Serling's account of the "Noon on Doomsday" episode can be found in Barnouw, *The Television Writer*, p. 28; "The Weary Young Man," p. 81; Mannes, *The Relation of the Writer*, p. 12.

36. FCC, *Second Interim Report*, pp. 376-77, 402.

37. "Billion Dollar Whipping Boy," *Television Age*, November 4, 1957, p. 90, emphasis in original; Winick, *Taste and the Censor*, p. 18; see also Mannes, *The Relation of the Writer*, p. 9.

38. Brodkin's comments can be found in FCC, *Second Interim Report*, p. 574; Frankenheimer's in "Television's Wealthy, Angry Young Men," *Broadcasting*, October 17, 1960, p. 56; Representative Celler's in "Billion Dollar Whipping Boy," p. 30.

39. FCC, *Interim Report*, p. 146; U.S., Congress, House, Committee on Interstate and Foreign Commerce, *Television Network Program Procurement, Report of the House Committee on Interstate and Foreign Commerce*, 88th Cong., 1st sess. (Washington, D.C.: U.S. Government Printing Office, 1963), p. 372; Winick, *Taste and the Censor*, p. 5; Shelby Gordon, "Traitor to My Class," *Mass*

Media, July 1959, reprinted in *Problems and Controversies in Television and Radio,* ed. Harry J. Skornia and Jack William Kitson (Palo Alto: Pacific Books, 1968), p. 106.

40. Mannes, *The Relation of the Writer,* pp. 11, 12; "The Millionaire Class of Young Writers," *Cosmopolitan,* August 1958, p. 41.

41. Jack Gould, *Television* interview by Donald McDonald (Santa Barbara: Center for the Study of Democratic Institutions, 1961), p. 6; FCC, *Second Interim Report,* pp. 27, 542.

42. FCC, *Interim Report,* pp. 162, 167.

43. "TV Lays an Egg," *Sponsor,* November 17, 1957, pp. 25-27; "New Season a Dud," *Variety,* October 2, 1957, p. 1; "Is There a Programming Crisis?," *Television,* February 1957, pp. 50, 52, 93.

44. "Success Secrets Bared to FCC," *Broadcasting,* October 9, 1961, p. 21.

45. "Rating Madness—An Editorial," *Sponsor,* November 30, 1951, pp. 30-31; Sylvester (Pat) Weaver, "What's Wrong with Television?," *Tide,* April 12, 1957, pp. 11, 14; Thomas E. Weakley, "Pat Weaver Sounds Off on the Ad Business," *Printer's Ink,* April 12, 1957, p. 28.

46. Richard W. Jencks, "How Network Television Programming Decisions Are Made," in *Network Television and the Public Interest,* ed. Michael Botein and David M. Rice (Lexington: D.C. Heath, 1980), p. 39; *Sponsor,* December 21, 1957, pp. 32-33; FCC, *Second Interim Report,* p. 535.

47. Hubbell Robinson, "TV: Myopia of the Widescreen," *Esquire,* July 1958, p. 21; "Another 'Meat and Potatoes' Year for Network TV?," *Sponsor,* June 1, 1957, pp. 38-39; "Television 1959," *Television,* January 1959, p. 33; Robert E. Dunville, "TV's Need for Self-Criticism," *Television,* January 1959, p. 41.

48. John P. Cunningham, " 'Creeping Mediocrity' Bringing Boredom to TV: It's Advertiser's Worry, Cunningham Warns," *Advertising Age,* December 2, 1957, pp. 65-67.

49. William N. McPhee, "Working Paper Suggested Research on the Potentialities of Television for CBS," quoted in National Broadcasting Company, *Television and Modern Marketing,* November 1960, n.p., collection of NBC Research Department, New York; "Videotown Ten Years Later," *Sponsor,* December 7, 1957, pp. 35, 43; "How TV's 'Program Mess' Hits the Sponsor," *Sponsor,* July 12, 1958, p. 29; Edward R. Murrow, "A Broadcaster Talks to His Colleagues," *Reporter,* November 13, 1958, pp. 32-36; *TV Guide,* December 13, 1958, pp. 22-27.

50. National Broadcasting Company, "Television Trends," *Research Bulletin,* November 25, 1959, p. 2, collection of NBC Research Department, New York; Roger G. Noll, Merton J. Peck, and John J. McGowan, *Economic Aspects of Television Regulation* (Washington, D.C.: Brookings Institution, 1973), p. 15; "TV's Program Mess," pp. 29, 36.

51. Robert Austin Smith, "TV: The Light That Failed," *Fortune,* December 1958, p. 81. Also see "How *Fortune* Tipped Off the New Anti-TV 'Party Line,'" *Sponsor,* November 29, 1958, p. 33; "*Fortune*'s Unfortunate TV Guess," *Sponsor,* November 19, 1962, p. 39.

52. Smith, "TV: The Light That Failed," p. 161.

12

TV's Public Relations
Crisis of the Late 1950s

Concern over rising critical complaints, talk of regulatory reform in Congress, expected plateaus in receiver sales and viewing levels, and a faltering advertising market in 1956-58 led to a mood of uncertainty and defensiveness in the network television industry. In the final two years of the decade, these problems were exacerbated by spectacular public revelations of commercial and regulatory misconduct within the industry. The result was a bitter debate that set the tone for public discussion of television far beyond the late 1950s.

There were occasional expressions of concern about the FCC's regulation of television throughout the 1950s, particularly regarding the commission's high-stakes station licensing decisions. After lifting the extended freeze on station licenses in 1952, the FCC faced the task of allocating a limited number of extremely valuable large-market VHF licenses in what *Broadcasting* called "the biggest land rush for facilities since the advent of electrical communication." In 1952, *Business Week* described the situation facing the commission: "In effect the FCC has to stand in a corner with a strictly limited number of million dollar bills in its hand, ask everybody who wants one to line up—and then decide who gets one and who doesn't." The history of the FCC and its predecessor, the Federal Radio Commission, is replete with examples of prima facie conflicts of interest and bias toward established broadcast interests nominally regulated by the independent federal agency. As one former FCC chairman described the commission in the 1950s: "Let's face it.

This was the 'Whorehouse Era' of the Commission. When matters were *arranged,* not adjudicated." In a 1976 report to the Senate Commerce Committee on appointments to federal regulatory agencies, researchers James Graham and Victor Kramer described the station licensing policies of the commission as "the Great Giveaway": "The story of the 'Great Giveaway' began in July 1952 when Truman was still President, but it had a long way to go when Truman left the White House. Essentially, the give-away years would be the Eisenhower years."[1]

The FCC, like other independent regulatory commissions associated with the New Deal, was a special target of Republican party activists when, after a long absence, the party regained control of the White House under Eisenhower, whose administration was assertive in proclaiming a new relationship with business. As the chair of the President's Council of Economic Advisors told the press: "The ultimate purpose is to produce more consumer goods. This is the goal. This is the object of everything we are working at: to produce things for consumers." Eisenhower's first secretary of the interior announced after his appointment: "We're here in the saddle as an administration representing business and industry." For historian David Frier, the story of the Eisenhower administration was "characterized by moral pronouncements and amoral responses to many of crucial ethical problems of the fifties." Eisenhower's first term witnessed seven separate major high-level staff scandals in what Frier characterizes as an "ethically perverted administration." According to Graham and Kramer, from 1953-60 all the appointees for chairman of the FCC "were fully acceptable" to AT&T; three of the four Eisenhower appointments to the commission (including Chairman John Doerfer) were drawn from state utility commissions, "and those appointments have been traced to the efforts of the officers of AT&T."[2]

Concern about ex parte contacts and conflicts of interest at the FCC in television licensing cases began to be expressed around 1957. In an essay entitled "The FCC: Who Will Regulate the Regulator?," Robert Bendiner argued that "The FCC seems to have fallen into such a morass of inconsistency and ad hoc judgments that there now seems to be almost no rule of law in parceling out these fabulously valuable public assets." A study by the Library of Congress of fifty-seven licensing cases before the commission found the FCC overruled its own hearing examiner twenty times; the study deduced thirteen criteria involved in the commission's decisions, but also found "almost no discernible consistency in applying" the criteria. The study concluded that "Not a single person at the Commission who is concerned with broadcast work will even pretend to demonstrate that the Commission's decisions in its broadcast cases have followed a consistent policy." Harvard Law professor Louis L. Jaffe argued in 1957 that the FCC's stated licensing criteria of the public interest, local management, and ownership diversity were ill defined and misused, and had become no more than "spurious criteria, used to justify results otherwise arrived at." Emanuel Celler also warned in a 1957 law review article that the FCC "must more closely conform its adjudicative practices to the dictates of due process of law."[3]

Growing reports of FCC misconduct in television licensing led to a short-lived special House of Representatives investigation in 1957-58 organized by House Speaker Sam Rayburn. The House Legislative Oversight Committee, established under the Communications Subcommittee of the Commerce Committee, uncovered evidence of FCC misconduct sufficient to bring about the immediate resignation of one commissioner from office and the subsequent resignation of the commission's chair. A thirty-four-year-old law professor, Bernard Schwartz, was selected by Commerce Committee Chair Oren Harris to direct what Schwartz quickly learned was intended to be a captive, nonthreatening investigation controlled by Representative Harris, considered friendly to the broadcast industry. When the Communications Subcommittee under Harris voted to suppress Schwartz's interim report and deny his request for hearings into FCC conduct, Schwartz leaked a copy of the report to the *New York Times.*

The published excerpts recounted FCC commissioners' double-billing for business travel (Chairman Doerfer actually triple-billed one trip), acceptance of gifts from industry groups, and widespread ex parte contacts between commissioners and those involved in proceedings before the FCC. Schwartz examined sixty comparative license cases which, he concluded, revealed a consistent commission bias toward large, nonlocal applicants and a regulatory record "more of whim and caprice than of application of settled law to the facts of the case." As Jack Gould observed dryly: "Many people in Washington are interested in television and if the lid ever comes off the sundry affairs of the Commission, it could lead to a rather varied spectacular." After noting that the ranking members of the congressional committees concerned with television, Senator Warren Magnuson and Representative Harris, were both part-owners of television stations, Gould concluded that "The chance for a really searching inquiry into the whole matter of television licensing is probably rather slim . . . On the other hand the [Schwartz] memorandum may be the spark to set a Washington fire that could take quite a while to put out."[4]

In retaliation for the news leak, Harris's committee voted to dismiss Schwartz and served him with a subpoena to appear the following morning as a committee witness. Schwartz responded in the *New York Times* the next day: "I accuse the majority of this Subcommittee of joining an unholy alliance between big business and the White House to obtain a whitewash. I accuse Mr. Harris of hypocritically posing publicly as a supporter of an investigation which he has done everything in his power to suppress. . . . I have nothing but contempt for most members of the Committee."[5]

Representative Harris's decision to subpoena Schwartz turned out to be a political miscalculation: Schwartz's testimony was attended by five hundred spectators and seventy reporters, in what *Newsweek* called the biggest congressional press turnout since the Army-McCarthy hearings. Schwartz was a very effective witness, and the subcommittee was forced to call for an FBI investigation of FCC misconduct. Chairman Harris also publicly called on Commissioner Richard Mack to resign because of allegations of bribe-taking. Schwartz produced a legal memorandum from the U.S. solicitor general advising that Chairman Doerfer broke the law in billing the government for trips paid by private broadcast interests.

In March 1958, *Sponsor* editorially worried that the probe could lead to the resignation of three commissioners, the reopening of ten licensing cases, and a new way of doing business at the commission. The next week the magazine reported Commissioner Mack's resignation and noted that "the consensus of the knowledgeable is that others will follow." Mack was later indicted by a Miami grand jury for bribery, and one congressman told *Sponsor* that twenty-five television license awards could be overturned in the investigation of influence peddling at the FCC. Schwartz reported that he had uncovered evidence of at least twelve other cases of ex parte contacts between commissioners and those with business before the FCC. Five of the seven commissioners admitted accepting gifts from broadcasters and manufacturers.[6] Doerfer, who had become FCC chair in 1958, was accused in the Schwartz hearings of accepting favors from large broadcasters and defrauding the government, but when he staunchly refused to admit wrongdoing and when President Eisenhower continued to support him, demands for his resignation faded. In the 1959-60 crises of programming complaints, the quiz show scandals, and revelations of illegal business practices in the industry, Doerfer came to play an important role as a defender of the television industry.

The most notorious public scandal in the television industry of the late 1950s concerned revelations about the rigging of popular quiz programs. Following the success of "The $64,000 Question" as a summer replacement in 1955, quiz shows crowded network prime-time schedules, reaching a peak in the 1958-59 season with twenty-four network quiz programs representing an estimated $100 million investment in time and talent costs. The programs were characterized by large cash prizes and elaborately staged matches between colorful "real people" contestants. Quiz shows were attractive to sponsors because they offered the possibility of reentering the market of direct program licensing at a low cost because the frequently highly rated programs were inexpensive to produce, requiring no writers, professional actors, or multiple sets. Following the rapid success of the genre, quiz show producer Louis Cowan became head of the CBS television network, and NBC announced a $4,800,000 purchase of four quiz shows from producers Jack Barry and Dan Enright.[7]

In 1957 a contestant of one program, "Twenty-One," began telling the press that the program's producers routinely coached contestants about the questions to be asked. In 1958, allegations of fraud caused Colgate and CBS quietly to cancel one show, while denying any impropriety in the program. In September 1958, a New York grand jury began investigating allegations of quiz show fraud, and in the 1959 season networks canceled several quiz programs, all for publicly stated reasons of ratings or commercial considerations. Meanwhile, producers of the rigged programs coached contestants called before the grand jury in perjured testimony; the prosecutor in the case later estimated that only 50 of 150 sworn witnesses before the panel told the truth. In June 1959, the grand jury finished its work, but in an unusual move, the judge blocked release of its twelve-thousand-word report.[8] The following month Representative Harris announced a probe into the quiz show charges, and on November 2, 1959, the popular contestant Charles Van Doren admitted his complicity in the program fraud. President Eisenhower spoke at a national press conference of his feelings of shock and bewilderment at the revelations and ordered his attorney general to prepare a report on fraud in the television industry. In the fall of 1959, the FCC directed the Office of Network Study to widen its inquiry into network television practices to include quiz show rigging and "plugola," the on-air promotion of products in exchange for material considerations.

The year 1959 brought other unethical commercial practices in broadcasting to the public's attention. Hal Roach, Jr., flush with his studio's telefilm profits, acquired the Mutual Broadcasting System in 1958, and in January 1959, he and his partners negotiated an agreement —that became public by spring—with Dominican Republic dictator Rafael Trujillo: in exchange for $750,000, Mutual guaranteed 425 minutes a month of favorable news and commentary for the dictator. Later that year, national attention was captured by charges of payola and conflicts of interest in the radio and television industry, and of promotional "tie-ins," cases in which uncredited sponsors paid to have their products displayed on network programs. *U.S. News and World Report* in December 1959 warned that "the radio-television industry, already under heavy fire, is heading for more investigations and more trouble in the months just ahead." It quoted a House Committee Staff Report that investigated commercial bribery in broadcasting and described "a situation that bordered on racketeering." Public reaction to the quiz show fraud and commercial scandals of 1959 was immediate and powerful: industry-sponsored polls indicated that between 87 and 95 percent of the American public was aware of the quiz scandals. The congressional hearings, which culminated in Van Doren's confession, were "the most publicized hearings of 1959," according to the *Congressional Quarterly.*[9]

The revelations of quiz show fraud focussed popular and critical discontent over a number of aspects of network television, especially the influence of the sponsor and the decline of quality drama on network schedules. In November 1959, NBC Board Chairman Robert Sarnoff protested to a meeting of network affiliates that "dishonesty is being equated with dull programming and with a supposed low level of creativity." CBS network head Frank Stanton told the Academy of Television Arts and Sciences in December 1959 that "The quiz show scandals triggered the explosion of pent-up discontents with television of large segments of the American people that go far beyond phony and deceitful practices and include everything from irritating commercials to program content."[10] In October 1959, Jack Gould called the quiz show fraud "the final phoniness of a troubled decade," and linked the scandal to rising commercial censorship, an exodus of major TV writers, and "the spreading virus of materialism" represented by "the awesome competitive pressures that everyone in the business feels." As the *New York Times* editorialized in November 1959: "The Van Doren episode, bad as it is, is but symptomatic of a disease in the radio and television world."[11]

With the exception of Louis Cowan's resignation at CBS, the industry managed to contain the damage of the quiz show scandals to low-ranking personnel and peripheral practices of the industry. Of the total of twenty-three persons indicted for perjury in the quiz show scandal, all but one were contestants. As the broadcast researcher and critic Charles A. Siepmann commented sardonically before the Office of Network Study in 1959 on the public attention and assorted federal investigations of television misconduct:

> That a Committee of the Congress and the entire press should, of late, have found the moral jungle of broadcasting a rich game preserve and happy hunting ground is no matter of surprise to anyone acquainted with the industry. One might, though, question the genuine concern for the public interest of either group on this safari as one observes the particular wildlife on which they seem to have chosen to concentrate fire. The bag, to date, seems to comprise a large number of frightened rabbits, not a few skunks, and innumerable rats. But the big game seems, by some odd coincidence, to have escaped as targets of the noisy gunfire—if in fact this was ever aimed in their direction.[12]

One direct effect of the quiz show scandal was a $600,000 public relations campaign directed by the National Association of Broadcasters' new Television Information Office. The new organization commissioned a survey of public attitudes toward the industry in the wake of the quiz scandals, placed advertisements in "highbrow" magazines highlighting cultural and public-service programs, and generally "helped put the quiz scandal storm in perspective," according to *Broadcasting.* An article in *Printer's Ink* explained that the organization "has been concentrating on reaching the so-called intellectual audience," via funded research, public information, and print advertising.[13]

Doerfer played a key role in mitigating the attacks on the television industry in the fall and winter of 1959-60, when it became clear that no federal action would threaten fundamental broadcast interests. In an action *Broadcasting* described as a "way of cooling television's hot seat," Doerfer offered a plan of self-regulation through the National Association of Broadcasters' Television Code, explaining, "A penny's worth of prevention is worth thousands of dollars spent in attempting to retrieve the confidence of the American public—even though besmirched by the mistakes of a few." A January 1960, *Broadcasting* editorial began: "In these troubled times broadcasters should be thankful for one stroke of good fortune, for which they were in no wise responsible. That is the presence on the FCC of its chairman, John Doerfer." In November 1959, *Variety* wrote more dispassionately of Doerfer that "Although it is unfair to call Doerfer an industry 'apologist,' he seldom parts company in major issues with broadcast interests, particularly the networks."[14]

Doerfer's public statements in the period provide a catalogue of industry defenses to the rising criticism of commercial television. In an interview in *U.S. News and World Report* in October 1959, he defended the industry from charges of program imitation and mediocrity and commercial corruption: "I don't think there's much wrong with TV. It's an infant industry and it's going through growing pains . . . it's a stage." Complaints of prime-time programming mediocrity were unfair, according to the FCC chair: "What people don't realize is that the television set has a voracious appetite. . . . Now, there just isn't enough good talent available. A lot of armchair experts say there is. Well, they're missing a good bet. All they have to do is produce them and they'd be gobbled up overnight." Moreover, the public was not a victim of fraud in the quiz show scandals, Doerfer argued, because it didn't directly purchase anything from the shows' producers or the networks. "There's no sense in pulling down the roof over our heads just because of some abuses," Doerfer told the magazine. "I would rather—and I am sure the American people would rather—put up with some abuses, startling and disappointing and disheartening as they are, rather than jeopardize what has been very, very close to their hearts. . . ."[15]

Responding to complaints from television writers of increasing commercial censorship in the medium, Doerfer offered a definition of censorship that excluded commercial pressures on writers, limiting the term's meaning to direct governmental direction of programming: "Censorship, when self-imposed, is a peculiar term to apply to self-discipline. Censorship is the official action of a government undertaking to enforce the morals or the conduct of a community in all forms of expression. Voluntary agreements to abide and implement codes of good standards are not censorship." This narrowly framed consideration of program censorship was part of a general industry response to calls for regulatory reform, a response that construed the public policy alternatives for American television as a stark choice between the commercial status quo and the direct federal dictation of program content. *Broadcasting*, reporting on Doerfer's remarks at a meeting of the New York Bar Association in January 1960, wrote that: "Congress must decide in the months ahead whether television will operate under a minimum of government control or whether it will function under an FCC superstructure with powers of national censorship.... Mr. Doerfer was outspoken in his view that he much preferred a minimum of governmental intrusion into broadcasting."[16]

Two weeks of testimony before the FCC in early 1960 by public interest advocates produced several proposals for restructuring American television, including the establishment of a public television network, the installation of spectrum or license fees to support public-interest programming, public utility regulation of broadcasting, and stricter enforcement of the FCC's "Blue Book" of 1946. The witnesses faced hostile questioning from Doerfer, who *Broadcasting* described as "outspoken in championing the broadcasting cause for self-regulation." The magazine reported that he "repeatedly warned against the concept of government regulation and questioned closely—at times almost antagonistically—government control proponents. . . ."[17] Such tribute from the trade press to the chair of a federal regulatory agency who "repeatedly warned against the concept of government regulation" suggests the nature of the relationship between Doerfer and the industry he was legally charged to oversee.

By February 1960, the industry enjoyed new confidence in its public relations battles and was less fearful of reform moves from Congress or from Doerfer's FCC. A *Broadcasting* editorial indicated the industry's sanguine new attitude toward criticism of the industry, described as "a superabundance of loose talk and shallow thinking." The editorial admitted that "some broadcasters and some advertisers and agencies were caught napping on quiz program trickery or payola or misleading commercials, . . . [but] The FCC, although it may have dawdled before, acted as expeditiously as the law permitted. . . . The fast and loose era is over."[18] Unfortunately for the industry, television's public relations problems and scandals were not over, but instead were shortly to claim the industry's most influential defender, Chairman Doerfer.

At a CBS Affiliates Association meeting on February 29, 1960, Doerfer and Oren Harris engaged in a "free-swinging display of bitter charges and counter-charges, causing great embarrassment and distress among top CBS brass who fear the legislator may seek reprisals," according to *Broadcasting*. Fuel for reprisal was close at hand: Doerfer's admission that he spent "one or two nights" as a guest on the yacht of broadcaster George Storer. In acrimonious questioning before Representative Harris's Legislative Oversight Subcommittee on March 4, Doerfer changed his account of the Storer trip, admitting that the favors he received from the broadcaster were more extensive than he had earlier stated while still denying any impropriety. A few days after Doerfer's appearance before the House Subcommittee, President Eisenhower asked him to resign. On March 7, Doerfer agreed to give the White House his resignation on the following morning. *Broadcasting* reported, however, that Doerfer reconsidered overnight and planned a weekend of network television appearances to fight for his job; concerned, the White House sent a car to Doerfer's home during a snowstorm to collect his resignation.[19]

The resignation of the FCC chair brought to a head the criticism of the television industry that had been stirred by rising complaints of sponsor censorship, concern over program mediocrity, and disgust over the quiz show scandals. In a speech in March 1960, CBS executive Richard Salent warned that "We are going to pay for these mistakes for a long time, and we are paying for them now. All sorts of dissatisfactions about television crystalize as a result of these miserable events." According to John Crosby: "The moral squalor of the quiz mess reaches clear through the whole industry. . . . The heavy hand of the advertiser suffocates truth, corrupts men and women. . . . the worst crumbs in the business are now in the saddle and the best and the most idealistic and creative men in the business either can't get work or they quit in disgust and go on to better things."[20]

Dalton Trumbo in the *Nation* denounced "the arrogant greed of men who have appropriated the free air and turned it into a witch's bazaar of howling peddlers hawking trash." During the quiz shows hearings, the *New Republic* called the FCC commissioners the "Seven Dwarfes" who "parcel it [the airwaves] out free to money grubbers. . . . " The *Reporter* argued: "Not until the bubble burst did it occur to anyone that there was a significant connection between public morals and public entertainment. . . . The FCC, which has long regarded its function as helping the networks make money, remained supremely indifferent."[21]

After Doerfer's resignation, the industry, with loud promises of self-regulation, concentrated on holding back legislation authorizing FCC licensing of networks, commission monitoring of program content, and the enforcement of the FCC's "Blue Book" provisions. The broadcast industry, one of the most powerful industry lobbies in Washington, also put enormous pressure on lawmakers to block reform legislation. Ranking members of the House and Senate Commerce committees were largely sympathetic to the industry's wishes, and most legislators courted station owners in their local districts. In November 1959, veteran *New York Times* political columnist James Reston wrote: "Congress in an election year is not going to want to punish the TV industry too hard."[22]

A 1972 study of broadcast policy, *The Politics of Broadcast Regulation,* estimated that 60–70 percent of members of Congress received free air time from local broadcasters, and quoted the NAB's vice president and general counsel Paul B. Comstock: "Most of our [lobbying] work is done with Congressional Committees. We concentrate on Congress. We firmly believe that the FCC will do whatever Congress tells it to do, and will not do anything Congress tells it not to do." Krasnow and Longley conclude their case studies of five regulatory issues with the observation that any successful FCC policy required the support of Congress and the broadcast industry; "Since Congress will generally oppose FCC policy only when the united industry does, the Commission can usually satisfy Congress by satisfying the lobby." The ranking Democrat on the Senate Commerce Committee, Senator Warren Magnuson, was described in a 1960 *Variety* article as "one of broadcasting's special friends on Capitol Hill." Committee chair John Pastore kept a network licensing bill in committee for several months while public pressure for reform subsided; the bill that finally emerged largely followed the guidelines suggested by network executives in earlier testimony. NAB chief lobbyist Vincent Wasilewski called the bill "ninety-five percent acceptable or even desirable."[23]

The leadership of the House Commerce Committee refused to schedule hearings on a bill sponsored by Representative Henry Reuss to authorize FCC public service programming standards for television networks. Another House bill calling for licensing of television networks, local license hearings, and criminal penalties for television fraud was defeated on a 13-5 vote in the Commerce Committee. One committee member of sixteen years' seniority said the broadcast lobby "really put the heat on the committee.... I've never seen such pressures exerted by a lobbying group in all the years I've been in Congress."[24]

The prospect of a new Congress and the Democratic administration of John F. Kennedy in 1960 did not overly concern broadcasters; as Wasilewski told NAB members: "For broadcasters, there won't be any traumatic changes." In January 1960, undeclared presidential candidate John Kennedy reassured the Association of Radio and Television Directors that the quiz show scandals reflected "the mistakes or misjudgments of a comparatively few," and asserted that "In time, we will look back at the present difficulties as merely a misstep in a long climb to usefulness in the public interest." The industry was therefore stunned by the first major speech by Kennedy's new FCC chair, Newton N. Minow. Speaking before the annual meeting of the National Association of Broadcasters on May 9, 1961, Minow complimented broadcasters for several worthwhile television programs, then continued:

> But when television is bad, nothing is worse. I invite you to sit down in front of your television set when your station goes on the air and stay there without a book, magazine, newspaper, profit-and-loss sheet or rating book to distract you—and keep your eyes glued to that set until the station signs off. I can assure you that you will observe a vast wasteland. You will see a procession of game shows, violence, audience participation shows, formula comedies about totally unbelievable families, blood and thunder, mayhem, violence, sadism, murder, Western badmen, Western goodmen, private eyes, gangsters, more violence and cartoons. And, endlessly, commercials—many scream-

ing, cajoling and offending. And most of all, boredom. True, you will see a few things you will enjoy. But they will be very, very few. And if you think I exaggerate, try it.[25]

Minow's phrase—"vast wasteland"—crystalized the accumulated public and critical disenchantment with commercial television and immediately entered the vocabulary of public debate. Minow's speech provoked an unprecedented amount of public reaction, including nearly ten thousand pieces of mail to the FCC, and his programming complaints were taken up by newspaper editorialists and reformers around the country. Industry reaction to the speech was swift and negative, including an attempt to uncover derogatory personal materials on Minow's past. One immediate effect of the speech was an intense industry lobbying campaign against President Kennedy's proposal to reorganize the commission and strengthen the powers of the chair. The reform bill was defeated 323–77 in the House, prompting the *New York Times'* Washington correspondent to remark: "Nobody . . . would discount the broadcasting industry's ability to write its own ticket on Capitol Hill."[26]

Meanwhile, as the television industry was going through its most serious public relations crisis in 1959-60, it was also enjoying unprecedented prosperity, rebounding from the effects of the national recession of 1958 with booming advertising revenues, an increased share of national advertising expenditures, and burgeoning foreign program revenues. *Broadcasting* noted in December 1959 that "Broadcasters can cope with the great ethical and moral issues of the times without having also to worry about unusual economic troubles." The FCC reported that pre-tax profits of the broadcasting industry rose nearly 30 percent in 1959, from $172 million to $222 million, and *Variety* estimated that industry profits on sales rose from 11.4 percent in 1958 to 14.3 percent in 1959. A January 1960 *Television Age* article, "TV Future Bright," argued that "In television the financial picture must be considered a rosy one. . . . As 1960 begins, television has reason to feel confidence in its future. In spite of the unfavorable publicity from the quiz scandals and the payola investigations, viewing continues at a very high scale." Looking ahead to the next decade, *Television Age* reported strong confidence of large television advertisers, equipment manufacturers, and networks: "The opinion seems unanimous—the future for

America is a bright one, and television will have the most important of roles in fulfilling that future."[27]

Even the individual sponsors who supported and often controlled the tainted quiz programs seemed unscathed by the scandals; an article in *Sales Management* reassured television advertisers that "it seems extremely unlikely that the sponsor's products will suffer in any direct fashion." *Broadcasting* pointed to a public opinion survey revealing the "startling result" of television's undisturbed public popularity despite the quiz show scandals. The article quoted one respondent: "My only regret is that I didn't have a chance to get on one of the shows before they were discovered rigged."[28]

The early and mid 1960s were a period of uninterrupted high profitability for network television, so much so that the networks made sizable investments outside of the broadcast industry: CBS purchased a toy company, a major publishing house, and the New York Yankees; ABC bought amusement parks; and all three networks made substantial direct investments abroad. ABC President Oliver Treyz told *The Saturday Evening Post* in 1961: "Television has a great future. ABC is out in front on the international front. We have acquired a minority interest in twenty-two stations abroad. 'The Untouchables', '77 Sunset Strip', 'Maverick' are the most popular programs in Australia. In Bangkok they watch 'Wyatt Earp'. Half the people in the world are illiterate. Television can penetrate that barrier ... Television is a worldwide medium. You have to think globally. If you own a show, you own it worldwide."[29]

Despite the scare given broadcasters by Minow's "vast wasteland" speech, network programming, economics, and regulation remained undisturbed in their established routines. As network executive Michael Dann later explained: "The ritual dance between, before Congressional committees and FCC members was something that everybody dressed for, rehearsed for and never had any impact at any time. . . . I would say that to my knowledge, in the history of network broadcasting, no program appeared on the network as the result of any action taken by the FCC. . . . Programming decisions are made solely on the basis of circulation, demographics and for profit."[30]

Only six weeks after predicting a 50-100 percent increase in "serious" network programs, a March 1960 *Sponsor* article described the upcoming 1960-61 television season as "tried and true. . . . By and large, the three newtorks' offerings will stick with . . . Westerns, adventure, mystery, and the musical-variety format. . . ." In July 1960, Jack Gould commented that "the chief emphasis of the 1960-61 season is not going to differ markedly from 1959-60 . . . the world of network video is standing pat." In October 1960, Gould concluded: "The answer of TV to the supposed crisis has been just business as usual. The volume of tripe has grown." Eighteen months after the first revelations about the rigged quiz programs, television columnist Harriet Van Horne wrote: "Boy, was I a fool to believe the pious declarations made by the networks." *Variety*'s television editor, George Rosen, wrote bitterly: "An exciting medium is going down the drain. . . . This is the 'year of the Nielsen'—all that matters is the number of homes reached."[31]

After the resounding legislative defeat of Kennedy's FCC reorganization plan and the release of the relatively mild *First Interim Report* of the FCC's Office of Network Study in 1960, broadcasters had fewer fears of unsettling moves from the federal government. Minow himself made several conciliatory gestures to the industry in 1961, telling *Variety* that the programming of the 1961-62 season signaled significant new hope for the industry: "Television is hardly a vast wasteland. There is in television programming a growing sense to be conscientious. . . . The trends are all pretty good. Progress is being made." Meanwhile, George Rosen commented on the same season: "The tragedy of the current season, hep tv showmen concede, is that it's just as bad, if not worse than last season." By early 1963, *Variety* wrote that "The truth is that broadcasters have learned to live with Minow, the way you do with a shrewish wife." In February 1962, Jack Gould complained in the *New York Times:* "The fact is that for all the controversy over TV in the last year . . . the caliber of theatre has been static and monotonous and in many respects has grown worse." Broadcast critic Meyer Weinberg concluded in 1963: "The Kennedy administration has succeeded in labeling the 'wasteland' but it has also helped maintain the desolation."[32]

NOTES

1. "Thaw July 1," *Broadcasting,* April 14, 1952, p. 23; "High Stakes in a Big Giveaway," *Business Week,* March 22, 1952, p. 21, quoted in U.S. Congress, Senate, Committee on Foreign and Interstate Commerce, *Appointments to the*

Regulatory Commissions: The FCC and FTC, 1949-74, Committee Print, James M. Graham and Victor H. Kramer, 94th Cong. 2d sess. (Washington, D.C.: U.S. Government Printing Office, 1976), p. 27 (hereafter referred to as Graham and Kramer); Sterling Quinlan, *The Hundred Million Dollar Lunch* (Chicago: J. Philip O'Hara, 1974), p. 4, emphasis in original.

2. David A. Frier, *Conflict of Interest in the Eisenhower Administration* (Ames: Iowa State University Press, 1969), pp. 204, 205, 25, 130; Graham and Kramer, p. 34.

3. Robert Bendiner, "The FCC: Who Will Regulate the Regulator?," *Reporter,* September 19, 1957, p. 27; report of James P. Radigan, Jr., Legislature Reference Service, Library of Congress, quoted in Victor G. Rosenblum, "How to Get into Television: The FCC and Miami's Channel 10" in *The Uses of Power: Seven Cases in American Policy,* ed. Alan F. Western (New York: Harcourt Brace World, 1962), p. 224; Louis F. Jaffe, "The Scandal in TV Licensing," *Harper's,* September 1957, p. 79; Emanuel Celler, "Antitrust Problems in the Television Broadcast Industry," *Law and Contemporary Problems* 22 (Autumn 1957): 570.

4. Bernard Schwartz, *The Professor and the Commissions* (New York: Alfred A. Knopf, 1959), pp. 4, 88; *New York Times,* January 23, 1958, p. 14; Jack Gould, "TV: Why All the Fuss?," *New York Times,* January 24, 1958, p. 47.

5. Schwartz is quoted in "Text of the Statement by Dr. Schwartz," *New York Times,* February 12, 1957, p. 20; also see Jay Walz, "Schwartz Ousted After Charges 'Whitewash' Move," *New York Times,* February 11, 1958, pp. 1, 20. Walz reported that Schwartz's probe had implicated members of President Eisenhower's cabinet and family in FCC misconduct. Also see Frier, *Conflict of Interest,* pp. 159, 174.

6. *Newsweek* is quoted in ibid., p. 159. For accounts of the Schwartz investigation, see "Washington Talk," *Sponsor,* March 1, 1958, p. 61; "Washington Week," *Sponsor,* February 8, 1958, p. 69, March 8, 1958, p. 78, October 11, 1958, p. 75; Rosenblum, "How to Get into Television," p. 225; Bob S. Lewis, "An Analysis of the Influence of Newton Minow on Broadcasting," master's thesis, University of Missouri, 1966, p. 22.

7. Quiz shows amounted to 18 percent of NBC's overall schedule in the 1957-58 season; see "Quiz Shows Stalked by Mr. DA," *Broadcasting,* September 1, 1958, p. 42; Kent Anderson, *Television Fraud: The History and Implications of the Quiz Show Scandals* (Westport: Greenwood Press, 1978), pp. 38, 105; Meyer Weinberg, *TV in America: The Morality of Hard Cash* (New York: Ballantine, 1962), p. 8.

8. Anderson, *Television Fraud,* pp. 117, 166, 134.

9. "More Charges on Radio-TV: 'Payola' . . . Rigged 'Inteviews' . . . Fraud . . . Deceit . . . 'Freebies,'" *U.S. News and World Report,* December 28, 1959, pp.

40-41; Erik Barnouw, *The History of Broadcasting in the United States,* vol. 3: *The Image Empire* (New York: Oxford University Press, 1970), pp. 127-28; "Grand Jury Indicts Guterma Trio: Charged with Selling MBS as Dominican Propaganda Vehicle," *Broadcasting,* September 7, 1959, pp. 68-70; "Dominicans File MBS Suit: Seek to Recover $750,000 from Guterma et al," *Broadcasting,* September 14, 1959, p. 48; for an account of the payola scandals in radio see Peter Fornatale and Joshua E. Mills, *Radio in the Television Age* (Woodstock: Overlook Press, 1980), pp. 47-54. As Erik Barnouw concluded: "It was a bad year for broadcasting" (*Image Empire,* p. 128); "A Statement by Elmo Roper Before the Federal Communications Commission," December 17, 1959, p. 9, and Frank Stanton, speech to the Academy of Television Arts and Sciences, New York City, p. 2, both in collection of the Television Information Office, New York; *Congressional Quarterly 1959 Almanac,* p. 744; also see "Hardly a Scratch in TV's Image," *Broadcasting,* November 2, 1959, pp. 41-44, 48.

10. "NBC Chairman Would Keep Honest Quizes," *New York Herald Tribune,* November 13, 1959, p. 15.; Stanton, Academy of Television Arts and Sciences, p. 1.

11. Jack Gould, "Quiz for TV: How Much Fakery?," *New York Times Magazine,* October 25, 1959, p. 74; *New York Times,* November 3, 1959, the editorial is quoted in William P. Rogers, *Report to the President by the Attorney General on Deceptive Practices in the Broadcast Industry,* reprinted in the *New York Times,* January 1, 1960, p. 10. For a discussion of the role of the quiz show scandals in defining the new relations between American intellectuals and popular culture, see Andrew Ross, *No Respect: Intellectuals and Popular Culture* (New York: Routledge, 1989), chap. 4.

12. Charles A. Siepmann, "Moral Aspects of Television," *Public Opinion Quarterly* 24 (Spring 1960): 12-13.

13. "TIO's First Year: An Appraisal," *Broadcasting,* September 26, 1960, pp. 27-30; Philip N. Schugler, "TV Industry's PR Office Undertakes Rebuilding Task," *Editor and Publisher,* January 2, 1960, pp. 11, 47; "TV Goes After the Intellectuals—but Gently," *Printer's Ink,* March 16, 1962, p. 44.

14. For a discussion of Doerfer's role, see Weinberg, *TV in America,* pp. 78, 85; "Doerfer for Clipp Review Plan," *Broadcasting,* February 8, 1960, p. 29; "The Man Doerfer," *Broadcasting,* January 18, 1960, p. 30; Les Brown, "Proposal for an Industry-Wide Testing Laboratory," *Variety,* November 29, 1959, p. 32.

15. "The Uproar over Television—Are Tighter Controls Needed?," *U.S. News and World Report,* October 26, 1959, pp. 47-50.

16. "Doerfer for Clipp Review Plan," p. 29; "Congress' Job," *Broadcasting,* February 1, 1960, p. 40.

17. "FCC Inquiry Hears Roper Data," *Broadcasting,* December 21, 1959, pp. 36-37; "Week of Shock, Sorrow," *Broadcasting,* March 14, 1960, p. 38.

18. "He Who Throws Stones," *Broadcasting,* February 15, 1960, p. 166.

19. "Live, Spontaneous, Unrehearsed," *Broadcasting,* March 7, 1960, pp. 60-61; "Week of Shock, Sorrow," pp. 31-33.

20. Speech by Richard Salant, March 15, 1960, copy in file 12-VI-A Broadcast Pioneers Library, quoted in James L. Baughman, *Television's Guardians: The FCC and the Politics of Programming 1958-1967* (Knoxville: University of Tennessee Press, 1985), p. 31; *New York Herald-Tribune,* October 14, 1959; quoted in "Is TV in Trouble?," *U.S. News and World Report,* October 26 1959, p. 44.

21. Dalton Trumbo, "Hail Blithe Spirit! . . . ," *Nation,* October 24, 1959, p. 245; *New Republic,* November 9, 1959, p. 7; "Quizzlings," *Reporter,* October 29, 1959, p. 2, quoted in Anderson, *Television Fraud,* p. 136. Doerfer's admission of receiving favors from the industry focused press criticism on the FCC leadership. A March 6 *Washington Post* editorial on Doerfer's House testimony was entitled "Payola at the Top," and the *Hartford Courant* wrote that "so long as Mr. Doerfer heads the FCC, not much is going to happen to force television to clean house," quoted in "Week of Shock, Sorrow," p. 38. The *Washington Post* editorialized in March 1960: "At this stage the FCC is a disorganized body, its morals in disarray from top to bottom," *Washington Post,* March 14, 1960, quoted in Lewis, "An Analysis of the Influence," p. 22. Representative John Moss, a member of the House Legislative Oversight panel, reacted to Doerfer's resignation by describing the former chair as someone with "a reluctance to grapple with the problems of the industry. He seemed to be far more concerned with the industry's interest than with the public's," "Week of Shock, Sorrow," p. 40.

22. Reston's comments can be found in the *New York Times,* November 11, 1959, quoted in Baughman, *Television's Guardians,* p. 49.

23. Erwin G. Krasnow and Lawrence D. Longley, *The Politics of Broadcast Regulation,* 2d ed. (New York: St. Martins Press, 1978), pp. 71, 184; Senator Magnuson is characterized in Les Carpenter, "Week the Senate Ganged Up: FCC, Industry Get a Drubbing," *Variety,* May 4, 1960, p. 44; also see Carpenter, "The Big Payoff—A Congress-Inspired TV Law in '60?," *Variety,* May 4, 1960, p. 29; Weinberg, *TV in America,* pp. 166-68; *Variety,* May 4, 1960, p. 29; Wasilewski is quoted in Weinberg, p. 168.

24. Congressman John B. Bennett's remark can be found in the *New York Times,* June 12, 1960, quoted in Weinberg, *TV in America,* p. 164.

25. "Broadcasters' Prestige Highest Ever," *Advertising Age,* November 21, 1960, p. 134; John F. Kennedy, speech to the Association of Radio and Television Directors, January 12, 1960, collection of the Museum of Broadcasting, New York. For a discussion of the new president's relations with the broadcast industry, see Weinberg, *TV in America,* pp. 272-74; Minow's NAB speech can be found in Newton Minow, *Equal Time* (New York: Atheneum, 1964), p. 52.

26. Lewis, "An Analysis of the Influence," p. 52; for trade reaction to Minow's NAB speech, see "Black Tuesday at the NAB Convention," *Broadcasting,* May 15, 1961, p. 36; Tom Wicker, "Lobbies Defeat Reform for the FCC," *New York Times,* June 18, 1961, sec. 4, p. 6.

27. "Happy New Year," *Broadcasting,* December 28, 1959; p. 74; "Average TV Station's 10% Biz Hike in '59; Radio's 5% Increase," *Variety,* July 6, 1960, p. 29; CBS reported its highest earnings in its thirty-two-year history for 1959, see Columbia Broadcasting System, *Annual Meeting of Stockholders Report of the President,* April 2, 1960, p. 1, collection of the Television Information Office, New York; "TV Future Bright," *Television Age,* January 11 1960, pp. 21, 23.

28. Sidney J. Levy, "The Sponsor: More to Be Pitied then Censured," *Sales Management,* November 6, 1959, p. 46; "Hardly a Scratch in TV's Image," pp. 41, 48.

29. Herbert H. Howard, "Multiple Ownership in Television Broadcasting," (Ph.D. diss., Ohio University, 1973, New York: Arno Press, 1973), p. 170; John Bartlow Martin, "Television USA," part 1: "Wasteland or Wonderland?," *The Saturday Evening Post,* October 21, 1961, p. 24.

30. Michael Dann interview, Federal Communications Commission File, Oral History Collection, Columbia University, New York, pp. 7, 4.

31. "What's Ahead on Network TV?," *Sponsor,* March 12, 1960, p. 35; Jack Gould, "Forecast of TV Ahead: Far from Fair," *New York Times,* July 3, 1960, sec. 2, p. 11; Jack Gould, "TV Quiz Aftermath," *New York Times,* October 23, 1960, sec. 2, p. 13; Van Horne is quoted in Harold Mehling, *The Great Time-Killer* (Cleveland: World Publishing, 1962), p. 53; George Rosen, " '60-'61 TV Season —Ratings," *Variety,* November 2, 1960, p. 1.

32. Minow's comments can be found in Les Carpenter, "TV Out of 'Wasteland': Minow," *Variety,* December 13, 1961, p. 1; George Rosen, "The New TV Season: Help," *Variety,* October 4, 1961, p. 27; "Getting to Know You Themes B'casters Vox Pop on Minow," *Variety,* April 3, 1963, p. 24; Gould's comments can be found in the *New York Times,* February 4, 1961, quoted in Weinberg, *TV in America,* p. 281; ibid., p. 277.

13

The Critics and the Wasteland: Redefining Commercial Television

The economic effects of the quiz show scandals within the industry reinforced the same trends toward film programming and network control seen by industry critics to be the root of the problem of declining program quality. The networks reacted to revelations of fraud in the television quiz shows, many of which were licensed directly to sponsors, with declarations of ignorance and victimization, arguing that the scandals demonstrated the necessity of even stronger network control of program production and procurement. NBC President Robert Kintner told the Office of Network Study: "We were merely taken in by a small group of deceitful people," and told the House Commerce Committee that "NBC was just as much a victim of the quiz show frauds as was the public." Despite network claims of victimization at the hands of unscrupulous sponsors and independent producers, Jack Gould concluded that "their plea that they were 'deceived' along with everyone else is not persuasive." Nevertheless, the continued efforts of the networks to control the market in prime-time programming, now given a reformist gloss with the quiz show scandals, exacerbated the competitive disadvantage of program producers, network affiliates, and independent stations apparent earlier in the decade.[1]

The quiz show scandals also served to accelerate and justify network power over television advertisers concerning the licensing, scheduling, and sponsorship of programs. Again, the effect was to consolidate long-term changes advantageous to the networks. The historian Kent Anderson concluded, "As a result of the furor created by the quiz show scandals, the strong sponsor gave way and the networks increased their power enormously." In 1960, *Variety* reported widespread anger and bitterness among advertisers and program suppliers at the increased concessions that networks demanded for access to program slots and advertising time, and noted the irony of the networks' enhanced power on the heels of their recent public relations thrashing in Washington. The quiz show revelations also accelerated the shift from live drama to the filmed series already underway in the late 1950s. Erik Barnouw argued in 1970: "Perhaps the most telling result of the scandals was that the networks scrapped big-prize quiz programs and filled the gaps mainly with telefilms. Thus, one of the principal remnants of New York television disappeared, yielding further hours to Hollywood."[2]

The extensive public hearings into fraud in quiz programs highlighted a new set of industry attitudes toward television critics and the public responsibilities of commercial television. Like their effects on the economic practices of network television, the scandals hardened industry responses to a half-decade of rising critical attacks on the medium. In the process, the television industry, under the leadership of the three networks, offered new public definitions of its programs, its creative workers, and its audience. The new positions mark the end of a trajectory that began in the mid-1950s, one dramatically opposed to that offered by writers and critics of the Golden Age.

Industry attitudes toward television critics underwent a sharp and continuous estrangement after the optimism of the first half of the decade, which had culminated in network leaders reading Jack Gould's defenses of live television into the *Congressional Record* in the mid-1950s. The growing critical complaints about prime-time programming provoked a steady and escalating counterattack from industry leaders. Broadcast historian Frank Jakes wrote that television critics "had naturally been challenged in the past, but at no previous time had censures been hurled from so many different sources in such a sustained attack." An early signal of industry impatience with television critics was a 1956 article in *Sponsor* by Evelyn Konrad, "The Critics Be Damned!," which complained that television critics "have done their best to cry panic as this TV season unfolded." Konrad argued that critics "seem to have, as a group, an almost built-in penchant for the live theatre character play and a degree of contempt for 'escape' entertainment." Noting the ratings success of several new series scorned by television critics, Konrad claimed that critics were increasingly irrelevant to a program's popularity and poor predictors of its audience success. While admitting that there was less novelty in prime-time programming, she argued that the programming shifts made television more effective and attractive to sponsors.[3]

A common industry response to the complaints of television critics was to note the popular success of the disparaged new program forms; an NBC Research Department publication argued in October 1957 that "Once more the TV critics, both professional and amateur, are weighing the merits of the new season's programming and lashing out with adjectives like 'unexciting,' 'mediocre,' and 'unimaginative.' And again the public is ignoring these pessimists."[4]

In May 1961, an NBC affiliate placed a full-page advertisement captioned "Malice in Wonderland" in *Broadcasting* that depicting a primitive-looking creature identified as "TV Critic" wielding a hatchet. A 1961 *Television Age* article argued that "*The New York Times,* for instance, has been close to carelessness in its reporting of television programs. The *Times* makes the primary mistake of assuming that American television viewers are *Times* readers. . . . It is probable that Jack Gould will despise anything that is popular. . . . He doesn't understand the work he is doing, . . . the needs of the people for whom the bulk of programming is built. He doesn't give a damn for the public; nor a tin kopec for America's semi-literate multitudes."[5]

In 1958, the Fund for the Republic commissioned a study of television criticism by Patrick McGrady, who observed that "the critics found themselves the target of terrible invective, most it from people in the television industry who denigrated the the critics' qualifications as unimpressive, their reviewing methods as erratic and their opinions as worthless." McGrady reported that network executives told him that although there were hundreds of television critics across the country, those in New York were the only important ones; "In fact, there are only three critics who are *really* important at all: Jack Gould, George Rosen and John Crosby. And, if you *really* want to know the truth, even *they're* not important. All that's important are money and ratings."[6]

The network leaders' dismissal of the qualifications and importance of television critics accompanied an attack on the program values associated with the earlier era of live drama. CBS President Frank Stanton told the FCC's Office of Network Study: "There were many turkeys in the good old days of live drama. If these programs were to be put on the air today, we would be shocked at what we considered good programming ten . . . years ago." In 1957, Kintner, who had been ABC's programming chief under President Leonard Goldenson from 1954-57 before becoming head of programming at NBC, scorned the earlier era of live television drama: "I think it was great for the beginning of the medium but I certainly don't think there was enough product, enough production know-how and ability to program for the home—where people want constant service, hour after hour. Those early shows like 'Studio One' and 'Robert Montgomery Presents,' 'Philco,' 'Kraft' and all the others—they simply couldn't survive today. Film shows would knock them off very fast. Those shows didn't have any dimension, no movement—they were mostly talk. They were fine for their time, but not for today." Goldenson explained the new program philosophy to *Forbes* in 1959: "People like what we're giving them. First we build a habit factor, get them used to watching us, then we can do something about upgrading programming. We're not interested in the critics."[7]

In a 1961 *Saturday Evening Post* article NBC Board Chairman Robert Sarnoff denounced "phoney social philosophy in plays about beatniks and characters full of self-pity." He also criticized "serious dramas that are arty and pretentious," admitting that in NBC's recent schedules, "social drama has had a rough time—maybe because it hasn't been good. . . . " Sarnoff offered a familiar explanation of the decline of serious drama on television by citing the medium's "tremendous drain" on creative talent, and argued that the live dramas presented on such programs as "Robert Montgomery Presents" and "Philco Playhouse" were overrated in retrospect, and that "most of them were pure soap operas in content and technique." He also attacked television critics as "dilettantes who bemoan the deterioration of TV since the early days."[8]

The industry's attack on television critics was accompanied by a shift in its representation of the television audience, setting the "elitist" critics against viewers' democratic tastes. A 1957 *Television Age* article complained that the television industry, "with all its undeniably efficient public relations setup, . . . had done very little to combat the half-truths, one-sided generalities, dogmatic pontification and double-domed doubletalk contained in most of the charges hurled against it." The magazine scorned what it called the "blatherings about the 'trite and vulgar' on TV and the medium's appeal to 'the lowest common de-nominator.'" It declared: "Television is a mass medium—a medium for the masses, not for that minority of superior gentry with spherical crania who dwell in ivory towers of pseudo-intellectualism and drool over Strindberg and Christopher Fry. . . . [T]elevision's . . . primary function is not to instruct or dictate or elevate its audience's taste in entertainment but to appeal to it on its widest existing level." According to the magazine, "Tossing a bundle" of the sponsor's money "into a TV program with little or no chance to induce a sales payoff because of its appeal to no one but the egghead contingent" would be an abdication of the sponsor's responsibility to mass audience.[9]

In March 1959, Sarnoff told the National Association of Broadcasters that the critics' complaints of program mediocrity represented "a minority distaste for programs chosen by the majority . . . and we must label this . . . for what it really is, . . . an effort of the few to impose tastes upon the many." According to Goldenson, critics were not only cultural elitists, but they also betrayed antidemocratic political tendencies. Thus, he told the Office of Network Study in 1960: "Since we are a medium of mass communication, it seems to me that we should primarily be concerned with majority programming. What puzzles me a great deal about the critics of TV is their persistent attack on the fundamental concept of the vote of the majority. . . . " In a similar vein, *Variety* quoted a TV station owner's warning of "autocrats who would set up a cultural tyranny within the framework of democracy," and the newspaper commented that "The attack may be expected to be sounded more frequently in the future. It has the appeal of championing plain folk versus the intellectual snobs who take a patronizing view, allegedly, toward what they call the tastes of the 'masses.'"[10]

Frank Stanton, in testimony before the FCC, argued that nothing less than American democracy was at stake: "perhaps the government could see to it that the trains of TV run on time—that only what is good for the people, in the government's view, goes over the air. But then we turn our back on democracy." In a famous reformulation of the language of the Communications Act, Stanton told the Office of Network Study: "Appeal to most of the people most of the time . . . is an inescapable part of the nature of television. . . . I suggest that a program in which a large part of the audience is interested is by that very fact a program in the public interest." Paraphrasing Stanton's "the public interest is what the public is interested in" philosophy, Sarnoff told the Office of Network Study that "[t]he Commission should operate on the basic premise that by attracting and maintaining an audience in competition with other broadcast services and other media, the licensee has met a public need."[11]

By the end of the 1950s it was no longer possible to find substantive differences among the three networks regarding procurement practices, program philosophies, or audience strategies. In the late 1950s, the heads of programming at all three networks were alumni of the Goldenson years at ABC, with Kintner moving to NBC in 1957 and James Aubrey to CBS in 1958. When Sarnoff used an FCC hearing in 1960 to denounce ABC as a "narrow-gauge" network, "watering the stock of broadcasting," *Broadcasting* reported widespread industry cynicism about his remarks. "None of the networks is clean," it quoted an unnamed industry official remarking. Parallel to the strong Warner Brothers-ABC program production tie, the telefilm producer MCA formed a strong association with NBC in the late 1950s. *Fortune* reported a meeting Sarnoff attended in early 1957, during which a network executive turned to an MCA vice president and said "Here are empty spots, you fill them." As differences among the three networks became increasingly cosmetic, a pattern emerged where network figures like Stanton served as industry statesman before congressional committees and FCC hearings, while program heads like Aubrey pursued the new network programming strategies. As Aubrey explained to *The Saturday Evening Post* in 1961: "Stanton is acknowledged to be the symbol of a respectable broadcaster. You have to maintain respectability though it's difficult and costly. At the same time you have to maintain leadership in audience. Competition is fierce. The eggheads, they criticize no matter what, because in general they just don't like television. I'm a businessman. I have to be. We have to give the public what it wants to stay solvent." Fred Friendly recalled Aubrey's explanation of the relationship between his role as CBS network president and Friendly's as news president. Aubrey told Friendly: "They say to me, 'Take your soiled little hands, get the ratings, and make as much money as you can.' They say to you, 'Take your lily-white hands, do your best, go the high road and bring us prestige.'" When television producer William Froug was hired as Hollywood executive in charge of drama, he told Erik Barnouw, a CBS executive instructed him, "Your job is to produce shit."[12]

RCA Chairman David Sarnoff was quoted by John Crosby: "We're in the same position of a plumber laying a pipe. We're not responsible for what goes through the pipe." Robert Sarnoff told the *Chicago Sun-Times* in March 1960 that "I'm not sure I know what it is that has to be reformed. I don't think anyone has proved that bad television is harmful." Responding to critics of television programming, Goldenson asked the Office of Network Study in 1960: "Can we legislate taste? Can we make it a criminal offense to be mediocre? Shall we set up a commissar of culture?" Network and advertising executive Max Wylie remarked blandly: "There is nothing wrong with mediocrity if you are mediocre. Mediocrity is exactly right. Most television critics never take this into account."[13]

Many of television's major critics responded to the new climate with expressions of frustration, impotence, and disillusionment. In 1958, John Crosby looked at the short history of television criticism and remarked grimly: "Actually, the very seriousness of the criticism leveled at television and the amount of space given to TV are both complimentary to the medium. When I first started writing a column about radio, radio coverage was almost entirely non-critical, because radio wasn't considered worthy of criticism and there was a negligible amount of space devoted to it. If television gets any blander, TV coverage is going to revert to that of radio days." Crosby argued that the commonplace debate over the influence of television critics was becoming pointless because television criticism itself had become passe, pointing to several critics who had recently given up writing about the medium. In a 1958 *Television* interview Jack Gould observed that TV critics now found less and less to say about the medium's programming. According to the broadcast historian Bob S. Lewis, by the end of 1959 several newspapers across the country closed their television columns "because the editors said there was nothing to write about and they were tired of continually damning television." In 1961, Gould noted Crosby's departure and argued: "That's what's happening you see. John has left; others around the country have left. I think this is exactly what television would like— for all of us simply to drop out so they could go on their merry way."[14]

The disillusionment of television critics in the late 1950s paralleled that of television's most prominent playwrights, and the change in industry attitudes toward writers of television drama suggests the larger shift in the industry's cultural position. In 1957, CBS Vice President of Programming Hubbell Robinson, after acknowledging the "soft underbelly" of mediocre television programming, maintained that there was still hope for the medium: "It lies in continuing to make television creatively challenging and financially rewarding to the kind of men who have consistently given television its greatest moments. They are men like Fred Coe, Frank Herridge, Rod Serling. . . . " Robinson called such men "realists . . . [who] understand that big budgets must deliver comparable ratings; but they have a built-in compulsion to deliver proud ratings too."[15] By the end of the 1950s, however, there is little evidence that network leaders were interested in the distinction between ordinary ratings and "proud ratings."

The industry's attitude toward TV playwrights who complained publicly of network television's retreat from anthology drama and social controversy was suggested in a series of hostile articles in the trade press with such titles as "Television's Wealthy, Angry Young Men," "Creators Turn on the Created," "Billion Dollar Whipping Boy," "Sniping at Radio-TV: New National Pastime," "Writers Blast *Sponsor*, Agency for Damaging TV," and "Ad Men Retort Sharply to TV Writers' Diatribe." Most of the writers' complaints concerned increasing censorship in the medium, and their charges were echoed by many of television's most influential critics. A 1960 *Sponsor* article, "Critics Blast TV Advertisers," complained that the censorship complaints of Rod Serling and other TV playwrights were "gleefully re-echoed in Broadway columns and in the pages of intellectual-type magazines." While dismissing such charges as inconsequential, *Sponsor* warned that "the criticism is dangerous because of its emotional appeal and the passion of its advocates."[16]

A 1960 article in *Sponsor* claimed that popular concern over the quiz show scandals and writers' complaints of censorship were spurred by the "yelps and squeals of certain newspaper TV columnists" and complained that "nearly everybody has been getting into the act." In 1960, a number of prominent television playwrights participated in a panel discussion on "the relation of writer to television," including Serling, who argued: "If the sponsor chooses the play as a kind of piggy back on which he wants to use his commercial, then he has to respect the form he has chosen." *Printer's Ink*, labeling the panel discussion "a diatribe," quoted several advertising executives who responded to Serling's complaints. Young and Rubicam executive Max Weiner declared: "The report doesn't contain any startling revelations. They were saying the same thing about radio in 1934." Robert L. Foreman, executive vice president of Baton, Barton, Durstein and Osborn, told the magazine: "These comments of a few misanthropes who can't get along with the rest of the world and still do their work leads me to suspect their ability." Max Banzhof, a board member of Association of National Advertisers, wrote of the writer-critics: "What's their motive? Why are they trying to discredit the American businessman? Who will gain from it?"[17]

The new industry attitude toward television writers was summarized in the testimony of sponsor and agency executives to the FCC's Office of Network Study in 1960. Banzhof, advertising director for Armstrong Cork Company, sponsor of "Armstong Circle Theatre," put the position of the television writer most starkly. He noted that some television writers "view television as their personal medium for the expression of their art," and "resent any influence the sponsor tries to exercise and cry loudly that the public has a right to see what they have created and that art is being prostituted for commercial gain." Banzhof testified that Armstrong was "careful to avoid employing such irresponsible persons," and told the panel: "Those who disagree with his [the sponsor's] policy have the recourse of seeking other sponsors who may hold different views, or they can turn to other mediums of expression." Following a round of testimony from writers, producers, and actors before the FCC panel, *Broadcasting* wrote: "Because of the statements made by writers and producers at this time, the FCC felt constrained to warn the industry not to attempt any retaliatory action against these witnesses."[18]

NOTES

1. Kintner is quoted in Fairfax M. Cone, *With All Its Faults: A Candid Account of Forty Years in Advertising* (Boston: Little, Brown, 1969), p. 267; the claim of victimization can be found in National Broadcasting Company, Press Release, November 5, 1959, p. 3, collection of the NBC Records Administration Library, New York; expressions of skepticism about network victimization can be found in Jack Gould, "A Plague on TV's House," *New York Times*, October 12, 1959, p. 39.

2. Kent Anderson, *Television Fraud: The History and Implications of the Quiz Show Scandals* (Westport: Greenwood Press, 1978), p. 167; Bill Greeley, "Agencies on Network Treatment: 'It's the Last Time They'll Give Us This Sort of Kicking Around,'" *Variety*, April 27, 1960, p. 30; Erik Barnouw, *The History of Broad-*

casting in the United States, vol. 3: *The Image Empire* (New York: Oxford University Press, 1970), p. 128.

3. Frank Henry Jakes, "A Study of Standards Imposed by Four Leading Television Critics with Respect to Live Television Drama," Ph.D. diss., Ohio State University, 1960, p. 50; Evelyn Konrad, "The Critics Be Damned!," *Sponsor,* October 19, 1957, pp. 32, 90.

4. National Broadcasting Company, *Research and Planning Bulletin,* October 14, 1957, p. 1, collection of NBC Research Department, New York.

5. *Broadcasting,* May 22, 1961, p. 2, cited in Mary Ann Watson, "Commercial Television and the New Frontier: Resistance and Appeasement," Ph.D. diss., University of Michigan, 1983, p. 27; "Who Knows Programming?," *Television Age,* December 25, 1961, p. 31.

6. "The TV Study That Nobody Saw," *Variety,* June 8, 1960, p. 27.

7. Stanton is quoted in "NBC Ruffles Calm as Hearing Continues," *Broadcasting,* February 5, 1962, p. 46; Kintner in "The TV Fan Who Runs a Network," *Sponsor,* June 8, 1957, p. 45; Goldenson in "The abc of ABC," *Forbes,* June 15, 1959, p. 15.

8. Robert Sarnoff, "What Do You Want from TV?," *The Saturday Evening Post,* July 1, 1961, pp. 14-15, 44.

9. "Billion Dollar Whipping Boy," *Television Age,* November 4, 1957, pp. 30, 91-92.

10. Quoted in Harold Mehling, *The Great Time-Killer* (Cleveland: World Publishing, 1962), p. 17; Goldenson is quoted in "Curtain Falls on FCC Hearings," *Broadcasting,* February 8, 1960, p. 60; "Haynes Blasts TV's 'Cultural Tyranny,'" *Variety,* February 14, 1962, p. 34. For reaction to Mehling's book, see Maurine Christopher, "Mehling's *Great Time-Killer* Finds TV Blameworthy in Practically All Respects," *Advertising Age,* June 4, 1962, p. 109, and Jack Gould, "What's with TV?," *New York Times,* May 27, 1962, sec. 7, p. 14; Sarnoff's NAB speech is quoted in Solomon Simonson, *Crisis in Television* (New York: Living Books, 1966), p. 148.

11. "Stanton: Gaps and Imperfections," *Broadcasting,* February 1, 1960, p. 43; U.S. Federal Communications Commission, Office of Network Study, *Interim Report: Responsibility for Broadcast Matter,* Docket no. 12782 (Washington, D.C.: Government Printing Office, 1960), p. 91; "Sarnoff: Let's Be Reasonable," *Broadcasting,* February 1, 1960, p. 42; "Just About All There Is to Say About TV," *Television,* February 1963, p. 49.

12. "Sarnoff Buries the Hatchet—in ABC-TV," *Broadcasting,* November 21, 1960, pp. 89-90; "Anyone Hurt by Sarnoff Blast?," *Broadcasting,* November 28, 1960, p. 28; Edward T. Thompson, "There's No Show Business Like MCA's Business," *Fortune,* July 1960, p. 117; John Bartlow Martin, "Television USA: Wasteland or Wonderland?," part 2: "Battle of the Big Three," *The Saturday Evening*

The Critics and the Wasteland **243**

Post, October 28, 1961, p. 60; Fred W. Friendly, *Due to Circumstances Beyond Our Control* (New York: Vintage Books, 1967), pp. xi-xii; Froug is quoted in Barnouw, *The Image Empire,* p. 244.

13. David Sarnoff is quoted in Robert Austin Smith, "TV: The Light That Failed," *Fortune,* December 1958, p. 16; Robert Sarnoff's remark can be found in *Chicago Sun Times,* March 21, 1960; quoted in Meyer Weinberg, *TV in America: The Morality of Hard Cash* (New York: Ballantine, 1962), p. 51; Goldenson is quoted in "Curtain Falls on FCC Hearing," p. 62; Wylie is quoted in Mehling, *The Great Time-Killer,* p. 27.

14. John Crosby, *New York Herald-Tribune,* July 6, 1958; quoted in Jakes, "A Study of Standards," p. 72; Leon Morse, "Inside Jack Gould," *Television,* November 1958, p. 49; Bob S. Lewis, "An Analysis of the Influence of Newton Minow on *Broadcasting,*" master's thesis, University of Missouri, 1966, p. 23; Jack Gould, *Television* interview by Donald McDonald (Santa Barbara: Center for the Study of Democratic Institutions, 1961), p. 26.

15. Hubbell Robinson, "TV's Myopia of the Widescreen," *Esquire,* July 1958, p. 23.

16. "Critics Blast TV Advertiser," *Sponsor,* February 6, 1960, pp. 34-35.

17. "TV Criticism: How Much of It Makes Sense?," *Sponsor,* January 30, 1960, p. 22; "Ad Men Retort Sharply to TV Writers' Diatribe," *Printer's Ink,* July 29, 1960, pp. 13-14.

18. U.S., Federal Communications Commission, Office of Network Study, *Second Interim Report: Television Network Program Procurement, Part 2,* Docket no. 12782 (Washington, D.C.: U.S. Government Printing Office, 1965), p. 86; "FCC's Network Program Hearing Continues," *Broadcasting,* January 22, 1962, p. 43.

14

The Death of the Networks as Reformist Heroes

The hearings around the quiz show scandals provide a summation to a final important theme in the rise and fall of television's Golden Age: the role of the networks as special guardians of free expression, experimentation, and program balance in television. Faced with widespread complaints of sponsor censorship of program content, part of the networks' strategy of presenting themselves as the unwitting victims in the quiz show fraud was promises of reform in relations with television advertisers. Typical was CBS President Frank Stanton's statement that "We shall be masters in our own house in program acceptance and scheduling and . . . making the ultimate decisions on what goes into our programming schedule." The network's resolution to become "masters in our own house" during the quiz show hearings evoked again the reformist image the networks had adopted in the earlier era of live drama. As Erik Barnouw described the reactions to the networks' 1960 statements: "The pronouncement were welcome by many. The network obviously had a broader constituency that any sponsor, and were considered far more likely to rise above merchandising considerations."[1]

That the network might not, in fact, be more tolerant of controversial material than sponsors or advertising agencies became clear as the network won control of program procurement and scheduling from sponsors in the 1950s. The dilution of the power of a single sponsor often led to even greater conservatism on the part of network program executives. Pat Weaver told *Broadcasting* in 1962 that television sponsors were responsible for only 5 percent of the interference in programming matters: "The networks are responsible for 85 percent and you can split the other 10 percent any way you like." Despite the substantial financial stakes of the networks' successful struggle to gain program control from sponsors and advertising agencies in the late 1950s, the implications for free expression in the medium pointed to a convergence of interests, all hostile to controversial programming. In 1961, Jack Gould looked back at the noisy battle for program control and concluded: "It has always seemed to me very academic, this perennial controversy over whether advertising agencies or the networks should control the programming. As a practical matter and how things stand, it doesn't make any difference."[2]

The Office of Network Study's 1965 *Second Interim Report* likewise concluded that the narrow issue of "sponsor interference" was largely a red herring because sponsors typically maintained the same rights of involvement in scripts, casting, and theme in network-controlled shows that they did in advertiser-licensed programs. "In sum," the report concluded, "if there is a difference in 'advertiser influence' on the programs produced by network managers as against those produced by independents, it appears to be slight and a difference of degree rather than kind." An unsigned article in *Variety* in 1959, "Magazine Concept a Panacea for Program Evils? Hardly," cited the "Playhouse 90" Nuremburg case as evidence that the shift to multiple sponsorship and network licensing merely increased the number of advertiser-censors without diluting their power.[3]

Indeed, network executives frequently took pains to assure television advertisers that they kept the commercial interests of the sponsor foremost in their minds. CBS Network President James Aubrey told the Office of Network Study in 1960:

There is relatively little that is incompatible between our objectives and the objectives of the advertisers. . . . Before sponsorship of a program series commences there is often a meeting between production personnel and representatives of the advertiser at which time the general areas of the advertiser's interest and general attitudes are discussed. A breakfast food advertiser may, for example, wish to make sure the programs do not contain elements that make breakfast distasteful. A cigarette manufacturer would not wish to have cigarette smoking depicted in an unattractive manner. Normally, as long as these considerations do not limit creativity, they will be adhered to.[4]

Mort Weiner, NBC's vice president of programming, also told the FCC's Office of Network Study:

> In entertainment, where public issues are not at stake, we have always gone on the theory that the man who pays the bills has a right to some voice in shaping the product. Nearly every advertiser who buys television advertising reserves a measure of control in terms of "corporate policy." For the most part, changes suggested or insisted upon because of this reservation are not significant insofar as basic program content is concerned. A cigarette sponsor bans cigar smoking; an automobile manufacturer doesn't want an automobile accident in the story; a manufacturer of bathroom fixtures sold through plumbing supply dealers specifies that no jokes about plumbers are to be used. These requirements do not really interfere with the entertainment objectives of the programs or with their creative integrity. We have learned to accommodate our operations to this type of request. . . .[5]

ABC executives also testified to their eagerness to accommodate sponsor censorship concerns, telling the Office of Network Study: "If the advertiser makes a reasonable suggestion from the orientation of business or advertising policy, that doesn't go to the essence of creative control, we attempt to be reasonable about it."[6] The evidence suggests the three networks defined the legitimate business concerns of television advertisers quite broadly and the areas of creative integrity exempt from sponsor censorship quite narrowly.

Independent telefilm producers had long demonstrated their willingness to align programming to sponsor and network specifications. For example, at the 1952 House hearings into objectionable television programming, which resulted in the establishment of the Television Code, a representative of an association of telefilm producers declared an eagerness for an explicit pre-clearance procedure for program approval before production began. In 1956, *Broadcasting-Telecasting* reported that a group of telefilm producers, led by an executive of Desilu, were at work on a telefilm supplement to the Television Code; the producers' group called the NAB code "a very good one," but argued that film producers needed a more "streamlined" censorship code for efficiency. The group formed to devise the code included William H. Mooring, a prominent syndicated conservative Catholic columnist. In 1958, Hubbell Robinson blamed the "welter of mediocrity" on independent producers "who place the mere fact of rating above the means by which they achieve it." A year later, after Robinson left CBS to become an independent television producer himself, he told the press that responsibility for imitative programming belonged not to the producer, but to the sponsor: "Producers are there to service sponsors. They give them what they want. They give them what they think they can sell. One of the reasons we have so many formula shows today is that they're salable. If sponsors encourage originality, that's what they'll get. If they encourage formula, that's what they'll get."[7]

In testimony before the Office of Network Study, Gore Vidal named advertising agencies as the most conservation group influencing program content. Robert Alan Aurthur told the Fund for the Republic that agencies were concerned about maintaining good relations with their clients and nervous about justifying their 15 percent commissions in the absence of any direct agency role in program production; under the circumstances, the agency dealt sternly with writers over censorship issues in order to justify the agency's role in programming. Rod Serling told the fund that agency representatives often told writers that they privately agreed with them in battles over script changes, but that because the sponsor was paying for the program, its objections must prevail. "They are frightened people, who are desperate, who have to have a feeling of functioning, of doing something all the time," he said of agency personnel. In the 1960 Office of Network Study hearings, Barnouw saw rising advertising costs reinforcing economic concentration and conservatism among television sponsors, and argued that the only solution was the assertion by the networks of programming control in the interests of program balance.[8]

Not surprisingly, executives from other sectors of the television industry came to different conclusions about the source of the problems with television programming in the late 1950s. Advertising executive Fairfax M. Cone, a prominent commentator on television in the 1950s, wrote in 1969: "The failure of television in the nasty business of the blacklist and the quiz show scandals was a failure of the networks." The networks, he argued, found it easy to scapegoat the television sponsor as "a soothing accompaniment to the march of the broadcasters to the vaults." Max Banzhof denied that television advertisers were responsible for the rise of the telefilm action-adventure shows of the late 1950s: "You may wonder why sponsors buy them and if you do, you have only to look at what else is offered to them to buy."[9]

In 1960, Serling argued that at some point in the 1950s, the networks could have insisted upon the insulation of the writer and program content from sponsor interference but instead ceded censorship rights to the sponsor and agency. After describing the current network schedules as "shockingly bad," Paddy Chayefsky placed the blame at network executives who "know right from wrong . . . but perceive wrong for the benefit of profit and commerce." Independent producer David Susskind called network schedules, "a travesty, a waste, a gigantic comic strip," and argued that "the principal cause has been the 'death grip' on programming held by the television networks to further the interests of mass advertisers." Susskind told the Office of Network Study in 1960 that the networks "used the national horror at the quiz show scandals as the excuse for establishing complete and absolute control of the programming. . . . [T]he myth that they can not control or be responsible for what's on the air if they don't own or control it is the myth that allows this kind of control and ownership."[10]

The question of who was responsible for creative censorship often provoked confused responses in the TV industry. In 1960, Vidal described his experience as a television writer a few years earlier: "The world of television—at least then, I suppose now—it's sort of a Kafka world; you can never tell exactly who is responsible for what. The agency will you tell you it's the sponsor; the sponsor will tell you it's the agency or the show itself, and sometimes everyone blames the network. It's very difficult to determine where the blame lies."[11]

Much of the equivocation was generated by network executives, who attempted to draw subtle distinctions between the advertiser's right to control content and the network's insistence on schedule and formal program control. ABC, for example, told the Office of Network Study that the network's independent telefilm producers maintained creative control over programming, while also admitting that the network supplied sponsors with scripts before production and told advertisers to come to ABC, not to the production company, with complaints. "If the advertiser makes a reasonable suggestion from the orientation of business or advertising policy, that doesn't go to the essence of creative control, we attempt to be reasonable about it," the network told the panel.

Stanton was quoted in the *New York Times* in 1960: "The advertiser may participate in the creative process and to the extent that his suggestion is constructive, it will be accepted. . . . The advertiser may object to a program or an element thereof, if he believes it will be detrimental to his product or his goodwill." "The ultimate responsibility is ours, but the ultimate power has to be to the sponsor's because without him you couldn't afford to run a network," Kintner told *Time* in 1959. A year later NBC's Sarnoff told the Office of Network Study that it was an "impractical suggestion" to seek to separate sponsors from programming; an advertiser's influence was helpful, not detrimental, Sarnoff argued. Answering what he described as "the double-barreled charge that it [programming] is degraded by conformity to advertisers' objectives and by the worship of ratings," Sarnoff argued that the sponsor was merely anticipating and responding to consumer wishes, and that the public via its surrogate therefore exercised actual control. Stanton's three-hour testimony before the Office of Network Study in 1960 sought to diffuse criticism of commercial censorship while at the same time reassure television sponsors that their desires would continue to be respected by the network; Jack Gould reported: "Dr. Stanton so effectively boxed the compass that it was not immediately clear in which direction he was going." The reductio ad absurdum of such network equivocation on the question of program control came from CBS network head Aubrey, who told *The Saturday Evening Post* in 1961: "Ultimately the network must decide. But it's a result of a lot of pulling and hauling among the networks, the station, the advertisers, talent, the agencies, everybody. Really no one decides."[12]

The spectacle of confusion and disingenuousness over program responsibility in the late 1950s points to what by then was the essential irrelevance of the question of formal program control to matters of freedom of expression. By the end of the decade there were no significant differences among sponsors, producers, advertising agencies, and networks in their sensitivity to the public interest values of free expression, program diversity, or aesthetic experimentation in the medium. One advertising agency executive told the FCC in 1960 that "The line of demarcation between the program 'responsibility' of the agencies and that of the networks is not always clear and is seldom precisely defined." Dan Seymour, vice president of J. Walter Thompson, explained to the Office of Network Study: "*We are not very concerned about the matter of who has control over the programming, as long as it is compatible to us, and we are able to continue in partnership in the production of shows."[13]*

A remarkable special editorial in the December 1959 issue of *Television* summarized the systematic nature of the commercial constraints on the television medium, which guided sponsor, agency, and network alike:

> The reverberations of the television quiz show scandals have struck home throughout the entire advertising business. Television, because of its tremendous hold on the American public, its power as a communications medium, has merely highlighted the symbolic ills of advertising. . . .
>
> Today, mass production is made possible by mass media . . . and today, all mass media are completely dependent on advertising revenue. . . . [The sponsor] survives only in his ability to make sufficient sales to turn a profit for his company. And these days, sufficient sales for those advertisers using mass media are BIG. This in turn means intensive and continued pressure for ever-larger sales. And with this pressure arises one serious problem, a problem so apparent and yet so deep that the entire advertising business: there is almost a complete similarity among many of the low-tab, competitive products. Advertisers, to capture their share of the market, must convince the public that their products *do* differ from competitors'. . . .
>
> And the partner to this approach is the advertising agency. Either it aids and abets the advertiser in deluding the public into thinking one product is better than another or it won't get the business. . . .
>
> Now the third step in the process—mass media. . . . Media must cater to the widest possible common denominator in terms of taste, if they wish to serve such advertisers. And media have lowered their standards and gone along with deceptive advertising practices. They cannot be absolved from blame, nor can they hide behind their large circulations and "giving the public what it wants."[14]

The sense of a systematic impasse within commercial television was pervasive at the end of the 1950s. In a 1960 *Broadcasting* article, David Susskind denounced the forthcoming television season as the worst ever and argued: "If the point of television is to sell products what we have now is inevitable." Max Enelow, the director of advertising for Philco, told *Advertising Age* in December 1959: "All the moralizing and preaching . . . won't convince the advertiser that he should pay the same millions for a ten rating that he does for a thirty, not as long as we have a system of commercial sponsorship. And what's more, all the laws and regulations that Congress and the FCC may pass won't do it either." The advertising executive explained that although "the airlanes belong to the people of the United States . . . the people have decided to sell those airlanes to the advertisers of the United States for commercial purposes. . . . Don't blame the advertiser for using every legitimate means to get full value for the millions he invests. . . . [If] this produces dull, sterile, imitative programming, don't blame the sponsors, blame the system."[15]

By the late 1950s, few would-be reformers of commercial television had much hope for significant change under the prevailing commercial and regulatory structures. Barnouw told the Office of Network Study in 1960 that sponsor fear of controversy and its interference in the writer's work in television were rational, if selfish, business decisions: "The question is whether such decisions should be put to them in the first place. The real question is whether we can afford to have our culture and artistic life become a byproduct of advertising. My answer is that we can't." Reacting to the quiz show scandals, veteran columnist Walter Lippmann began one 1959 newspaper column with: "Television has been caught in perpetuating a fraud which is so gigantic that it calls into question the foundation of the industry." Lippmann argued that "[T]here is something radically wrong with the fundamental national policy under which television operates. . . . [W]hile television is supposed to be 'free,' it has in fact become the creature, the servant, and indeed the prostitute, of merchandising."[16] Lippman called for the creation of a publicly subsidized television network to compete with the commercial networks.

Veteran broadcast critic Charles Siepmann told the Office of Network Study in 1960 that the preceding twenty-five years had witnessed "a significant and disastrous sea change" in industry perception and performance of public service responsibilities in broadcasting. He argued that "Service . . . has been progressively subordinated to profitmaking and the satisfaction of advertisers. There has been . . . [a] . . . narrowing, to a near vanishing point, of areas of controversy, and the spawning of stereotyped programs."[17]

Broadcast researcher Paul Lazarsfeld testified "with mixed feelings of hope and doubt" before the Office of Network Study in 1959, confessing, "for three decades I was professionally involved in discussions of the kinds of problems which are on the docket today, and nothing much ever came of them." Nevertheless, Lazarsfeld called for the creation of a television advisory committee comprising artists, psychologists, and research technicians to improve programming; a voluntary agreement by the three networks to offer public affairs and minority programming in prime time and share the financial sacrifice; and the use of the Lazarsfeld-Stanton "program analyzer" to "find out how serious programs could be made more entertaining."[18]

Perhaps the most striking criticism of the prosperous new era of network television came from former leaders in television program production, network management, and manufacturing. In 1959, independent telefilm producer Frederick Ziv sold his company to United Artists, and later described his motives for leaving the program production business: "The reason I sold my business is because I recognized that the networks were taking command of everything and were permitting the independent producers no room at all. The networks demanded a percentage of your profits, they demanded script approval, cast approval. You practically were no longer an independent producer. You were just doing whatever the networks asked you to do. And that was not my type of operation. And I didn't care to become an employee of the networks." Network domination of program production and procurement so restricted the market for first-run syndicated programming, *Broadcasting* reported in 1961, that "the time is already approaching when stations will be dependent on the networks for virtually all new programming except what the stations produce themselves." The magazine quoted a station operator who warned: "If we have a wasteland in television programming now then what we're doing is freezing the wasteland for a long time to come."[19]

In November 1960, Pat Weaver told the *Sunday Denver Post:* "Television has gone from about a dozen forms to just two—news shows and the Hollywood stories. The blame lies in the management of NBC, CBS, and ABC. Management doesn't give the people what they deserve. I don't see any hope in the system as it is." In June 1961, television inventor and former network operator Allen B. DuMont addressed the American Institute of Electrical Engineers and called for a federally funded public television network to mitigate against the "crassly commercial Frankenstein" of network commercial television: "All my life I have advocated as little government as possible in the personal and economic life of America. My friends—both in and out of the TV industry—may be shocked, but I believe that the Government of the United States is the only possible sponsor for programming of a non-commercial, intellectual and informative type."[20] The devaluation of television writers and critics, the shrinking of the aesthetic promise of the medium they had celebrated just a few years earlier, and the growing rigidity of program formats, acceptable dramatic subjects, and desired audience targets convinced many critics inside and outside the industry that prime-time television's weaknesses were inherent in the commercially supported system of broadcasting.

In a warmly received speech before the Radio and Television Executives Society in 1959, writer Patrick McGrady outlined the new impasse between the television industry and its increasingly strident critics: "Each side accuses the other of prejudicial subjectivity. Television's peculiar subjectivity is more easily ascertained than the critics': it is simply an abiding, over-riding concern with making money—the abiding, overriding concern of television. If television and criticism are going to make more sense than they do now, this fundamental issue will have to be resolved."[21]

This contradiction at the heart of American commercial broadcasting is suggested in the conclusions of a 1969 law review article by Ashbrook P. Bryant, who led the second phase of the Office of Network Study's inquiry into program practices: "We must, in our evaluation of television service, accept the inevitable subject matter restrictions imposed by the essential nature of our communications system. But we must also be certain that unnecessary further restriction of the sources and subjects of programs are not imposed purely to maximize profits."[22]

The "violent, often confused refusal to countenance money-making as an abiding, overriding concern of television" displayed by many observers of the television industry by 1960 reflects the general disillusionment of a generation of critics and creative talent who were unhappy with the political and aesthetic costs of the spectacular commercial success of a new mass medium. Their rejection of the tight control of ideas and entertainment exercised by a grossly imperfect marketplace may be conceptually more consistent than granting the existence of a fundamentally restrictive communications structure and hoping that its profit-seeking actors will operate in ways contrary to their individual self-interest. Since the 1950s, the major economic changes and programming innovations in American television would come from *outside* the network industry, particularly from cable television and a chronically underfunded public television system. Moreover, the continued theorizing and agitation over minority programming, free expression, and the public interest in American television since 1960 have most often been founded precisely and productively on the "violent, often confused refusal to countenance money-making as an abiding, overriding concern of television."

NOTES

1. U.S., Federal Communication Commission, Office of Network Study, *Interim Report: Responsibility for Broadcast Matter*, Docket no. 12782 (Washington, D.C.: U.S. Government Printing Office, 1960), p. 86; Erik Barnouw, *The Sponsor: Notes on a Modern Potentate* (New York: Oxford University Press, 1978), p. 57.

2. "TV Experts Roast, Roasted in Hollywood," *Broadcasting,* December 24, 1962, p. 36; Jack Gould, *Television* interview by Donald McDonald (Santa Barbara: Center for the Study of Democratic Institutions, 1961), p. 3.

3. U.S., Federal Communications Commission, Office of Network Study, *Second Interim Report: Television Network Program Procurement Part 2*, Docket no. 12782 (Washington, D.C.: Government Printing Office, 1965), p. 27; "Magazine Concept a Panacea for Program Evils? Hardly," *Variety*, November 25, 1959, p. 32.

4. FCC, *Second Interim Report*, p. 239.

5. Ibid., pp. 276-77.

6. FCC, *Interim Report*, p. 98.

7. U.S. Congress, House Committee on Interstate and Foreign Commerce, *Investigation of Radio and Television Programs, Hearings Before the Communications Subcommittee of the House Committee on Interstate and Foreign Commerce on H. Res. 278*, 82nd Cong., 2d sess. (Washington, D.C.: U.S. Government Printing Office, 1952), p. 155; J. Frank Beatty, "Sniping at Radio-TV: New National Pastime," *Broadcasting-Telecasting,* April 9, 1956, p. 123; Hubbell Robinson, "TV's Myopia of the Widescreen," *Esquire,* July 1958, p. 24; Leon Morse, "Hubbell Robinson Evaluates TV Programming Today," *Television,* December 1959, pp. 49-50.

8. Vidal is quoted in FCC, *Second Interim Report,* p. 625; Aurthur and Serling in Marya Mannes, "The TV Pattern: Signs of Revolt," *Reporter,* May 2, 1957, p. 14; Barnouw in *Second Interim Report,* p. 548.

9. Fairfax M. Cone, *With All Its Faults: A Candid Account of Forty Years in Advertising* (Boston: Little, Brown, 1969), p. 267; *Advertising Age,* November 16,

1959, quoted in Meyer Weinberg, *TV in America: The Morality of Hard Cash* (New York: Ballantine, 1962), p. 80.

10. Serling is quoted in Mannes, "The TV Pattern," p. 16; Chayefsky and Susskind in FCC, *Interim Report*, pp. 27, 549-50.

11. Ibid., p. 265.

12. ABC's testimony can be found in ibid., pp. 86, 98-100; Stanton's remarks in Jack Gould, "CBS and the Sponsors," *New York Times*, May 4, 1960, sec. 2, p. 15; Kintner's in "The Tarnished Image," *Time*, November 16, 1959, p. 80; Robert Sarnoff's in "Sarnoff: Let's Be Reasonable," *Broadcasting*, February 1, 1960, p. 4; Jack Gould, "TV: Sarnoff's Panacea," *New York Times*, January 30, 1960, p. 43; "Stanton: Gaps and Imperfections," *Broadcasting*, February 1, 1960, p. 46; John Bartlow Martin, "Television USA: Wasteland or Wonderland?," Part 2: "Battle of the Big Three," *The Saturday Evening Post*, October 28, 1961, p. 60.

13. FCC, *Interim Report*, p. 86; *Second Interim Report*, p. 751, emphasis in original.

14. "A Special Editorial," *Television*, December 1959, pp. 42-43.

15. "Television's Wealthy Angry Young Men," *Broadcasting*, October 17, 1960, p. 56; letter to *Advertising Age*, December 14, 1959, p. 88.

16. FCC, *Second Interim Report*, p. 751; Walter Lippmann, "Television: Whose Creature, Whose Servant?," *New York Herald Tribune*, October 27, 1959, reprinted in *The Essential Lippmann*, ed. Clinton Rossiter and James Lare (New York: Random House, 1963), pp. 411-12.

17. Charles A. Siepmann, "Moral Aspects of Television," *Public Opinion Quarterly* 24 (Spring 1960): 15.

18. Paul Lazarsfeld, "A Researcher Looks at Television," *Public Opinion Quarterly* 24 (Spring 1960): 24, 27, 29.

19. Interview with F.W. Ziv, July 16, 1973 in Morleen Getz Rouse, "A History of the F.W. Ziv Radio and Television Syndication Companies 1930-1960," Ph.D diss., University of Michigan, 1976, p. 243; "Program Sources Drying Up?" *Broadcasting*, September 18, 1961, pp. 19-20.

20. Larry Ingram, "Network TV Faces Day of Reckoning," *Sunday Denver Post*, November 20, 1960, p. AA1; "DuMont: 'Created a Frankenstein,'" *Variety*, June 21, 1961, p. 23.

21. Patrick McGrady, speech to the Radio and Television Executives Association, January 28, 1959, quoted in Frank Henry Jakes, "A Study of Standards Imposed by Four Leading Television Critics with Respect to Live Television Drama," Ph.D. diss., Ohio State University, 1960, p. 53.

22. Ashbrook P. Bryant, "Historical and Social Aspects of Concentration of Program Control in Television," *Law and Contemporary Problems* 34 (Summer 1969): 635.

Bibliography

I. Books and Pamphlets

Abramson, Albert. *The History of Television, 1880 to 1941.* Jefferson, N.C.: McFarland, 1987.

Ace, Goodman. *The Book of Little Knowledge: More Than You Want to Know About Television.* New York: Simon and Schuster, 1955.

Adams, Charles. *Producing and Directing for Television.* New York: Henry Holt, 1953.

Allen, Robert C., ed. *Channels of Discourse: Television and Contemporary Criticism.* Chapel Hill: University of North Carolina Press, 1987.

————. *Speaking of Soap Operas.* Chapel Hill: University of North Carolina Press, 1985.

American Business Consultants. *Red Channels: The Report on the Communist Influence in Radio and Television.* New York: American Business Consultants, 1950.

Anderson, Kent. *Television Fraud: The History and Implication of the Quiz Show Scandals.* Westport, Conn.: Greenwood Press, 1978.

Ang, Ien. *Watching Dallas: Soap Opera and the Melodramatic Imagination.* London: Methuen, 1985.

Arthur D. Little, Inc. *Television Program Production, Procurement and Syndication.* Cambridge: Arthur D. Little, Inc., 1966.

Averson, Richard, and David Manning White, eds. *Electronic Drama: Television Plays of the 1960s.* Boston: Beacon Press, 1971.

Balio, Tino, ed. *The American Film Industry.* Madison: University of Wisconsin Press. 1976.

Barnouw, Erik. *The History of Broadcasting in the United States.* Vol. 1, *A Tower in Babel.* New York: Oxford University Press, 1966; Vol. 2, *The Golden Web.* New York: Oxford University Press, 1968; Vol. 3, *The Image Empire.* New York: Oxford University Press, 1970.

———. *The Sponsor: Notes on a Modern Potentate.* New York: Oxford University Press, 1978.

———. *The Television Writer.* New York: Hill and Wang, 1962.

Bauer, George. *Government Regulation of Television.* New York: New York University Graduate School of Public Administration, 1956.

Baughman, James L. *Television Guardians: The FCC and the Politics of Programming 1958-1967.* Knoxville: University of Tennessee Press, 1985.

Bennett, Tony, Susan Boyd-Bowman, Colin Mercer, and Janet Woollacott, eds. *Popular Television and Film: A Reader.* London: British Film Institute/Open University Press, 1981.

Bernstein, Irving. *The Economics of Television Film Production and Distribution.* Los Angeles: Screen Actors Guild, 1960.

Besen, Stanley M, Thomas G. Krattenmaker, Richard A. Metzger, Jr., and John R. Woodbury. *Misregulating Television: Network Dominance and the FCC.* Chicago: University of Chicago Press, 1984.

Bilby, Kenneth. *The General: David Sarnoff and the Rise of the Communications Industry.* New York: Harper and Row, 1986.

Bluem, William. *Documentary in American Television.* New York: Hastings House, 1965.

Bluem, William, and Roger Manvell, eds. *TV: The Creative Experience: A Survey of Anglo-American Progress.* New York: Hastings House, 1965.

Botein, Michael, and David M. Rice, eds. *Network Television and the Public Interest.* Lexington, Mass.: D.C. Heath, 1980.

Boucheron, Pierre. "Advertising Radio to the American Public," in *The Radio Industry: The Story of Its Development*, pp. 260-70. Chicago: A. W. Shaw, 1928

Britton, Florence, ed. *Best Television Plays 1957.* New York: Ballantine, 1957.

Broughton, Irv. *Producers on Producing: The Making of Film and Television.* Jefferson, N.C.: Mcfarland, 1986.

Brunsdon, Charlotte, and David Morley. *BFI Television Monograph 10: Everyday Television:* Nationwide. London: British Film Institute, 1978.

Leo Burnett, Inc. *Report Number 2: Progress of Television: Where the Industry Stands Today Viewed as an Advertising Medium.* New York: Leo Burnett, 1946.

Castleman, Harry, and Walter Podrazik. *Watching TV: Four Decades of American Television.* New York: McGraw-Hill, 1982.

Center for the Study of Democrate Institutions. *Television.* Santa Barbara, Calif.: Fund for the Republic, 1978.

Chayefsky, Paddy. *Television Plays.* New York: Simon and Schuster, 1955.

Cole, Barry, and Moe Oettinger. *Reluctant Regulators: The FCC and the Broadcast Audience.* Reading Mass.: Addison-Wesley, 1978.

Collins, James, James Curran, Nicholas Garnham, Paddy Scannell, Philip Schlesinger, and Colin Sparks. *Media, Culture and Society: A Reader.* Beverly Hills: Sage Publications, 1988.

Columbia Broadcasting System, Inc. *An Analysis of Sentor John W. Bricker's Report Entitled "The Network Monopoly."* New York: Columbia Broadcasting System, 1956.

———. *Annual Meeting of Stockholders Report of the President.* New York: Columbia Broadcasting System, April 2, 1960.

———. *Forecasts in FM and Television.* New York: Columbia Broadcasting System, 1945.

———. *Is Pre-War Television Good Enough?* New York: Columbia Broadcasting System, n.d. (1944?).

———. *Network Practices: Memorandum Supplementing Statement of Frank Stanton, President, Columbia Broadcasting System, Inc.* New York: Columbia Broadcasting System, 1956.

———. *Opinion of Counsel and Memorandum Concerning the Applicability of Antitrust Laws to the Television Broadcast Activities of Columbia Broadcasting System, Inc.* New York: Columbia Broadcasting System, 1956.

———. *Television Audience Research.* New York: Columbia Broadcasting System, 1945.

Conant, Michael. *Antitrust in the Motion-Picture Industry: Economic and Legal Analysis.* Berkeley: University of California Press, 1960.

Cone, Fairfax M. *With All Its Faults: A Candid Account of Forty Years in Advertising.* Boston: Little, Brown, 1969.

Cook, Jim, ed. *BFI Dossier 17: Television Sitcom.* London: British Film Institute, 1982.

Coughie, John, ed. *BFI Television Monograph 9: Television: Ideology and Exchange.* London: British Film Institute, 1978.

Crosby, John. *Out of the Blue.* New York: Simon and Schuster, 1952.

Curtis Publishing Company. *The Television Industry.* Philadephia: Curtis Publishing, 1948.

Czitrom, Daniel J. *Media and the American Mind: From Morse to McLuhan.* Chapel Hill: University of North Carolina Press, 1982.

D'Agostino, Peter, ed. *Transmission: Theory and Practice for a New Television Aesthetics.* New York: Tanam Press, 1985.

DeForest, Lee. *Television Today and Tomorrow.* New York: Dial Press, 1942.

Dinsdale, Alfred. *First Principles of Television.* London: Chapman and Hall, 1932.

Donner, Stanley T., ed. *The Meaning of Commercial Television.* Austin: University of Texas Press, 1967.

Drummond, Philip, and Richard Paterson, eds. *Television in Transition: Papers from the First International Television Studies Conference.* London: British Film Institute, 1986.

Dunlap, Orrin E., Jr. *The Future of Television.* New York: Harper and Brothers, 1942.

Dupuy, Judy. *Television Show Business.* Schenectady, N.Y.: General Electric, 1945.

Dyer, Richard. *BFI Television Monograph 2: Light Entertainment.* London: British Film Institute, 1973.

Dyer, Richard, Christine Geraghty, Marion Jordan, Terry Lovell, Richard Paterson, and John Stewart. *BFI Television Monograph 13:* Coronation Street. London: British Film Institute, 1982.

Ellis, John. *Visible Fictions: Cinema Television Video.* London: Routledge and Kegan Paul, 1982.

Erickson, Don V. *Armstrong's Fight for FM Broadcasting: One Man vs Big Business and Bureaucracy.* University: University of Alabama Press, 1973.

Everson, George. *The Story of Television: The Life of Philo Farnsworth.* New York: Norton, 1949.

Feuer, Jane, Paul Kerr, and Tise Vahimagi. *MTM: "Quality Television."* London: British Film Institute, 1984.

Fiske, John. *Television Culture.* New York: Methuen, 1978.

Fiske, John, and John Hartley. *Reading Television.* London: Methuen, 1978.

Fornatale, Peter, and Joshua E Mills. *Radio in the Television Age.* Woodstock N.Y.: Overlook Press, 1980.

Friendly, Fred W. *Due to Circumstances Beyond Our Control.* New York: Vintage Books. 1967.

Frier, David A. *Conflict of Interest in the Eisenhower Administration.* Ames: Iowa State University Press, 1969.

Gitlin, Todd. *Inside Prime Time.* New York: Pantheon Books, 1985.

———, ed. *Watching Television.* New York: Pantheon Books, 1986.

Goldmark, Peter C., with Lee Edson. *Maverick Inventor: My Turbulent Years at CBS.* New York: Saturday Review Press/E. P. Dutton, 1973.

Gould, Jack. Interview by Donald McDonald. *Television.* Santa Barbara: Center for the Study of Democratic Institutions, 1961.

Greene, Robert S. *Television Writing.* New York: Harper, 1952

Grote, David. *The End of Comedy: The Sit-Com and the Comedic Tradition.* Hamden Conn.: Shoestring Press, 1983.

Gurevitch, Michael, Tony Bennett, James Curran, and Janet Woollacott, eds. *Culture, Society and the Media.* London: Methuen, 1982.

Hanhardt, John, ed. *Video Culture: A Critical Investigation.* Rochester, N.Y.: Visual Studies Workshop Press/Peregrine Smith Books, 1986.

Harvard University, Graduate School of Business Administration. *The Radio Industry: The Story of Its Development as Told by the Leaders of the Industry.* Chicago: A. W. Shaw, 1928.

Hawes, William. *American Television Drama: The Experimental Years.* University: University of Alabama Press, 1986.

Hess, Gary Newton. *An Historical Study of the DuMont Television Network.* New York: Arno Press, 1979.

Howard, Herbert H. *Multiple Ownership in Television Broadcasting: Historical Development and Selected Case Studies.* New York: Arno Press, 1979.

Hubbell, Richard W. *Four Thousand Years of Television.* New York: G. P. Putnam and Sons, 1942.

———. *Television Programming and Production.* New York: Murray Hill Books, 1945.

Hylander, C. J., and Robert Harding, Jr. *An Introduction to Television.* New York: Macmillan, 1941.

Johnson, Nicholas, and Kenneth Cox. *Broadcasting in America and the FCC's License Renewal Process: An Oklahoma Case Study.* Washington, D.C.: FCC, 1968.

Jolliffe, C. B. *An Engineer's Report on Television.* New York: Radio Corporation of America, 1945.

Kaplan, E. Ann, ed. *Regarding Television: Critical Approaches—An Anthology.* Frederick Md.: American Film Institute/University Publications of America, 1983.

Kaufman, William I., ed. *The Best Television Plays, 1950-1951.* New York: Hastings House, 1952.

———. *The Best Television Plays.* New York: Merlin Press, 1952.

———. *The Best Television Plays,* vol. 3. New York: Merlin Press, 1954.

———. *The Best Television Plays 1957.* New York: Harcourt Brace, 1957.

———. *How to Write for Television.* New York: Hastings House, 1955.

Kaufman, William I., and Robert S Colodzin. *Your Career in Television.* New York: Merlin Press, 1950.

Kerby, Philip. *The Victory of Television.* New York: Harper and Brothers, 1939.

Kesten, Paul. *Postwar Shortwave, FM, and Television.* New York: Columbia Broadcasting System, 1944.

Kindem, Gorham, ed. *The American Movie Industry: The Business of Motion Pictures.* Carbondale: Southern Illinois University Press, 1982.

Kittross, John M. *Television Frequency Allocation Policy in the United States.* New York: Arno Press, 1979.

Konecky, Eugene. *The American Communications Conspiracy.* New York: People's Radio Foundation, 1948.

Krasnow, Erwin G., and Lawrence D. Longley. *The Politics of Broadcast Regulation,* 2d ed. New York: St. Martin's Press, 1978.

Lee, Chin-Chuan. *Media Imperialism Reconsidered.* Beverly Hills: Sage Publications, 1980.

Lessing, Lawrence. *Man of High Fidelity: Edwin Howard Armstrong.* New York: Bantam Books, 1969.

Levin, Harvey J. *The Invisible Resource: Use and Regulation of the Radio Spectrum.* Baltimore: Johns Hopkins University Press, 1971.

Levinson, Richard, and William Link. *Off Camera: Conversations with the Makers of Prime-Time Television.* New York: New American Library, 1986.

———. *Stay Tuned: An Inside Look at the Making of Prime-Time Television.* New York: St. Martin's Press, 1981.

Lippmann, Walter. *The Essential Lippmann: A Political Philosophy for Liberal Democracy.* Edited by Clinton Rossiter and James Lare. New York: Random House, 1963.

Litman, Barry Russell. *The Vertical Structure of the Television Broadcasting Industry: The Coalescence of Power.* East Lansing: Michigan State University Press, 1979.

Lohr, Lenox R. *Television Broadcasting: Production, Economics, Technique.* New York: McGraw-Hill Book Company, 1940.

Long, Stuart Lewis. *The Development of the Television Network Oligopoly.* New York: Arno Press, 1979.

Lyons, Eugene. *David Sarnoff.* New York: Harper and Row, 1966.

MacCabe, Colin, ed. *High Theory/Low Culture: Analysing Popular Television and Film.* Manchester: Manchester University Press, 1986.

Mannes, Marya, ed. *The Relation of the Writer to Television.* Santa Barbara: Center for the Study of Democratic Institutions, 1960.

———. *Demographic Vistas: Television in American Culture.* Philadelphia: University of Pennsylvania Press, 1984.

Marc, David. *Comic Visions: Television Comedy and American Culture.* Boston: Unwin Hyman, 1989.

Masterman, Len, ed. *Television Mythologies: Stars, Shows and Signs.* London: Comedia Publishing Group/MK Media Press, 1984.

McArthur, Colin. *BFI Television Monograph 8: Television and History.* London: British Film Institute, 1978.

McLaurin, W. Rupert. *Invention and Innovation in the Radio Industry.* New York: Macmillan, 1949.

Mehling, Harold. *The Great Time-Killer.* Cleveland: World Publishing, 1962.

Miller, Mark Crispin. *Boxed In: The Culture of TV.* Evanston, Ill.: Northwestern University Press, 1988.

Minow, Newton. *Equal Time.* New York: Atheneum, 1964.

Modleski, Tania. *Loving with a Vengeance: Mass-Produced Fantasies for Women.* Hamden Conn.: Archon Books, 1982.

_____. ed. *Studies in Entertainment: Critical Approaches to Mass Culture.* Bloomington: Indiana University Press, 1986.

Morganstein, Steve, ed. *Inside the TV Business.* New York: Sterling Publishing, 1979.

Morley, David. *BFI Television Monograph 11: The Nationwide Audience: Structure and Decoding.* London: British Film Institute, 1982.

Mosco, Vincent. *Broadcasting in the United States: Innovative Challenge and Organizational Control.* Norwood N.J.: Ablex Publishing, 1979.

Mosel, Tad. *Other People's Houses.* New York: Simon and Schuster, 1956.

Museum of Broadcasting. *Columbia Pictures Television: The Studio and the Creative Process.* New York: Museum of Broadcasting, 1987.

_____. *KTLA: West Coast Pioneer.* New York: Museum of Broadcasting, 1985.

_____. *Lucille Ball: First Lady of Comedy.* New York: Museum of Broadcasting, 1984.

_____. *Metromedia and the DuMont Legacy.* New York: Museum of Broadcasting, 1985.

_____. *Produced by . . . Herb Brodkin.* New York: Museum of Broadcasting, 1985.

_____. *Rod Serling: Dimensions of Imagination.* New York: Museum of Broadcasting, 1984.

_____. *Television Syndication: Seminars at the Museum of Broadcasting.* New York: Museum of Broadcasting, 1986.

National Broadcasting Company. *NBC Television Profile April 1950.* New York: National Broadcasting Company, 1950.

Newcomb, Horace, ed. *Television: The Critical View,* 4th ed. New York: Oxford University Press, 1987.

Newcomb, Horace, and Dick Adler. *The Producer's Medium: Conversations with Creators of American TV.* New York: Oxford University Press, 1983.

Noll, Roger C., Merton J. Peck, and John McGowan. *Economic Aspects of Television Regulation.* Washington, D.C.: Brookings Institution, 1973.

O'Connor, John E., ed. *American History/American Television: Interpreting the Video Past.* New York: Frederick Ungar, 1983.

O'Meara, Carroll. *Television Program Production.* New York: Ronald Press, 1955.

Opotowsky, Stan. *TV: The Big Picture.* New York: E. P. Dutton, 1961.

Owen, Bruce, Jack Beebe, and Willard Manning. *Television Economics.* Lexington Mass.: D.C. Heath, 1974.

Paley, William S. *As It Happened.* New York: Doubleday, 1979.

Paper, Lewis J. *Empire: William S. Paley and the Making of CBS.* New York: St. Martin's Press, 1987.

Peatman, John Gray, ed. *Radio and Business 1945: Proceedings of the First Annual Conference on Radio and Business.* New York: City College of New York, 1945.

Porterfield, John, and Kay Reynolds, eds. *We Present Television.* New York: Norton, 1940.

Quinlan, Sterling. *The Hundred Million Dollar Lunch.* Chicago: J. Philip O'Hara, 1974.

———. *Inside ABC.* New York: Hastings House, 1979.

Radio Corporation of America. *Television Progress and Promise.* New York: Radio Corporation of America, 1941.

Read, William H. *America's Mass Media Merchants.* Baltimore: Johns Hopkins University Press, 1976.

Root, Jane. *Open the Box.* London: Comedia Publishing Group/Channel Four, 1986.

Rose, Reginald. *Six Television Plays.* New York: Simon and Schuster, 1956.

Ross, Andrew. *No Respect: Intellectuals and Popular Culture.* New York: Routledge, 1989.

Rowland, Willard D., Jr. *The Politics of TV Violence.* Beverly Hills: Sage Publications, 1983.

Rowland, Willard D., Jr., and Bruce Watkins, eds. *Interpreting Television: Current Research Perspectives.* Beverly Hills: Sage Publications, 1984.

Royal, John F., ed. *Television Production Problems.* New York: McGraw-Hill, 1948.

Schaffner, Franklin. *Worthington Miner.* Metuchen N.J.: Directors Guild of America Oral History/Scarecrow Press, 1985.

Schiller, Herbert I. *Mass Communications and American Empire.* Boston: Beacon Press, 1971.

Schwartz, Bernard. *The Professor and the Commissions.* New York: Alfred A. Knopf, 1959.

Seldes, Gilbert. *The Great Audience.* New York: Viking Press, 1950.

———. *The Public Arts.* New York: Simon and Schuster, 1956.

———. *Writing for Television.* New York: Doubleday, 1952.

Serling, Rod. *Patterns.* New York: Simon and Schuster, 1957.

Settel, Irving and Norman Glenn. *Television Advertising and Production Handbook.* New York: Thomas Y. Cronwell, 1953.

Shiers, George, ed. *Technical Development of Television.* New York: Arno Press, 1977.

Siepmann, Charles A. *Radio Second Chance.* Boston: Little, Brown, 1946.

———. *Radio, Television and Society.* New York: Oxford University Press, 1950.

Simonson, Solomon. *Crisis in Television.* New York: Living Books, 1966.

Skornia, Harry J., and Jack William Kitson, eds. *Problems and Controversies in Television and Radio.* Palo Alto: Pacific Books, 1968.

Slater, Robert. *This ... Is CBS.* Englewood Cliffs, N.J.: Prentice-Hall, 1988.

Sperber, A. M. *Murrow: His Life and Times.* New York: Freudlich Books, 1986.

Stasheff, Edward, and Rudy Bretz, eds. *The Television Program.* New York: A. Wyn, 1951.

Steiner, Gary A. *The People Look at Television: A Study of Audience Attitudes.* New York: Alfred A. Knopf, 1963.

Sterling, Christopher H., and Timothy R. Haight. *The Mass Media: Aspen Institute Guide to Communication Industry Trends.* New York: Praeger Publishers, 1978.

Sterling, Christopher H., and John Kittross. *Stay Tuned: A Concise History of American Television.* Belmont, Calif.: Wadsworth Publishing, 1978.

Stern, Robert H. *The FCC and Television: The Regulatory Process in an Environment of Rapid Technological Innovation.* New York: Arno Press, 1979.

Stuart, Frederick. *The Effects of Television on the Motion-Picture and Radio Industries.* New York: Arno Press, 1976.

Udelson, Joseph H. *The Great Television Race.* University: University of Alabama Press, 1982.

Verna, Tony. *Live TV: An Inside Look at Directing and Producing.* Boston: Focal Press, 1987.

Waldrop, Frank C., and Joseph Borkin. *Television—A Struggle for Power.* New York: William Morrow, 1938.

Weinberg, Meyer. *TV in America: The Morality of Hard Cash.* New York: Ballantine, 1962.

Western, Alan F., ed. *The Uses of Power: Seven Cases in American Policy.* New York: Harcourt Brace World, 1962.

Wicking, Christopher, and Tise Vahimagi. *The American Vein: Directors and Directions in Television.* New York: E. P. Dutton, 1979.

Wilk, Max. *The Golden Age of Television: Notes from the Survivors.* New York: Delacorte, 1976.

Williams, Raymond. *Television: Technology and Cultural Form.* New York: Schocken Books, 1975.

Wilson, H. H. *Pressure Group: The Campaign for Commercial Television in England.* New Brunswick: Rutgers University Press, 1961.

Winick, Charles. *Taste and the Censor in Television.* New York: Fund for the Republic, 1959.

Winston, Brian. *Misunderstanding Media.* Cambridge: Harvard University Press, 1986.

II. Periodicals

"ABC Crowds Out the Other TV Networks." *Business Week,* May 9, 1959, p. 46.

"The abc of ABC." *Forbes,* June 15, 1959, pp. 15-18.

"AB-PT 'Full Speed Ahead' Sets in Motion '30,000,000 Agenda.'" *Variety,* February 11, 1953, p. 1.

Adams, Charles. "The Stage Director in Television." *Theatre Arts,* October, 1951, pp. 46-48.

Adams, Jack. "Washington: The Scalpels Are Sharpened." *Television,* May 1957, p. 118.

Adams, Val. "Network Accuses Film Syndicators." *New York Times,* May 28, 1956. p. 51.

"Ad Men Pose Top Radio-TV Questions for 1955." *Sponsor,* January 10, 1955, p. 38.

"Ad Men Retort Sharply to TV Writers' Diatribe." *Printer's Ink,* July 29, 1960, pp. 13-14.

"The Agencies Still Have the Final Say in Programming." *Television,* June 1955, p. 39.

"Americans a Little Less Fascinated by Television Programs This Year." *Business Week,* October 27, 1956, p. 2.

"Another 'Meat and Potatoes' Year for Network TV?" *Sponsor,* June 1, 1957, pp. 38-39.

"Anyone Hurt by Sarnoff Blast?" *Broadcasting,* November 28, 1960, p. 28.

"Armstrong of Radio." *Fortune,* February 1948, pp. 88-91.

"As the Film Men See It." *Television,* July 1956, p. 51

Aurthur, Robert Alan. "Creative Rating-Zero." *TV Guide,* June 17, 1961, pp. 27-29.

"'Average TV Station's' 10% Biz Hike in '59; Radio's 5% Increase." *Variety,* July 6, 1960, p. 29.

Aylesworth, Merlin. "'Radio Is Movies' Best Friend.'" *Broadcasting,* August 1, 1936, pp. 9, 60-61.

"Backing for CBS." *Business Week,* November 4, 1944, p. 88.

Balten, Will. "Television Chaos Avoided." *Televiser*, Fall 1944, pp. 52, 64.

Barrow, Roscoe L. "Antitrust and the Regulated Industry: Promoting Competition in Broadcasting." *Duke Law Journal*, September 1964, pp. 282-306.

_____. "Network Broadcasting—The Report of the FCC Network Study Staff." *Law and Contemporary Problems* 22 (Autumn 1957): 611-25.

Baughman, James L. "'The Strange Birth of *CBS Reports*' Revisited." *Historical Journal of Film, Radio and Television* 2 (1982): 27-38.

"Be Careful on the Air." *Sponsor*, September 10, 1951, p. 30.

"Be Careful on the Air, Part II." *Sponsor*, September 24, 1951, p. 37.

Beatty, J. Frank. "Sniping at Radio-TV: New National Pastime." *Broadcasting-Telecasting*, April 9, 1956, p. 121.

Bendiner, Robert. "The FCC: Who Will Regulate the Regulator?" *Reporter*, September 19, 1957, pp. 26-30.

Bergerman, Jean. "One Party Television Too?" *New Republic*, February 23, 1953, pp. 17-18.

"Big Men on the Paper." *Newsweek*, April 15, 1957, p. 104.

"Billion Dollar Whipping Boy." *Television Age*, November 4, 1957, pp. 29-31.

Black, John. "What Television Offers as a Selling Medium." *Printer's Ink*, March 30, 1939, pp. 63-68.

"Black Tuesday at the NAB Convention." *Broadcasting*, September 15, 1961, p. 36.

Boddy, William. "Entering the 'Twilight Zone.'" *Screen* 25 (July-October 1984): 98-108.

_____. "Operation Frontal Lobes versus the Living Room Toy: The Battle Over Program Control in Early Television." *Media, Culture and Society* 9 (July 1987): 347-68.

_____. "The Rhetoric and the Economic Roots of the American Broadcasting Industry." *Cinetracts*, Spring 1979, pp. 37-54.

_____. "'The Shining Centre of the Home': Ontologies of Television in the Golden Age." in *Television in Transition: Papers from the First International Television Studies Conference*, edited by Phillip Drummond and Richard Paterson, pp. 125-34. London: British Film Institute, 1985.

Bodic, Ben, and Alfred J. Jaffee. "Talent Agents: Have They Won Control over TV Costs?" *Sponsor*, January 24, 1955, pp. 35-37.

_____. "Talent Agents: What's the Alternative to Paying Their Price?" *Sponsor*, February 7, 1955, p. 36.

Bourjaily, Vance. "The Lost Art of Writing for Television." *Harper's*, October 1959, pp. 151-57.

"Box Office's Job." *Business Week*, June 17, 1944, p. 90.

"Broadcasters' Prestige Highest Ever." *Advertising Age*, November 21, 1960, pp. 1, 134.

Brown, Les. "Proposal for an Industry-Wide Testing Laboratory." *Variety*, November 29, 1959, p. 32.

Browne, Nick. "The Political Economy of the Television (Super) Text." *Quarterly Review of Film Studies* 9 (Summer 1984): 174-82.

Bryant, Ashbrook P. "Historical and Social Aspects of Concentration of Program Control in Television." *Law and Contemporary Problems* 34 (Summer 1969): 610-35.

Buscombe, Ed. "Thinking It Differently: Television and the Film Industry." *Quarterly Review of Film Studies* 9 (Summer 1984): 196-203.

"The Busy Air." *Time*, December 9, 1957, pp. 79-80, 82.

"California as a Program Source." *Television*, April 1951, p. 38.

"Can the FCC End the Seller's Market in TV?" *Sponsor*, April 2, 1956, p. 26.

Carpenter, Les. "The Big Payoff—A Congress-Inspired TV Law in '60?" *Variety*, May 4, 1960, p. 29.

_____. "TV Out of 'Wasteland': Minow." *Variety*, December 13, 1961, p. 1.

_____. "Week the Senate Ganged Up: FCC, Industry Get a Drubbing." *Variety*, May 4, 1960, pp. 44.

"CBS Steals the Show." *Fortune*, July 1953, p. 79.

"CBS to Build World's Largest Video Plant." *Broadcasting*, February 23, 1948, p. 14.

Celler, Emanuel. "Antitrust Problems in the Television Broadcasting Industry." *Law and Contemporary Problems* 22 (Autumn 1957): 549-71.

Chalfin, L. N. "A Psychologist Looks at Television." *Televiser*, Winter 1945, p. 37.

Chandler, Bob. "TV Films: An Updated Version of Freewheeling Picture Pioneers." *Variety*, January 4, 1956, p. 9.

Christopher, Maurine. "Mehling's *Great Time-Killer* Finds TV Blameworthy in Practically All Respects." *Advertising Age*, June 4, 1962, p. 109.

Cohen, Ralph M. "Cycles Pass, Quality Stays." *Television*, January 1957, p. 45.

"Congress' Job." *Broadcasting*, February 1, 1960, p. 40.

Coulson, T. "Is Television Ripe for the Picking?" *Forum*, July 1933, pp. 35-39.

"Creators Turn on the Created." *Broadcasting*, June 26, 1961, p. 32.

"Critics Blast TV Advertiser." *Sponsor*, February 6, 1960, pp. 34-35.

"The Critics Choose." *Television*, December 1956, p. 111.

"The Critics' Viewpoint." *Television*, November 1955, p. 64.

Crosby, John. "It Was New and We Were Very Innocent." *TV Guide*, September 22, 1973, pp. 5-8.

Cuniff, Robert. "Selznick Talks About Television." *Television,* February 1955, p. 32.

Cunningham, John P. "'Creeping Mediocrity' Bringing Boredom to TV: It's Advertiser's Worry, Cunningham Warns." *Advertising Age,* December 2, 1957, pp. 65-67.

"Curtain Falls on FCC Hearings." *Broadcasting,* February 8, 1960, p. 60.

Davidson, Ross. "The New Television Playwright and His Markets." *Writer,* April, 1962, pp. 58-62.

"Delicacy and Violence." *Time,* June 26, 1950, p. 49.

"Disillusion Between the Lines." *Television,* June 6, 1961, p. 92.

"Disney: How Old Is a Child?" *Television,* December 1954, p. 72.

"Doerfer for Clipp Review Plan." *Broadcasting,* February 8, 1960, p. 29.

"Dominicans File MBS Suit: Seek to Recover $750,000 from Guerma et al." *Broadcasting,* September 14, 1959, p. 48.

Dominick, Joseph R., and Millard C. Pearce, "Trends in Network Prime-Time Programming, 1953-74." *Journal of Communication,* 26 (Winter 1976): 70-80.

"DuMont: 'Created a Frankenstein.'" *Variety,* June 21, 1961, p. 23.

Dunville, Robert E. "TV's Need for Self-Criticism." *Television,* January 1959, p. 41.

Eaton, Mick. "Television Situation Comedy." *Screen* 19 (1978): 61-89.

"Editorial." *Television,* Spring 1944, p. 1.

"Fall Film Outlook." *Television Age,* August 1955, p. 46.

"The FCC Allocation Controversy." *Television Century,* Spring 1945, pp. 20-21.

"FCC Inquiry Hears Roper Data." *Broadcasting,* December 21, 1959, pp. 36-37.

"FCC's Durr, Others Wonder Whether Radio Knows What the People Want." *Variety,* June 20, 1945, p. 30.

"FCC's Network Program Hearing Continues." *Broadcasting,* January 22, 1962, p. 43.

"Feature Film's Spectacular Impact." *Sponsor,* October 15, 1956, pp. 27-28.

"Film Basics." *Sponsor,* July 12, 1954, p. 186.

"Film for '52.'" *Newsweek,* August 11, 1952, p. 54.

Film: Its Supply and Demand." *Broadcasting-Telecasting,* November 21, 1955, p. 28.

"Film vs. Live Shows." *Time,* March 29, 1954, p. 77.

"Filmed TV." *Newsweek,* February 12, 1951, p. 78.

"Film's $100,000,000 Year." *Sponsor,* January 23, 1956, p. 31.

"First-run Film Series: Its Heyday Is Past." *Broadcasting,* May 8, 1961, pp. 84, 86, 88.

Fiske, Irving. "Where Does Television Belong?" *Harper's*, February 1940, pp. 265-69.

"500 TV Stations: How Major Agencies See the Picture." *Sponsor*, January 12, 1953, p. 23.

Flitterman-Lewis, Sandy. "All's Well That Doesn't End: Soap Operas and the Marriage Motif." *Camera Obscura*, no. 16 (January 1988): 119-28.

"Fly Urges Video in High Frequencies." *Broadcasting*, September 25, 1944, p. 13.

"*Fortune's* Unfortunate TV Guess." *Sponsor*, November 19, 1962, p. 39.

Garon, Jay. "Free-lancing for Television." *Writer*, July 1951, pp. 219-21.

"Getting to Know You Themes B'casters Vox Pop on Minow." *Variety*, April 3, 1963, p. 24.

Gilbert, Robert. "Television 1953—Wall Street." *Television*, January 1953, p. 36.

Gitlin, Todd. "Media Sociology: The Dominant Paradigm." *Theory and Society*, 6 (1978): 205-53.

Goldsmith, Alfred. "Stability vs. Chaos." *Television*, October 1948, p. 24.

———. "Theatre Television." *Television*, September 1947, p. 39.

Gomery, Douglas. "Failed Opportunities: The Integration of the U.S. Motion Picture and Television Industries." *Quarterly Review of Film Studies* 9 (Summer 1984): 219-29.

———. "Theatre Television: The Missing Link of Technological Change in the U.S. Motion Picture Industry." *Velvet Light Trap*, no. 21 (Summer 1985): 44-54.

Gould, Jack. "CBS and the Sponsors." *New York Times*, February 7, 1960, sec. 2, p. 15.

———. "Forecast of TV Ahead: Far from Fair." *New York Times*, July 3, 1960, sec. 2, p. 11.

———. "Forgotten Man Panel Concludes that Artistic Author Has Been Stymied by Television." *New York Times*, August 7, 1960, sec. 2, p. 11.

———. "Give and Take: Criticisms and Defense of TV Industry Can Pave Way to Improved Medium." *New York Times*, April 29, 1956, sec. 2, p. 13.

———. "Half-Act Drama." *New York Times*, February 10, 1952, sec. 2, p. 13.

———. "'Live' TV vs. 'Canned.'" *New York Times Magazine*, February 5, 1956, p. 27.

———. "NBC Leads the Field in Video Funny Men." *New York Times*, September 24, 1950, sec. 2, p. 11.

———. "A Plague on TV's House." *New York Times*, October 12, 1959, p. 39.

———. "A Plea for Live Video." *New York Times*, December 7, 1952, sec. 2, p. 17.

_____. "Quiz for TV: How Much Fakery?" *New York Times Magazine*, October 25, 1959, p. 74.

_____. "Television Today—A Critic's Appraisal." *New York Times Magazine*, April 8, 1956, pp. 12-13.

_____. "TV Faces Series of U.S. Inquiries, First Tomorrow." *New York Times*, June 1, 1956, p. 1.

_____. "TV Films Boom Hollywood into Its Greatest Prosperity." *New York Times*, July 3, 1955, p. 1.

_____. "TV: One Long Plug." *New York Times*, July 25, 1955, p. 41.

_____. "TV Quiz Aftermath." *New York Times*, October 23, 1960, sec. 2, p. 13.

_____. "TV: Sarnoff's Panacea." *New York Times*, January 30, 1960, p. 43.

_____. "TV: Why All the Fuss?" *New York Times*, January 24, 1958, p. 47.

_____. "Two Networks on the Spot." *New York Times*, April 8, 1956, sec. 2, p. 13.

_____. "The Vanishing Frontier." *New York Times*, June 17, 1956, sec. 2, p. 11.

_____. "Video Version of Broadway Play Cancelled in Dispute Over Theme." *New York Times*, January 13, 1953, p. 32.

_____. "What's with TV?" *New York Times*, May 27, 1962, sec. 7, p. 14.

"Grand Jury Indicts Guterma Trio: Charged with Selling MBS as Dominican Propaganda Vehicle." *Broadcasting*, September 7, 1959, pp. 68-70.

"The Great Debate on Network Show Control." *Sponsor*, October 31, 1955, p. 38.

Greeley, Bill. "Agencies on Network Treatment: 'It's the Last Time They'll Give Us This Sort of Kicking Around.'" *Variety*, April 27, 1960, p. 30.

_____. "Writers Blast Dearth of Quality TV, Blame 'Controls' & 'Cost-Per-M.'" *Variety*, June 21, 1961, pp. 1, 45.

Hanson, Victor R. "Broadcasting and the Antitrust Laws." *Law and Contemporary Problems* 22 (Autumn 1957): 572-83.

"Happy New Year." *Broadcasting*, December 28, 1959, p. 74.

Haralovich, Mary Beth. "Sitcoms and Suburbs: Positioning the 1950s Homemaker." *Quarterly Review of Film and Video* 11 (1989): 61-84.

Harbord, J. G. "Commercial Uses of Radio." *Annals of the American Academy of Political and Social Science* 142 supplement (March 1929): 57-63.

"Hardly a Scratch in TV's Image." *Broadcasting*, November 2, 1959, pp. 41-44.

Harris, Leslie. "The Thorny Side of Syndicated Film." *Broadcasting-Telecasting*, November 8, 1954, p. 94.

Hart, Walter. "Directing for TV." *Theatre Arts*, February, 1951, p. 51.

"Have Sponsors Stopped Taking Program Risks in TV?" *Sponsor,* December 1, 1952, p. 24.

"Have TV Show Costs Reached Their Ceiling?" *Sponsor,* September 21, 1953, p. 106.

Hawley, Lowell S. "Looking What TV's Doing to Hollywood." *The Saturday Evening Post,* February 7, 1953, p. 34.

"Haynes Blasts TV's 'Cultural Tyranny.'" *Variety,* February 14, 1962, p. 34.

Heath, Dick B., and J. Raymond Hutchinson. "Making Motion Pictures for Television." *Televiser,* Spring 1945, p. 29.

"He Who Throws Stones." *Broadcasting,* February 15, 1960, p. 166.

"High Stakes in a Big Giveaway." *Business Week,* March 22, 1952, pp. 21-22.

"Hollywood Cameras Grind Out Film Fare for TV." *Business Week,* November 24, 1951, p. 125.

"Hollywood Digs In." *Business Week,* March 24, 1945, p. 92.

"Hollywood Learns to Live with TV." *Business Week,* August 9, 1952, pp. 43-48.

"Hollywood Report." *Television,* August 1948, p. 55.

"Hollywood and TV." *Life,* February 25, 1952, p. 20.

Horowitz, Murray. "Vidfilm-Webs % Marriage." *Variety,* April 27, 1960, p. 27.

Houseman, John. "Battle Over Television: Hollywood Faces the Fifties." *Harper's,* May 1950, pp. 50-59.

"How Film Distributors Would Change Network Television." *Sponsor,* June 11, 1956, pp. 30-31.

"How *Fortune* Tipped Off the New Anti-TV 'Party Line.'" *Sponsor,* November 29, 1958, p. 33.

"How Hollywood Hopes to Hit the Comeback Trail." *Newsweek,* January 12, 1953, p. 108.

"How TV's 'Program Mess' Hits the Sponsor." *Sponsor,* July 12, 1958, p. 29.

"How to Use TV Films Effectively." *Sponsor,* June 19, 1950, p. 33.

Hunter, Mary. "The Stage Director in Television." *Theatre Arts,* May 1949, pp. 46-47.

Ingram, Larry. "Network TV Faces Day of Reckoning." *Sunday Denver Post,* November 20, 1960, p. AA1.

"Is the Programming Subsidy Era Over in Network TV?" *Sponsor,* September 8, 1952, p. 83.

"Is the Rush to Film Shows Economically Sound?" *Sponsor,* July 28, 1952, pp. 66-70.

"Is There a Programmming Crisis?" *Television,* February 1957, p. 50.

"Is TV in Trouble?" *U. S. News and World Report,* October 26, 1959, pp. 44-45.

Jaffe, Alfred J. "Are Agencies Earning Their Fifteen Percent on Network TV Shows?" *Sponsor*, October 18, 1954, p. 29.

Jaffe, Louis F. "The Scandal in TV Licensing." *Harper's*, September 1957, pp. 79-84.

James, T. F. "The Millionaire Class of Young Writers." *Cosmopolitan*, August 1958, p. 40.

Jowett, Garth. "The Machine in the Text: Technology in Introductory Mass Communication Texts." *Critical Studies in Mass Communication* 1 (December 1984): 442-46.

Joyrich, Lynne. "All That Television Allows: TV Melodrama, Postmodernism and Consumer Culture." *Camera Obscura*, no. 16 (January 1988): 129-54.

"Just About All There Is to Say About TV." *Television*, February 1963, p. 49.

Kass, Robert. "Radio and TV." *Catholic World*, June 1956, p. 225.

"Keep It Clean." *Newsweek*, November 17, 1952, p. 68.

Kennedy, Roger. "Programming Content and Quality." *Law and Contemporary Problems* 22 (Autumn 1957): 541-48.

"Kintner Rejects Huckster Charge." *New York Times*, April 18, 1956, p. 63.

Konrad, Evelyn. "The Critics Be Damned!" *Sponsor*, October 19, 1957, pp. 31-31, 90, 92.

――――. "Will 'Outside' Packagers Reshape TV?" *Sponsor*, April 20, 1957, pp. 27-28.

Kroeger, Albert R. "Dark Days in Syndication." *Television*, October 1961, pp. 36-39.

――――. "Programming: Short Supply, Big Demand." *Television*, April 1964, p. 72.

Kugel, Frederick. "The Economics of Film." *Television*, July 1951, p. 45.

――――. "L'Affaire Firestone." *Television*, May 1959, p. 112.

――――. "Thank You Senator Benton and Mr Rubicam!" *Television*, November 1951, p. 11.

――――. "Threat to our Economy." *Television*, February 1950, p. 11.

Land, Herman. "After the Western—What?" *Television*, July 1958, p. 55.

――――. "The Spectacular: An Interim Report." *Sponsor*, November 15, 1954, p. 31.

Lane, Stanley R. "Films as a Source of Programming." *Television*, May 1946, p. 14.

Lazarsfeld, Paul. "A Researcher Looks at Television." *Public Opinion Quarterly* 24 (Spring 1960): 24-31.

Lessing, Lawrence. "The Electronics Era." *Fortune*, July 1951, pp. 78-83.

――――. "The Television Freeze." *Fortune*, November 1949, pp. 123-27.

Levey, Arthur. "Who Will Control Television?" *Television*, Spring 1944, p. 25.

Levin, Harvey J. "The Economic Effects of Broadcast Licensing." *Journal of Political Economy* 72 (April 1964): 151-62.

_____. "Federal Control of Entry in the Broadcast Industry." *Journal of Law and Economics* 5 (October 1962): 49-67.

Levy, Sidney J. "The Sponsor: More to Be Pitied then Censured." *Sales Management,* November 6, 1959, pp. 46-47.

Lincoln, Freeman. "Comeback of the Movies." *Fortune,* February 1955, pp. 127-31.

"Lining Up for TV's Big Battle." *Business Week,* March 10, 1956, p. 66.

Lipsitz, George. "The Meaning of Family, Class and Ethnicity in Early Network Television Programs." *Camera Obscura,* no. 16 (January 1988): 79-118.

Litman, Barry R. "The Affiliation Agreement in U. S. Broadcasting: The Tie That Binds." *Telecommunications Policy,* June 1979, pp. 116-25.

_____. "The Economics of the Television Market for Theatrical Movies." *Journal of Communication* 29 (Autumn 1979): 20-33.

_____. "The Television Networks, Competition, and Program Diversity." *Journal of Broadcasting* 23 (Fall 1979): 393-409.

"Live, Spontaneous, Unrehearsed." *Broadcasting,* March 7, 1960, pp. 60-61.

"'Live' TV: It Went Thataway." *Variety,* May 4, 1960, p. 23.

Longley, Lawrence D. "The FM Shift in 1945." *Journal of Broadcasting* 12 (Fall 1968): 353-65.

MacKaye, Milton. "The Big Brawl: Hollywood vs. Television." *The Saturday Evening Post:* Part 1, January 19, 1952, pp. 17-19, 70-72; Part 2, January 26, 1952, pp. 30, 119-22; Part 3, February 2, 1952, pp. 30, 100-02.

MacLauren, W. Rupert. "Patents and Technical Progress—A Study of Television." *The Journal of Political Economy* 58 (April 1950): 142-57.

"Magazine Concept a Panacea for Program Evils? Hardly." *Variety,* November 25, 1959, p. 32.

"Majors Worry Syndicators." *Variety,* May 11, 1955, p. 39.

"The Man Doerfer." *Broadcasting,* January 18, 1960, p. 30.

Mann, Denise. "The Spectacularization of Everyday Life: Recycling Hollywood Stars in Early Television Variety Programs." *Camera Obscura,* no. 16 (January 1988): 49-78.

Mannes, Marya. "The TV Pattern: Signs of Revolt." *Reporter,* May 2, 1957, pp. 19-22.

Marlowe, Harvey. "Drama's Place in Television." *Television,* March 1946, p. 17.

Martin, John Bartlow. "Television USA": Part 1: "Wasteland or Wonderland?" *The Saturday Evening Post,* October 21, 1961, pp. 19-25; Part 2: "Battle of the Big Three." *The Saturday Evening Post,* October 28, 1961, pp. 56-58, 60-62; Part 3: "The Master Planners." *The Saturday Evening Post,* November 4, 1961, pp. 34, 36-39; Part 4: "Conclusion: The Big Squeeze." *The Saturday Evening Post,* November 4, 1961, pp. 62, 64, 66, 68, 71-72.

Mayer, Martin. "ABC: Portrait of a Network." *Show,* September 1961, pp. 59-63.

———. "TV's Lords of Creation." *Harper's,* November 1956, pp. 26-32.

———"MCA—Putting the Business in Show Business." *Forbes,* November 15, 1965, pp. 20-25.

McGannon, Donald. "There's Room for Features, Network Too." *Television,* January 1957, p. 41.

"Measuring the Giant." *Time,* November 9, 1959, pp. 77-78.

Meehan, Eileen R. "Critical Theorizing on Broadcast History." *Journal of Broadcasting* 30 (Fall 1986): 393-411.

"The Millionaire Class of Young Writers." *Cosmopolitan,* August 1958, p. 41.

Millstein, Gilbert. "'Patterns' of a Television Playwright." *New York Times Magazine,* December 2, 1956, p. 24.

"Minow Observes 'A Vast Wasteland.'" *Broadcasting,* May 15, 1961, pp. 58-60.

"More Charges on Radio-TV: 'Payola'...Rigged 'Interviews'...Fraud... Deceit...'Freebies.'" *U. S. News and World Report,* December 28, 1959, pp. 40-41.

Morse, Leon. "Hubbell Robinson Evaluates TV Programming Today." *Television,* December 1959, pp. 49-50.

———. "Inside Jack Gould." *Television,* November 1958, p. 49.

"Movies—End of an Era?" *Fortune,* April 1949, pp. 98-102.

"The Movie Makers Look for Gold in the TV Screen." *Business Week,* April 23, 1955, p. 156.

Murray, Lawrence L. "Complacency, Competition and Cooperation: The Film Industry Responds to the Challenge of Television." *Journal of Popular Film* 6 (1977): 47-70.

Murrow, Edward R. "A Broadcaster Talks to His Colleagues." *Reporter,* November 13, 1958, pp. 32-36.

"Mysteries: They Love 'em on TV!" *Sponsor,* October 23, 1950, p. 32.

"NBC Chairman Would Keep Honest Quizes." *New York Herald Tribune,* November 13, 1959, p. 15.

"NBC Ruffles Calm as Hearing Continues." *Broadcasting,* February 5, 1962, p. 46.

"Network Accuses Film Syndicators." *New York Times,* May 28, 1956, p. 51.

"Network Regulation Bill Appears Doomed." *Editor and Publisher,* June 23, 1956, p. 65.

"Network TV Lineup: Tear It Down, Build It Up." *Sponsor,* May 14, 1956, p. 28.

"New Season a Dud." *Variety,* October 2, 1957, p. 1.

"New Wave of Criticism." *Television Age,* December 11, 1961, p. 75.

"1939—Television Year." *Business Week,* December 31, 1938, p. 17.

"One Round to CBS." *Business Week,* September 3, 1949, p. 24.

Orme, Frank. "TV's Most Important Show." *Television,* June 1955, p. 34.

"Packagers (Not Nets) Lead in Building New Shows." *Sponsor,* January 28, 1952, p. 31.

"Packaging Returns to the Networks." *Sponsor,* January 16, 1950, p. 21.

"Paramount Enters Television; Would Utilize Motion Pictures." *Motion Picture World,* August 13, 1938, p. 17.

"People Are Talking About." *Vogue,* April 1, 1957, p. 138.

"Post-Freeze TV: What Advertisers Ask About It." *Sponsor,* June 2, 1952, p. 70.

"Program Sources Drying Up?" *Broadcasting,* September 18, 1961, pp. 19-20.

"The Programmers." *Television,* February 1950, p. 14.

"Programming." *Television,* Spring 1944, p. 21.

"Programming." *Television,* May 1947, p. 31.

"The Promise of Television." *Fortune,* August 1943, pp. 140-44.

Pryor, Thomas M. "Hollywood Dilemma: Fine Films Sold to TV Now Haunt Industry." *New York Times,* September 23, 1956, sec. 2, p. 7.

"Quiz Biz Starts New York Legal Fiz." *Editor and Publisher,* September 6, 1959, p. 47.

"Quiz Shows Stalked by Mr. DA." *Broadcasting,* September 1, 1958, p. 42.

"Radio and Filmdom Both Keep Eye on Television." *New York Times,* July 28, 1940, sec. 2, p. 10.

Raibourn, Paul. "Theatre Television Is Here!" *Television,* April 1948, p. 26.

Rand, Abby. "The Fall Programming Outlook." *Television,* June 1957, pp. 45-46, 115.

———. "Feature Film Goes Bigtime." *Television,* April 1956, p. 52.

———. "The Outlook for Film." *Television,* July 1957, p. 63.

———. "2500 Films—How Will They Change TV?" *Telelvision,* July 1956, p. 64.

"Rating Madness—An Editorial." *Sponsor,* November 30, 1951, pp. 30-31.

"RCA's Television." *Fortune,* September 1948, pp. 80-85.

"Reaction to the Barrow Report." *Television,* November 1957, p. 118.

"Report to Sponsors." *Sponsor,* July 25, 1955, pp. 1-2; August 6, 1956, pp. 1-2; August 20, 1956, pp. 1-2; September 3, 1956, pp. 1-2; September 17, 1956, pp. 1-2.

"Revolutionizing Radio: CBS Wants to Buy ABC and Hytron." *Business Week,* May 12, 1951, p. 21.

Rice, Elmer. "The Biography of a Play." *Theatre Arts,* November 1959, pp. 59-64.

Roberts, Edward B. "The Free-Lance Television Playwright." *Writer,* February 1954, pp. 39-43.

Robertson, Bruce. "CBS to Build World's Largest Video Plant." *Broadcasting,* February 23, 1948, p. 14.

Robinson, Hubbell. "TV: Myopia of the Widescreen." *Esquire,* July 1958, p. 21.

Rosen, George. "Newton Shootin': An Epilogue." *Variety,* June 7, 1961, p. 25.

––––––. "The New TV Season: Help." *Variety,* October 4, 1961, p. 27.

––––––. "'60-'61 TV Season—Ratings." *Variety,* November 2, 1960, p. 1.

Rowland, Willard D., Jr. "Deconstructing American Communications Policy Literature." *Critical Studies in Mass Communication* 1 (December 1984): 423-35.

––––––. "The Siren Song of Broadcasting Research." *Public Telecommunications Review* 3 (1978): 31-35.

Salent, Richard S., Thomas K. Fisher, and Leon R. Brooks. "The Functions and Practices of a Televison Network." *Law and Contemporary Problems* 22 (Autumn 1957): 584-611.

Sarnoff Buries the Hatchet—in ABC-TV." *Broadcasting,* November 21, 1960, pp. 89-90.

"Sarnoff: Let's Be Reasonable." *Broadcasting,* February 1, 1960, p. 42.

Sarnoff, Robert. "What Do You Want from TV?" *The Saturday Evening Post,* July 1, 1961, pp. 14-15.

Schaffer, Helen B. "Movie-TV Competition." *Editorial Research Reports,* January 18, 1957, p. 54.

Schiller, Herbert I. "The U.S. Hard Sell." *Nation* December 5, 1966, pp. 609-12.

Schmuhl, Robert. "American Communications and American Studies." *Critical Studies in Mass Communication* 2 (June 1985): 185-94.

Schugler, Philip N. "TV Industry's PR Office Undertakes Rebuilding Task." *Editor and Publisher,* January 2, 1960, pp. 11, 47.

Schwartz, Bernard. "Antitrust and the FCC: The Problem of Network Dominance." *University of Pennsylvania Law Review* 107 (April 1959): 753-95.

Seldes, Gilbert. "Can Hollywood Take Over Television?" *Atlantic,* October 1950, pp. 51-53.

––––––. "A Clinical Analysis of TV." *New York Times Magazine,* November 23, 1954, p. 13.

––––––. "The 'Errors' of Television." *Atlantic,* May 1937, pp. 531-51.

––––––. "Television: The Golden Hope." *Atlantic,* March 1949, pp. 34-37.

Serling, Rod. Interview with J. P. Shanley. *New York Times,* April 22, 1956, sec. 2, p. 13; September 20, 1959, sec. 2, p. 19.

————. Interview. *New York Daily News,* March 6, 1960, n.p.

————. Interview. *Playboy,* November 1961, p. 35.

————."TV in the Flesh vs. TV in the Can." *New York Times Magazine,* November 24, 1957, p. 49.

Shanley, J. P. "Notes on 'Patterns' and a Familiar Face." *New York Times,* February 6, 1955, II, p. 15.

Sharpe, Don. "TV Film: Will Economics Stifle Creativity?" *Television,* April 1955, p. 39.

Shayen, Robert Lewis. "Television as Hollywood Sees It." *Saturday Review,* November 1, 1952, p. 28.

Shepard, Richard F. "House Unit Hears TV Film Charges." *New York Times,* September 14, 1956, p. 47.

Shupert, George. "Film for Television." *Television,* August 1949, p. 22.

Siepmann, Charles A. "Moral Aspects of Television." *Public Opinion Quarterly* (Spring 1960): 12-18.

Sinclair, Charles. "Should Hollywood Get It for Free?" *Sponsor,* August 8, 1955, p. 32.

Smith, Bernard B. "Television—There Ought to be a Law." *Harper's,* September 1948, pp. 34-42.

Smith, Richard Austin. "TV: The Coming Showdown." *Fortune,* September 1954, p. 164.

————. "TV: The Light That Failed." *Fortune,* December 1958, pp. 78-81.

"A Special Editorial." *Television,* December 1959, pp. 42-43.

"Speed of Switch to CinemaScope Will Key 20th's Pix Flow to Video." *Variety,* April 15, 1953, p. 3.

Spigel, Lynn. "Installing the Television Set: Popular Discourses on Television and Domestic Space, 1948-1955." *Camera Obscura,* no. 16 (January 1988): 11-48.

"Sponsor-Agency-Station: Who Is Responsible for What in TV?" *Sponsor,* January 1948, p. 53.

"Sponsor Scope." *Sponsor,* December 15, 1956, p. 12; April 6, 1957, p. 9; April 27, 1957, p. 10; November 16, 1957, p. 11; November 27, 1959, p. 10.

"Sponsors Spell Out Their Do's, Don'ts." *Broadcasting,* October 9, 1961, p. 34.

Stahl, Bob. "What Good Are Television Critics?" *TV Guide,* January 24, 1959, pp. 8-11.

Staiger, Janet. "Individualism versus Collectivism." *Screen,* July-August 1983, pp. 68-79.

"Stanton: Gaps and Imperfections." *Broadcasting,* February 1, 1960, p. 43.

"Stars, Spectaculars—and Uplift?" *Newsweek,* July 18, 1955, p. 49.

Steffens, Mildred. "Postwar Television." *Telescreen,* September 1945, pp. 10-12, 28-31.

Stern, Robert H. "Regulatory Influences upon Television's Development: Early Years Under the Federal Radio Commission." *American Journal of Economics and Sociology* 22 (1963): 347-62.

———. "Television in the Thirties: Emerging Patterns of Technical Development, Industrial Control and Governmental Concern." *The Journal of Economics and Sociology* 23 (1964): 285-301.

"Success Secrets Bared to FCC." *Broadcasting,* October 9, 1961, p. 21.

"Syndicated Film." *Television,* July 1952, p. 27.

"Syndicators' New Programming for '59." *Sponsor,* November 8, 1959, pp. 44-46.

"The Tarnished Image." *Time,* November 16, 1959, pp. 72-74, 77-80.

Tebbel, John. "U.S. Television Abroad: Big New Business." *Saturday Review,* July 14, 1962, pp. 44-45.

"Television! Boom!" *Fortune,* May 1948, p. 78-83.

"Television Broadcasters Association." *Television,* Spring 1944, p. 9.

"Television—A Case of War Neurosis." *Fortune,* February 1946, pp. 104-9.

"Television—A Test Case for Free Enterprise." *Television,* Spring 1944, p. 36.

"Television I: A Three Million Dollar 'If.'" *Fortune,* April 1939, pp. 52-59.

"Television II: Fade in on Camera One!" *Fortune,* May 1939, pp. 67-74.

"Television 1959." *Television,* January 1959, p. 33.

"Television's Wealthy, Angry Young Men." *Broadcasting,* October 17, 1960, p. 56.

"Text of the Statement by Dr. Schwartz." *New York Times,* February 12, 1958, p. 20.

"That Tom . . . He Makes Money!" *Television,* September 1955, pp. 25-26.

"Thaw July 1." *Broadcasting,* April 14, 1952, pp. 23, 67-68.

Thompson, Edward T. "There's No Show Business Like MCA's Business." *Fortune,* July 1960, pp. 114-19.

"3D as TV's Sesame to Pix?" *Variety,* February 11, 1953, p. 21.

"TIO's First Year: An Appraisal." *Broadcasting,* September 26, 1960, pp. 27-30.

Trumbo, Dalton. "Hail Blithe Spirit! . . . " *Nation,* October 24, 1959, pp. 243-46.

"The Truth About *Red Channels.*" *Sponsor,* October 8, 1951, p. 76.

"TV Adds Support to Code of Ethics." *New York Times,* January 6, 1960, p. 71.

"TV Costs: Sponsor Pays More, Gets More." *Sponsor,* April 25, 1949, p. 58.

"TV Criticism: How Much of It Makes Sense?" *Sponsor,* January 30, 1960, p. 22.

"TV Critics Say Libel Laws Delayed Quiz Show Expose." *Editor and Publisher,* October 17, 1959, p. 13.

"TV Experts Roast, Roasted in Hollywood." *Broadcasting,* December 24, 1962, p. 36.

"The TV Fan Who Runs a Network." *Sponsor,* June 8, 1957, pp. 45-46.

"TV Feature Films: 1953." *Sponsor,* June 15, 19953, p. 48.

"TV-FM-FAX." *Sponsor,* November 1947, pp. 36, 75.

"TV and Film: Marriage of Necessity." *Business Week,* August 15, 1953.

"TV Future Bright." *Television Age,* January 11, 1960, pp. 21, 23.

"TV Goes After the Intellectuals—but Gently." *Printer's Ink,* March 16, 1962, p. 44.

"TV Lays an Egg." *Sponsor,* November 17, 1957, pp. 25-27.

"TV 1955: Big Spending, Big Programs." *Sponsor,* December 26, 1955, p. 96.

"TV Produces on Film." *Business Week,* October 15, 1949, p. 7.

"TV Shows Are Gold Mine, but Hard to Dig." *Business Week,* October 5, 1957, pp. 66-68.

"TV Show Costs: Why They Went Through the Roof." *Sponsor,* September 6, 1954, p. 40.

"The TV Study That Nobody Saw." *Variety,* June 8, 1960, p. 27.

"TV Writer Sizes Up His Craft." *Broadcasting,* January 4, 1960, p. 42.

"TV's Hottest Problem: Public Relations." *Sponsor,* June 16, 1952, p. 27.

"TV's Image Shines Untarnished: Roper's Two-Years-Later Survey Compares Standing with 1959." *Broadcasting,* February 12, 1962, pp. 27-29.

"TV's Time of Trouble." *Fortune,* August 1951, p. 75.

"Two Views on Sponsor Control." *Broadcasting,* October 2, 1961, p. 24.

Tynan, Kenneth. "The Electronic Theatre." *Holiday,* August 1960, pp. 83-84.

"The UHF Dilemma." *Television,* September 1954, p. 27.

"The Uproar over Television—Are Tighter Controls Needed?" *U.S. News and World Report,* October 26, 1959, pp. 47-50.

"U.S. Steel Makes Friends While it Sells." *Sponsor,* April 4, 1955, p. 39.

Vianello, Robert. "The Rise of the Telefilm and the Network's Hegemony Over the Motion Picture Industry." *Quarterly Review of Film Studies* 9 (Summer 1984): 204-18.

Vidal, Gore. "Notes on Television." *Writer,* March 1957, pp. 8-10.

_____. "Television Drama, Circa 1956." *Theatre Arts,* December 1956, pp. 65-66.

"Video's '50's Accent on Writing." *Variety,* December 21, 1949, p. 27.

"Videotape: The Revolution Is Now." *Television,* July 1957, p. 46.

"Videotown Ten Years Later." *Sponsor,* December 7, 1957, pp. 35, 43.

"Vitapix, Princess Plan First Runs Made for TV." *Broadcasting-Telecasting,* September 7, 1953, p. 34.

Walz, Jay. "Schwartz Ousted After He Charges 'Whitewash' Move." *New York Times,* February 11, 1958, pp. 1, 20.

"Washington Talk." *Sponsor,* June 8, 1957, p. 85; October 5, 1957, p. 79; March 1, 1958, p. 61; January 4, 1958, p. 77; January 18, 1958, p. 75; February 8, 1958, p. 69; March 8, 1958, p. 78; October 11, 1958, p. 75.

Waters, Norman D. "Has Daytime Video a Future? Of Course It Has!" *Televiser,* Fall 1944, p. 23.

Weakley, Thomas E. "Pat Weaver Sounds Off on the Ad Business." *Printer's Ink,* April 12, 1957, pp. 27-28.

"The Weary Young Man." *Newsweek,* September 28, 1959, p. 81.

"Weaver Scans the Way Ahead." *Broadcasting-Telecasting,* February 28, 1955, pp. 38-39.

Weaver, Sylvester. "What's Wrong with Television?" *Tide,* April 12, 1957, p. 11.

Webbink, Douglas W. "The Darkened Channels: UHF Television and the FCC." *Harvard Law Review* 78 (June 1962): 1578-607.

———. "The Impact of UHF Promotion: The All-Channel Television Receiver Law." *Law and Contemporary Problems* 34 (Summer 1969): 535-61.

"We Don't Care What Our Rating Is." *Television,* September, 1957, p. 55.

"Week of Shock, Sorrow." *Broadcasting,* March 14, 1960, p. 38.

Western, John. "Television Girds for Battle." *Public Opinion Quarterly* 3 (October 1939): 547-63.

"What About Hollywood?" *Television,* December 1944, p. 5.

"What Are Admen Telling the FBI About 'Divorcement'?" *Sponsor,* May 28, 1956, p. 32.

"What Are Your 'Rights' to a Time-Slot?" *Sponsor,* April 5, 1954, p. 29.

"What's Ahead on Network TV?" *Sponsor,* March 12, 1960, pp. 35-37, 66, 68.

"What's Wrong with Television Drama?" *Film Culture,* no. 19 (1959): 18-37.

"Where Are TV Shows Heading This Fall?" *Sponsor,* March 9, 1953, p. 27.

White, Owen P. "What's Delaying Television?" *Colliers,* November 30, 1935, p. 11.

Whiteside, James. "The Communicator I: Athens Starts Pouring In." *The New Yorker,* October 16, 1954, pp. 37-38.

———. "The Communicator II: What About the Gratitude Factor?" *The New Yorker,* October 23, 1954, pp. 43-44.

"Who Controls What in TV Films." *Broadcasting,* October 17, 1960, p. 34.

"Who Knows Programming?" *Television Age,* December 25, 1961, p. 31.

"Who Will Produce TV?" *Televiser,* Spring 1945, p. 9.

Wicker, Tom. "Lobbies Defeat Reform for the FCC." *New York Times,* June 18, 1961, sec. 4, p. 6.

Wilk, Max. "Writing for Television." *Theatre Arts,* February 1951, pp. 49-50.

"Will Feature Films Reshape TV?" *Business Week,* November 24, 1956, p. 131.

"Will Vitapix Create TV Film Revolution?" *Sponsor,* January 11, 1954, p. 42.

Winfield, Gilbert. "The Status of Theatre Television." *Television,* February 1946, p. 44.

Wolf, George. "New TV Programming Pattern." *Advertising Agency Magazine,* June 24, 1955, p. 27.

_____. "TV Program Outlook Bright as New Big Season Opens." *Advertising Agency Magazine,* October 28, 1955, p. 22.

"The Word from Washington: Relax." *Television,* April 1955, p. 35.

"Year End Report." *Sponsor,* December 27, 1954, pp. 29, 90, 110.

"You Can Crack the Hollywood Dam but You Have to Know How." *Sponsor,* February 6, 1956, p. 68.

III. Government Documents

Commission on the Organization of the Executive Branch of Government. *Staff Report on the FCC.* Washington, D.C.: Government Printing Office, 1948.

U.S., Congress House, Committee on Interstate and Foreign Commerce. *Investigation of Radio and Television Programs, Report by the Communications Subcommittee of the Committee on Interstate and Foreign Commerce, House.* 82nd Cong., 2d sess., 1952.

_____. Committee on Interstate and Foreign Commerce. *Network Broadcasting,* House Report no. 1297, Committee on Interstate and Foreign Commerce. 85th Cong., 2d sess., 1958.

_____. Committee on Interstate and Foreign Commerce, *Radio Frequency Modulation, Hearings on H.J. Res. 78.* 80th Cong., 2d sess., 1948.

_____. Committee on Interstate and Foreign Commerce. *Television Network Program Procurement, Report of the House Committee on Interstate and Foreign Commerce.* 88th Cong., 1st sess., 1963.

_____. Committee on the Judiciary. *Monopoly Problems in the Regulated Industries, Hearings before the Subcommittee on Antitrust.* 84th Cong., 2d sess., 1956.

U.S. Congress, Senate, Committee on Interstate and Foreign Commerce. *Appointments to the Regulatory Commission: The FCC and the FTC, 1949-79.* 94th Cong., 2d sess., 1976.

———. Committee on Interstate and Foreign Commerce. *Hearings: Development of Television.* 76th Cong., 3d sess., April 10, 11, 1940.

———. Committee on Interstate and Foreign Commerce. *Investigation of Television Networks and the UHF-VHF Problem.* 84th Cong., 2d sess., 1955.

———. Committee on Interstate and Foreign Commerce. *The Network Monopoly, Report for the Committee on Interstate and Foreign Commerce, U.S. Senate, by Senator John W. Bricker.* 84th Cong., 2d sess., 1955.

———. Committee on Interstate and Foreign Commerce. *Progress of FM Radio: Hearings on Certain Changes Involving Development of FM Radio and RCA Patent Policies.* 80th Cong., 2d sess., 1948.

———. Committee on Interstate and Foreign Commerce. *The Television Inquiry,* Volume 4: *Network Practices, Hearings before the Committee on Interstate and Foreign Commerce, Senate.* 84th Cong., 2d sess., 1956.

———. Committee on Interstate and Foreign Commerce. *Television Network Practices, Staff Report.* 85th Cong., 1st sess., 1957.

U.S., Department of Commerce. *Television as an Advertising Medium.* Washington, D.C.: Government Printing Office, 1949.

U.S., Federal Communications Commission. *Annual Report.* Washington, D.C.: Government Printing Office, 1939.

———. *Annual Report.* Washington, D.C.: Government Printing Office, 1940, 1946, 1947.

———. *Public Service Responsibility of Broadcast Licensees.* Washington, D.C.: Government Printing Office, 1946.

———. Office of Network Study. *Interim Report: Responsibility for Broadcast Matter.* Washington, D.C.: Government Printing Office, 1960.

———. Office of Network Study. *Second Interim Report: Television Program Procurement, Part II.* Washington, D.C.: Government Printing Office, 1965.

U.S., Federal Trade Commission. *Report on the Radio Industry.* Washington, D.C.: Government Printing Office, 1923.

U.S., Justice Department. *Report to the President by the Attorney General on Deceptive Practices in the Broadcast Industry.* December 30, 1959.

IV. Speeches and Oral Histories

Association of National Advertisers. "Planning TV's Tomorrow." Panel discussion, New York City, November 9, 1954, collection of the NBC Records Administration Library, New York.

Barrow, Roscoe L. "The Rigged Quiz Shows and Payola Deceptions—Symptoms of a Lack of Responsibility in Broadcasting." Speech to the Kiwanis Club,

February 1, 1960, collection of the Television Information Office, New York.

Dann, Michael. Interview, June 14, 1979. Federal Communications Commission File, Oral History Collection, Columbia University, New York.

Hooper, Richard H. "Television—The Post-War Sales Tool." Speech to the Federated Advertising Clubs of Chicago, December 7, 1944.

Jolliffe, C. B. "An Engineer's Report on Television." Speech to the Radio Executives Club of New York, November 15, 1945.

Joyce, T. F. "Television and Post-War Distribution." Speech to the Boston Conference on Distribution, October 17, 1944.

Kennedy, John. Speech to the Association of Radio and Television Directors. January 12, 1960, collection of the Museum of Broadcasting, New York.

Segal, Alex. "The Future of Television Drama." "Horizons," June 6, 1952, collection of the Museum of Broadcasting, New York.

Stanton, Frank. Speech to the Academy of Television Arts and Sciences, New York City. Collection of the Television Information Office, New York.

Weaver, Pat. Appearance on "Youth Wants to Know." NBC television, June 5, 1955, collection of the NBC Records Administration Library, New York.

———. "Selling in a New Era." Speech to the Advertising Club of New Jersey, May 24, 1955, collection of the NBC Records Administration Library, New York.

———. Speech at the Television Affiliates Meeting. Chicago, November 18, 1953, collection of the NBC Records Administration Library, New York.

V. Dissertations and Theses

Bailey, Robert Lee. "An Examination of Primetime Network Television Special Programs 1948 to 1966." Ph.D. dissertation, University of Wisconsin, 1967.

Bellamy, Robert V., Jr. "Zenith's Phonevision: An Historical Case Study of the First Pay Television System." Ph.D. dissertation, University of Iowa, 1985.

Bluem, Albert William. "The Influence of Medium upon Dramaturgical Method in Selected Television Plays." Ph.D. dissertation, Ohio State University, 1959.

Chisholm, Bradley. "The CBS Color Television Venture: A Study in Failed Innovation in the Broadcasting Industry." Ph.D. dissertation, University of Wisconsin-Madison, 1987.

Deihl, Ernest. "George Schaefer and the 'Hallmark Hall of Fame': A Study of the Producer-Director of a Live Television Drama Series." Ph.D. dissertation, Ohio State University, 1964.

Diskin, Marvin Newton. "A Descriptive and Historical Analysis of the Live Television Program, the 'United States Steel Hour,' 1953-1963." Ph.D. dissertation, University of Michigan, 1963.

Hawes, William Kenneth, Jr. "A History of Anthology Drama Through 1958." Ph.D. dissertation, University of Michigan, 1960.

Jakes, Frank Henry. "A Study of Standards Imposed by Four Leading Television Critics with Respect to Live Television Drama." Ph.D. dissertation, Ohio State University, 1960.

Larson, Alan David. "Integration and Attempted Integration Between the Motion-Picture and Television Industries Through 1956." Ph.D. dissertation, Ohio University, 1979.

Levott, Daniel Herbert. "The Radio and Television Production and Promotion of the Cisco Kid." Master's thesis, Ohio State University, 1970.

Lewis, Bob S. "An Analysis of the Influence of Newton Minow on Broadcasting." Master's thesis, University of Missouri, 1966.

Mayerle, Judine. "The Development of the Television Variety Show as a Major Program Genre at the National Broadcasting Company, 1946-56." Ph.D. dissertation, Northwestern University, 1983.

Moore, Barbara Ann. "Syndication of First-Run Television Programming: Its Development and Current Status." Ph.D. dissertation, Ohio University, 1979.

Ozersky, Richard. "Television and Imitations of Life: Social and Thematic Patterns in Top-Rated Television Dramatic Programs During the Period 1950-1970, a Descriptive Study." Ph.D. dissertation, New York University, 1976.

Rouse, Morleen Getz. "A History of the F. W. Ziv Radio and Television Syndication Companies, 1930-1960." Ph.D. dissertation, University of Michigan, 1976.

Salbach, Louis Carl. "Jack Gould: Social Critic of the Television Medium, 1947-72." Ph.D. dissertation, University of Michigan, 1980.

Schnapper, Amy. "The Distribution of Theatrical Feature Films to Television." Ph.D. dissertation, University of Wisconsin-Madison, 1975.

Shaw, Myron Berkley. "A Descriptive Analysis of the Documentary Drama Television Program, the 'Armstrong Circle Theatre,' 1955-1961." Ph.D. dissertation, University of Michigan, 1962.

Silverman, Fred. "An Analysis of ABC Television Network Programming from February 1953 to October 1959." Master's thesis, Ohio State University, 1959.

Sova, Harry W. "A Descriptive and Historical Survey of American Television, 1937-1946." Ph.D. dissertation, Ohio University, 1977.

Stewart, Robert Hammel. "The Development of Network Television Types to January, 1953." Ph.D. dissertation, Ohio State University, 1954.

Sturchen, Francis W. "An Historical Analysis of Live Network Television Drama from 1938 to 1958." Ph.D. dissertation, University of Minnesota, 1960.

Thiel, Jean Elizabeth. "Albert McCleery's Transfer of Theatre Practice to Live Television Drama." Ph.D. dissertation, University of Michigan, 1977.

Watson, Mary Ann. "Commercial Television and the New Frontier: Resistance and Appeasement." Ph.D. dissertation, University of Michigan, 1983.

VI. Memoranda

Herbert, J. K. Memorandum to Frank White. April 11, 1953. NBC Records Administration Library, New York.

National Broadcasting Company. *Bulletin Research and Planning.* July 15, 1955.

———. *Research Bulletin.* No. 8, 1950; April 30, 1958.

———. *Research Bulletin.* "Advertising and Marketing Highlights." July 14, 1958.

———. *Research Bulletin.* "An Analysis of ABC's 'Get Age' Campaign." May 16, 1958.

———. *Research Bulletin.* "National Television Advertising in 1958." April 13, 1959.

———. *Research Bulletin.* "National Television Advertising in 1958." May 4, 1959.

———. *Research Bulletin.* "Television Trends." November 25, 1959.

———. *Research Bulletin.* "National Television Advertising in 1959." April 22, 1960.

———. *Research Bulletin.* September 14, 1960; June 20, 1961.

———. *Research and Planning Bulletin,* April 3, 1953; July 15, 1955; November 8, 1955; September 24, 1956; April 26, 1957; October 14, 1957.

———. *Sales Facts Bulletin.* March 26, 1951.

———. *Television and Modern Marketing.* 1960.

Weaver, Pat. "Comments on the Billy Rose Plan for Film by NBC." 1951.

———. "Memorandum to Executive Group: NBC Television: Principles, Objectives, Policies." November 1949.

———. "Memorandum for Planning." 1952.

———. "Memorandum on the Spectaculars." March 8, 1954.

———. "Presentation to General Foods." 1952.

———. "Television's Destiny." 1950.

Index